More Advance Praise for
The eBay Seller's Tax and Legal Answer Book

"An apt subtitle might be 'Everything You Had No Idea You Needed to Know About Doing Business on eBay.' And who better to clarify the intricacies of taxes and the law in regard to this amazing auction site than Cliff Ennico? Cliff will keep you on the straight and narrow, pointed directly toward eBay success."

    —**Peter Kent, e-commerce consultant and author,** *Search Engine Optimization for Dummies*

"All eBay buyers and sellers could benefit greatly from this book. Cliff Ennico has written a comprehensive tax and legal 'Rules of the Road' for eBay success. Written in plain English with numerous practical examples, you will refer back to it again and again. I highly recommend it."

    —**Jack Waddick, eBay University instructor; President, OakviewTraining.com**

"In my over eight years as an eBay PowerSeller, I have never discovered a book that was more timely and germane to the issues of top eBay sellers than Cliff Ennico's *The eBay Seller's Tax and Legal Answer Book*. With governments rapidly seeking to throw a lasso around online sellers' profits, Cliff's book is true preventative enlightenment for all eBay and online entrepreneurs in today's rapidly evolving environment. I know first-hand that Cliff possesses the legal experience and prowess to connect readers with a predictable road map for success. You cannot risk missing this important and essential tool in your eBay arsenal. All questions are answered, and I wish this book existed wʰ I first started selling on eBay."

    —**Christopher Matthew Spencer, author,** *The eBay Entrepreneur* **and** *eBay Shooting Star,* **and eBay University instructor**

"Cliff delivers the essential ingredients to what all sellers should know and do to protect their eBay business, in the way only Cliff can . . . making you belly laugh through it all."
   —JP O'Brien, Founder and CEO, KeepMore.net

"If anyone can explain how to make a profit on eBay the right way, it's Cliff Ennico. Buy this book for all the answers to your toughest questions . . . and sleep better at night!"
   —Jane Applegate, marketing consultant and author of *201 Great Ideas for Your Small Business*

"A must-read for eBay sellers! No legalese—Cliff Ennico gives you practical tips for protecting your business online. Finally—a book that makes the legal side of running an eBay business easy to understand!"
   —Catherine Seda, Internet marketing strategist and author of *How to Win Sales & Influence Spiders*

"If you want to make money selling on eBay, then you have to stop treating it like a garage sale and start treating it like a real business. Sheer panic sets in as you realize this dream of success involves a corporate structure, taxes, business plans, and even hiring employees. Make that dream a reality and read this book. Cliff breaks down all of these required business rules by making them easy to understand in step-by-step guidelines that are filled with sheer genius, ingenuity, practical advice, and a huge dose of humor. This should be THE book that sits next to your computer."
   —Janelle Elms, eBay University instructor, Dean of eBay Business for L.A. College International, and creator of the eBay Stores Video Series www.StoresSuccessVideo.com

The eBay Seller's

• TAX AND LEGAL ANSWER BOOK •

Everything You Need to Know to Keep the Government
Off Your Back and Out of Your Wallet

CLIFF ENNICO

⋏MACOM

American Management Association
New York • Brussels • Chicago • Mexico City • San Francisco
Shanghai • Tokyo • Washington, D.C.

Special discounts on bulk quantities of AMACOM books are
available to corporations, professional associations, and other
organizations. For details, contact Special Sales Department,
AMACOM, a division of American Management Association,
1601 Broadway, New York, NY 10019.
Tel.: 212-903-8316. Fax: 212-903-8083.
E-mail: specialsls@amanet.org
Website: www.amacombooks.org/go/specialsales
To view all AMACOM titles go to: www.amacombooks.org

This publication is designed to provide accurate and authoritative
information in regard to the subject matter covered. It is sold with the
understanding that the publisher is not engaged in rendering legal,
accounting, or other professional service. If legal advice or other expert
assistance is required, the services of a competent professional person
should be sought.

Library of Congress Cataloging-in-Publication Data

Ennico, Clifford R.
    The eBay seller's tax and legal answer book : everything you need to
know to keep the government off your back and out of your wallet / Cliff Ennico.
        p.   cm.
    Includes index.
    ISBN-13: 978-0-8144-7425-9
    ISBN-10: 0-8144-7425-X
    1. eBay (Firm)   2. Internet auctions.   3. Electronic commerce—Taxation.
I. Title.

    HF5478.E576   2007
    658.8'7—dc22

                                                    2007001139

Printing number

10   9   8   7   6   5   4   3   2   1

To my wife, Dolores, for being quite simply the most beautiful woman on Earth, and for letting me keep (almost) all of the stuff I buy on eBay.

"It isn't the size of the dog in the fight that matters;
it's the size of the fight in the dog"
— Dwight D. Eisenhower

"Duffy," Photo courtesy of the DeFonzo family

Contents

Acknowledgments

Any book is a team effort, and *The eBay Seller's Tax and Legal Answer Book* would not have been possible without the support, friendship, inspiration, love, and occasional "noodging" of these individuals, among others. My many thanks to:

- ➤ Rieva Lesonsky, the editorial director of *Entrepreneur* magazine, for allowing me to tell the story at the beginning of this introduction and for making my involvement with the eBay community possible

- ➤ Janelle Elms, noted eBay author and my "partner in crime" on the eBay University tour, for being such a great resource on "all things eBay"

- ➤ Catherine Seda, Internet marketing columnist for *Entrepreneur* magazine, for teaching me the finer points of marketing a business online

- ➤ Jim "Uncle Griff" Griffith, Mike Rudolph, Sharon Guldner, Elisa Stern, and the rest of the eBay Education team, for having the courage to put a lawyer in a position where he can really do some good for a change

- ➤ Jacquie Flynn, my editor at AMACOM Books, for believing that a legal and tax guide can be both entertaining and informative

- ➤ The eBay community, for being so receptive and welcoming to a guy who's telling them to "eat their spinach" while keeping the government from "eating their lunch."

Introduction to "La Vida eBay"

In the sweltering summer of 2004, I received a telephone call from my good friend Rieva Lesonsky, the editorial director of *Entrepreneur* magazine, with the following request: "Cliff, what are you doing next weekend? I need you to fly to New Orleans to be on a panel."

She explained that *Entrepreneur* magazine had agreed to put together a panel on "Starting a Business on eBay" for eBay Live, the annual trade show, convention, and love-in for people who buy and sell on eBay. She asked if I could spend fifteen minutes talking about the "legal and tax aspects" of selling stuff on eBay. I had written a couple of legal and tax columns for *Entrepreneur* at that point, but more important, I had bought a ton of stuff on eBay, mostly "nineteenth-century American folk art and decorative items with whimsical, humorous, or politically incorrect themes"—which is what I lovingly call my collection (although my wife, Dolores, calls it something else). Rieva thought I would be a good fit for the job.

Hey, a free weekend in New Orleans (pre–Hurricane Katrina) to talk for fifteen minutes? No problemo.

On the plane, I thought to myself, "This is going to be a piece of cake. I know a lot of people buy stuff on eBay, but how many are going to attend a three-day convention on 'all things eBay'? I mean, how much can you say about being nice on the Feedback Forum? And a panel on legal and tax issues? If we get five people in that room, we'll be lucky."

The next day, wearing my finest "don't mess with me, I'm a

lawyer" suit, I walked into a room the size of an airplane hangar. There were close to a thousand people in that room, along with two gigantic video monitors on either side of the podium so that the large crowd could see every one of my nose hairs in living color. I was told that several thousand more were attending the convention, and that more than a hundred companies had signed up for booths at the trade show offering products and services specifically tailored to eBay buyers and sellers.

After my talk, these 1,000 people "rushed the podium" and flattened me and the other panelists against the wall, asking question after question about sales taxes and income taxes, incorporating in Nevada, dealing with crazy business partners, and crushing buyers who don't pay. Rieva and another panelist had to grab me by the arm and create a "flying wedge" formation to get us all out of the room in one piece.

Needless to say, it wasn't the sort of reception I get when I speak on legal or tax topics to bar associations, chambers of commerce, and venture capital clubs. For a few minutes in New Orleans in 2004, I knew exactly how it was to be Elvis.

I frankly had no idea back then just how big eBay was, but in the words of the old Monkees' song, "I'm a Believer" today. To anyone who doubts eBay is a major force in our economy, listen to some of the statistics CEO Meg Whitman laid down during her keynote address at the 2006 eBay Live! in Las Vegas (which attracted more than 15,000 attendees):

➤ eBay has more than 200 million unique registered users throughout the world. If eBay were a country, it would be the fifth largest in the world (after China, India, the United States, and Indonesia).

➤ There are more than 1.4 million people worldwide making a full-time or part-time living by selling on eBay.

➤ There are more than 100 million PayPal account holders worldwide, more than own American Express and Discover cards combined.

> ➤ More than 250,000 people have opened "eBay Stores" on the site.
> ➤ eBay sellers gave more than $20 million to charity last year using eBay's "Giving Works" program.

Shortly after my talk in New Orleans, I was invited to join the faculty of eBay University—a team of eBay employees, authors, and small business and e-commerce experts who travel the country helping eBay entrepreneurs get their businesses off the ground. As the unofficial "Defense Against the Dark Arts Professor" of eBay University (if you don't understand the inside joke, talk to anyone familiar with the "Harry Potter" books), I have spoken to thousands of "eBayers" in cities and towns throughout the United States about such scintillating, cutting-edge topics as sales tax compliance, customs regulations, the difference between accounting and book-keeping, and how to hire and fire employees.

And there's one thing I can tell all of you: If you're planning to sell anything on eBay more than occasionally, you really, really need this book.

What prevents even more people from selling professionally on eBay is cold, naked fear: People worry that they will be sued, that they will lose their homes to business creditors, that they will be accused of fraud if something they sell turns out not to be exactly as described, that a buyer will cancel a credit card transaction after the goods have shipped, or that they will run afoul of some obscure government regulation and pay a fortune in taxes, fines, and penalties. *The eBay Seller's Tax and Legal Answer Book* is the first book to help the eBay community deal with the legal, tax, and regulatory issues of doing business online.

SELLING ON EBAY? THERE ARE RULES

A lot of people buying and selling stuff online think they're living in an alternate universe, a Shangri-la where there are no rules, laws, or regulations governing business; a virtual Woodstock where people can bliss out and engage in capitalistic acts between con-senting adults without fear, anxiety, or stress.

Time to burst a big bubble, folks. When you are buying and sell-ing stuff on eBay, a website, a blog, or indeed anywhere on the Internet, *if you are making money, you are in business*. Specifically, you are running a "retail" business, one that sells goods to an end-consumer. As such, you are subject to the same federal, state, and local taxes that brick-and-mortar retail businesses in your commu-nity have to pay, and you must comply with the same laws, rules, and regulations that they do. There is no tax-free lunch on the In-ternet, and there never has been.

Just to give you some examples:

> ➤ You have to pay income tax on *every penny* of profit you make on eBay—even if you make just one dollar, and even if you think of your eBay selling as a hobby rather than a business.

> ➤ If you sell something to a buyer who lives in the same state you do, you must collect and pay sales taxes on the winning bid amount.

> ➤ If you sell something on eBay and it arrives in damaged condition, you are required by law to give the buyer a full refund unless (a) you re-quire the buyer to purchase insurance and (b) you put a notice on your auction pages warning buyers that you will not give refunds unless they purchase insurance.

JUST BUYING ON EBAY? THERE ARE RULES, TOO

Most of the tips in this book are for people selling on eBay, but there are quite a few legal and tax traps for buyers, too. For exam-ple, did you know that:

> ➤ If you buy something on eBay from an out-of-state or overseas seller, you are required in many states to pay a "use tax" on the winning bid amount. (A use tax is similar to a sales tax, but on stuff you buy for your own consumption.)

➢ You can go to jail if you contact someone bidding against you in an eBay auction and offer to do "something nice for him" if he stops bidding and lets you win the auction.

➢ If a seller offers a "genuine 100 percent original 1885 mechanical bank" and there is even one repaired or replaced part in that bank, however small or trivial (such as an internal screw that could not possibly have been produced before 1910), you can return the bank to the seller and get a full refund.

THE FOUR TYPES OF EBAY SELLERS

Generally, there are four types of eBay sellers, or, if you prefer, four distinct stages to an eBay business.

1. *The "Fun" Seller.* The fun seller, or eBay hobbyist, sells only occasionally on eBay, not more than ten times a year, as a "labor of love." Hobbyists sell items they personally own, and they are more interested in the fun of selling online than they are in making money. As a friend of mind puts it, "The goal here is to clean out the attic, the basement, and the garage and make a few bucks without having to go through all the trouble of hosting a tag sale."

    I personally estimate that the vast majority of eBay's 200 million registered users worldwide fall into this category, to the extent they are sellers at all and not just buying stuff on eBay.

2. *The "Opportunistic" Seller.* These individuals realize that eBay's more than just a way to clean out the attic. These folks generally:

    ➢ Make less than $25,000 a year selling on eBay.

    ➢ Complete between 10 and 500 transactions on eBay every year.

    ➢ Are generally savvy about eBay, having read at least one book or taken an online or community college course on eBay selling techniques.

    ➢ Are serious about selling, and are beginning to treat their eBay "hobby" as a real business.

    ➢ Have a full-time job and sell on eBay only during "evenings and weekends."

➤ Are thinking about making a full-time living selling on eBay.

I would estimate that between 1.5 million and 2 million eBay registered users fall into this category.

3. *The "Job" or "Business" Seller.* These folks are serious about treating their eBay selling experience as a business:

➤ They make more than $25,000 a year selling on eBay.

➤ They complete more than 500 transactions on eBay each year.

➤ They fall into one of eBay's PowerSeller categories.

➤ They generally are full-time sellers without "day jobs."

I would estimate that between 750,000 and 1,250,000 eBay registered users fall into this category, which is rapidly expanding.

4. *The "Enterprise" Seller.* These folks are the tip of the eBay selling pyramid, with more than $500,000 in sales and thousands of transactions on eBay each year. I would estimate their number to be only in the hundreds, but this category is growing rapidly as more and more people find profitable "niche categories" they can dominate on eBay.

While this book contains useful information for all four categories of eBay seller, it is targeted mainly at the "opportunistic" and "business" sellers who form the vast majority of eBay's selling community worldwide.

SHOULD YOU TREAT YOUR EBAY SELLING AS A "BUSINESS"?

At a recent eBay University program on the West Coast, an audience member got up during the Q&A for my "eBay for Business" program and asked the following question: "Earlier this year I started selling stuff on eBay, mainly to clean out my attic. I ran out of attic stuff a while back, so I've started selling stuff for some of my friends and relatives. So far I've made about $50,000 after expenses. I don't really look at this as a business, but I'm being told that I have to pay taxes on what I'm making. Is that right?"

Let me get this straight . . . you've made $50,000 in just a few months and you're not sure if you have a business? Are you kidding?

A lot of people are surprised to find out that their cherished hobbies have somehow morphed into real businesses overnight without their knowledge. Your good-faith belief that what you are doing is "only a hobby" doesn't count for much when it comes to the Internal Revenue Service and your state and local tax authorities. This is such an important topic for the eBay community that I've devoted the very first chapter of this book to the whole "hobby versus business" issue.

But my off-the-cuff answer to this question always is: Why shouldn't you treat your eBay selling as a real business, especially if you're making money at it? When you are running your own business . . . life is deductible! Well, at least some things are. If you are running a business, you are considered to be self-employed and can deduct a lot of things that people with hobbies just can't. According to IRS publications, there are more than 1,000 business, charitable, and "miscellaneous" other deductions self-employed people can legitimately take on their tax returns (the most common deductions for eBay sellers are discussed in Chapter 9). Not everything is deductible, of course, and the rules don't always follow logical patterns, but if you are making money on eBay and not treating it as a business, you are probably paying more in taxes than you should.

THE BAD NEWS ABOUT DOING BUSINESS ON eBAY

If you are serious about making money on eBay, or from e-commerce generally, you are simply going to have to learn a little bit about the law, pay your taxes, and figure out creative ways to comply with government regulations.

When you set up any kind of business in America, the government is your partner. Sometimes it regulates you, sometimes it tells you what you can and cannot do in your business, and it always requires you to pay taxes if you're successful.

While the vast majority of transactions on eBay (more than 99.9 percent, according to official eBay statistics) go through without a hitch, sooner or later you will encounter a "bad buyer" on eBay, or you'll get into a dispute with a supplier or have a cherished antique destroyed while being shipped to a buyer. These things happen in any retail business, and you have to know how to deal with them professionally.

The eBay Seller's Tax and Legal Answer Book is the first book to deal with the legal and tax issues of doing business on eBay, in language that won't require you to get a law degree or sit for your state CPA exam.

THE GOOD NEWS ABOUT DOING BUSINESS ON eBAY

A lot of folks are intimidated by the legal and tax aspects of doing business on eBay, but they really shouldn't be. A fair number of legal requirements (although not all) are "common sense with a Latin name," and it's fairly easy to learn the most important things you have to know so that you won't lose any sleep worrying about what "might happen" in your eBay business.

To those who still grumble "I really don't like having to deal with taxes when all I really want to do is sell on eBay," I say—look on the bright side: Taxes are the best kind of problem to have when you're running your own business. My wish to all of my new small business clients is, "May you have tax problems as soon as possible." Why? Because the only people who have tax problems are people who are succeeding and making money. If you were failing miserably, you wouldn't have to worry about taxes. No income, no taxes. So face it, folks—taxes are the government's way of telling you that you've got what it takes to succeed, you're doing a great job, and you should keep it up.

THERE'S THE LAW, AND THEN THERE'S eBAY

When reading this book, keep in mind that there are two sets of rules you need to know in order to sell effectively on eBay. You need to know the federal and state legal and tax rules that apply to an online commerce business such as eBay selling. But just because the law allows you to do something online doesn't mean that eBay will let you do it. eBay has a number of policies that are more restrictive than the law. Violating an eBay policy is not likely to get you sued or throw you in jail, as violation of a law will, but it will sure as heck get you kicked off of eBay, which is not a good thing.

A number of eBay's most important policies are described in this book (especially where they prohibit something the law would otherwise allow you to do), but there's no way to fit them all in. For a complete listing of eBay policies, go to the eBay home page, click on the Help tab, then scroll halfway down the page and click on Rules and Policies. This is probably the most important section of the eBay site and should be read carefully by anyone thinking about selling professionally on eBay.

I would estimate the vast majority of sticky situations eBay sellers get themselves into occur because they simply didn't spend enough time reading and understanding eBay's policies. Here's some free advice: At least once a year, take two hours out of your life, brew a strong pot of coffee, sit down at your computer, and reread the eBay Rules and Policies section. These two hours a year will save you an enormous amount of time and heartache if you ever get into a difficult situation on eBay.

"NOBODY ELSE IS FOLLOWING THE RULES AND THEY'RE GETTING AWAY WITH IT!"

It's no secret that some laws are more strictly enforced than others. For example, most of you have never before heard of a "use tax" and will be hearing about it for the first time in this book, even though it's been around for decades. Many of you will be shocked to learn that you have been ignoring or violating some laws and rules in your eBay business, and not only has nothing bad happened, but everyone you know is doing things exactly the same way.

No one in their right mind will ever tell you "not to worry, because everyone does it." Your goal in running any sort of business is to comply as much as is humanly possible with all laws, rules, and taxes that apply to that business—bar none. It may take you a while to get into "substantial compliance," but you should be taking steps every day to improve your track record and correct any deficiencies.

Why? Because nice people finish first? Nope. Because sooner or later, as information technology improves and enables us all to do things we couldn't dream of doing just a few years ago, the government will have the tools (or staff levels) it lacks today to enforce laws and taxes that have been "on the books" for years but are not being strenuously enforced.

For example, as this book is being written, the IRS has asked PayPal to disclose information about eBay users who have used credit cards issued by overseas (particularly Cayman Islands) banks for their eBay transactions in an effort to hide income from U.S. tax authorities. Now, you say to yourself, "Well, I guess that's okay, because I don't like tax cheats any more than the IRS does." Fair enough, but if the IRS request is successful, we have to ask another question: What's to prevent the IRS (or your state tax authority) from requesting information from eBay or PayPal about your selling or buying activities on eBay? Are you 100 percent sure you have paid every penny of tax due to the federal, state, and local governments on your eBay selling or buying activities? Enough said.

HOW THIS BOOK IS ORGANIZED

I really hate most "law for the layperson" books that throw the law at you and expect you to figure out how it applies to your business. As lawyers, we are taught to think about the law in specialized "compartments": The tax laws belong over there, the labor and employment laws are over here, and that pile in the corner is the commercial law section. That's how lawyers learn the law—in courses devoted to a single area of legal practice. But when you're running an eBay business, everything is all mixed up and problems get thrown at you in random order.

This book takes a more practical approach. First, I start by describing the "life cycle" of a typical eBay business and point out the issues you are most likely to confront at each stage of the process. And rather than tell you "what the law is" (I have never, in twenty-six years of practicing law, had any client ask me "what's the law?"), I hope to give you some practical advice about what you should do when you find yourself in a sticky situation on eBay.

I confess to being that most dangerous of creatures—a lawyer with a sense of humor. One of my early mentors in the legal profession gave me an invaluable piece of advice about public speaking, which will be true of this book as well: "If you can't keep them awake, Cliff, you won't be able to teach them anything." Whether you read this book cover to cover, or just "dip into it" every once in a while for specific advice, I promise to do everything I can to make the material as much fun as possible.

EVEN AFTER READING THIS BOOK, YOU WILL NEED A LAWYER

This book contains general information designed to help you figure out if there are any legal or tax issues you need to address when building a successful eBay selling business. It is no substitute for actual legal, tax, or accounting advice, which can be provided only by a qualified professional who is licensed to practice law or accounting in your state. The laws and tax issues you will encounter when selling on eBay vary widely from state to state, and from country to country, and nobody (myself included) knows them all. Use this book by all means to find out if there's something you should discuss with your lawyer, accountant, or tax adviser, but don't take any action based on anything you read in this book without talking to that person first.

A FINAL WORD BEFORE WE LAUNCH

This is a book about selling on eBay; this is not a book by eBay. I am not an eBay employee—I speak for eBay University as an independent consultant. Neither eBay, PayPal (an eBay company), nor any of their employees has reviewed, vetted, approved, or authorized anything in this book. *The eBay Seller's Tax and Legal Answer Book* is entirely my doing, and I am solely responsible for its contents.

Getting Started as an eBay Seller

CHAPTER 1

"Is This Really a Business?"

It's the most commonly asked question at my eBay University presentations around the country: "I've been selling on eBay for a while, but I don't know if I should treat it as a hobby or a business." Sooner or later, every eBay seller has to make the fateful decision: Should I sell online only occasionally, for the fun of it, or should I consider making a part-time or full-time living from selling on eBay? Sometimes the decision is made for you, as when so many people are asking you to sell their stuff on eBay that before you know it you've made $50,000 or more in profits and you almost have to treat it as a business.

YOU KNOW YOU HAVE AN eBAY BUSINESS WHEN . . .

Here are the top-twenty signs, counted down David Letterman–style, that your eBay selling activities are getting a wee bit beyond the "hobby" stage.

20. You've run out of things in your attic and basement to sell on eBay, but you're continuing to sell stuff from . . . somewhere.
19. After putting your garbage out by the curb on pickup day, you drive around the neighborhood to see if anybody is throwing away anything interesting.

18. You've taken out classified ads in the local newspapers and placed one-page "flyers" in all of your neighbors' mailboxes offering to help them clean out their attics and basements on eBay—for a fee, of course.

17. You begin haunting local funeral parlors, like Paul Newman in *The Verdict,* offering your eBay selling services to bereaved relatives who just can't bear the thought of cleaning out Mom's house.

16. You're personally acquainted with every estate, divorce, and bankruptcy attorney in your community.

15. A hedge fund wants to invest in what you're doing.

14. You consider building out the shed in your backyard, or adding a third story to your center-hall colonial, so you'll have more room to store your inventory.

13. You keep your Chihuahua chained to your eBay inventory at night so you can deduct him as a "guard dog."

12. The first things you read in the newspaper every morning are the liquidation and creditors' notices in the "legal" section of the classified ads page.

11. You carry rolls of hundred-dollar bills to garage sales, arriving just as the homeowners are putting out their stuff, and offer to buy everything they have, sight unseen.

10. You own the complete works of Janelle Elms, Marsha Collier, Joseph Sinclair, and Jim "Uncle Griff" Griffith. (If you don't know who these folks are, you probably aren't quite "there" yet.)

9. You're on a first-name basis with every employee of your town dump, the head of the local trucker's union, and every freight liquidator, customs broker, and factory outlet within a fifty-mile radius of your home.

8. You arrive at 6 A.M. for your local library's annual book sale with thirty-six empty liquor boxes and three illegal-immigrant "day laborers" to help you pack up your truck.

7. You have so many student interns helping you create eBay auction pages the local community college has named a faculty chair after you.

6. You know exactly where you can find motor vehicles that were "formerly owned by drug dealers."

5. You know which brands of perfume, housewares, and other consumer goods are being discontinued by their manufacturers within the next six months—and which distributors are likely to have overstocks of these items.

4. The talk show hosts on eBay Radio (www.wsradio.com) have your home phone number on speed-dial.

3. The local kids can't play basketball in the street anymore because they're too busy dodging UPS trucks going to and from your home office.

2. You're setting up a charitable foundation to teach convicts in your state prison system how to use Turbo Lister, Selling Manager Pro, and Blackthorne.

And last but not least . . . the number-one reason your eBay selling activities are getting beyond the "hobby" stage:

1. YOU MAKE AT LEAST ONE PENNY IN PROFIT EACH YEAR FROM YOUR EBAY SELLING ACTIVITIES.

EVEN A "HOBBY" CAN MAKE A PROFIT, AND IF IT DOES, YOU PAY TAXES!

When people ask, "Do I really have a business selling on eBay?" the question they often really want to ask is, "Do I have to pay taxes on the money I'm making on eBay?"

The short answer is: "Yes, if you are making a profit"—that is, you are selling stuff for more than you originally paid for it.

If you make money selling on eBay, the IRS really doesn't care if you're a "business" or a "hobby"—it wants you to report your income (i.e., profits) from whatever it is you're doing on your tax return and pay taxes on it. The amount of money you make on eBay doesn't matter—there is no "minimum threshold" for income taxes, so even if you made one dollar in profit last year on eBay, you have to cough up the federal, state, and local taxes due on that buck.

If you are *losing* money on eBay, then it does make a difference whether you are a hobby or a business, for IRS purposes.

. . . BUT IF YOU LOSE MONEY, YOU CAN'T DEDUCT THE LOSS UNLESS YOU ARE A "BUSINESS"

Why does it matter if you are a hobby or a business if you are losing money on eBay?

Because while the IRS allows you to deduct "business losses" from your other income (e.g., the salary from your "day job"), it *does not* allow you to deduct losses from a "hobby" against your other income. You can deduct "hobby losses" only from "gains" you realized in the same or a different hobby.

Example: You sell two rare coins to local coin dealers and make $200 in profit on the sales, but you lose $600 selling other items on eBay. If your eBay selling is considered a "business," you can deduct the entire $600 in losses. If your eBay selling is considered a hobby, however, you can deduct only $200 of your eBay losses to offset the profit you made on the two rare coins.

What if you are making money on eBay but want to treat it as a "hobby" anyway, because it's just too much trouble to deal with the discipline and paperwork of running a business? Fine, but you still have to report any profits you made from selling on eBay as "income" on your personal tax return (Form 1040). You do not fill out Schedule C.

• Where Do You Report Your Income from eBay Selling? •

- If you are pursuing a hobby and making money selling on eBay, you report your income (profit) from eBay selling on the "Other Income" line of your Form 1040.
- If you are a hobby, you lose money selling on eBay, and you do not have income from any other hobby to offset it, you do not report your loss at all on your tax return—it's a "personal" loss, and you just suck it up.
- If you are a hobby, you lose money selling on eBay, and you *do* have income from another hobby to offset it, you report the loss as a "capital loss" on your tax return.
- If you are a business, whether you make money or lose money selling on eBay, you fill out Schedule C (Income or Loss from a Trade or Business) and slap it onto your Form 1040.

DECIDING WHETHER YOUR eBAY SELLING QUALIFIES AS A "BUSINESS"

The IRS doesn't give you a whole lot of guidance here. The only hard-and-fast rule is that you will be considered to be in business if you made a profit in three out of the last five tax years (including the current one). That doesn't help you when you have been selling on eBay for less than three years, and of course the IRS won't wait three years for you to figure it out!

As long as you take your eBay selling seriously, keep proper records, create and update a written business plan, and spend an appropriate amount of time on your eBay selling, there's a good chance the IRS will look at your activities as a business rather than a hobby, even if you don't meet the "three out of five years" test.

While there can never be a 100 percent guarantee that the IRS will view your online selling activities as a business, if you answer "yes" to one or more of the following questions, you may be able to treat your eBay selling activities as a business:

➤ Do you keep accurate and proper records of your income and expenses?

➤ Have you hired an accountant or bookkeeper to help you with your business records?

➤ Are you ordering goods in bulk for sale on eBay, as opposed to occasional sales of unique items?

➤ Are you selling goods on a regular basis on eBay, as opposed to only occasional or intermittent sales?

➤ Have you formed a limited liability company (LLC) or corporation for your business?

➤ Are you disciplined in the way you conduct your eBay selling (e.g., do you devote regular hours each day or week)?

➤ Do you rent office space outside of your home that you use exclusively for selling on eBay?

➤ Is it likely that you will make a profit from your eBay selling activities next year?

If you sold anything on eBay this year and lost money, you may not have a business yet. If it was your first year on eBay and you lost money, and you think you will make a profit next year from selling on eBay, you should treat that selling as a business and fill out Schedule C.

If you continue to lose money from your eBay sales each year, the IRS may consider your eBay selling a hobby and not allow you

• "Oops! I've Been in Business for Years and Didn't Know It!" •

Here's a question I get a lot at eBay University seminars: "I started selling items on eBay last year and didn't think I had to pay taxes. I thought it was only a hobby. I have since learned that I had to start paying taxes, hobby or not. I plan to file Schedule C as a 'business' and pay all taxes due for this year, but what do I do about the income I made last year? Will the IRS come back to me about that?"

You could report last year's income by filing an amendment to last year's tax return. If you do, though, you will have to pay interest and penalties on the overdue taxes, which may trigger an IRS audit to see if you've got any other unreported income you need to pay taxes on. While you clearly want to do the right thing, you don't want to wake any sleeping Rottweilers, either.

Whenever you find out that you haven't complied with a legal or tax regulation because of simple ignorance, the best advice is to get yourself into compliance going forward. Even if the IRS finds out that you really started your business last year (unlikely, but no one can predict what the IRS will or won't find out if it ever audits you), it will be a lot gentler on those who voluntarily get themselves into compliance after the fact than on people who willfully do not comply and "wait to be caught."

By all means, fill out Schedule C on this year's tax return, and pay all taxes due on your eBay income for this year. Then, consider adding last year's income to your income for this year and pay taxes "as if" it was all earned this year. That way, if the IRS discovers that you had a business last year, it will also see that you paid the taxes on last year's income (although a bit late), and you will have to pay interest and penalties only from the date you started your business (sometime last year) to the date (April 15 of next year) you paid the taxes on last year's income.

to deduct your losses, except to the extent that you have gains from other hobbies.

Because there aren't a whole lot of start-up costs in getting an eBay selling business off the ground, it's unlikely you will incur a loss in your first year of selling on eBay. Since you're going to have to pay taxes on your eBay selling eventually, why not take the steps necessary to treat it as a "real" business? That way, you can claim deductions that people with hobbies simply can't, and you'll have an incentive to look for even more creative ways to make a ton of money on eBay. For a complete listing of deductible expenses for the typical eBay seller, go to Intuit Corp.'s eBay Tax Center, online at www.taxcenter.turbotax.com/ebaytaxtips/deductiblechecklist.

It isn't always clear whether an activity is a hobby or a business for tax purposes. If you have any questions, you should ask an accountant or tax adviser. Or, at the online eBay Tax Center, you can click on the "Ask an Expert" prompt, fill in a short question box, and transmit your question to one of Intuit's eBay tax experts in Omaha, Nebraska, who will call you and answer your question *without charge.*

WHAT DOES IT COST TO START AN eBAY SELLING BUSINESS?

An eBay business is similar to any small retail business. The costs of becoming an eBay seller depend on what you are planning to sell and whether you are committed to becoming a "serious player" on the world's leading auction website.

If you're planning to sell only occasionally on eBay, you will probably be a "sole proprietor" or an informal family partnership (see Chapter 2), so there will be no legal costs to set up your business. If you decide to set up a corporation or limited liability company (LLC) for your business, it will cost roughly $400 to $800 in legal and filing fees (for an LLC), or $800 to $1,500 (for a corporation). Since you will likely be working out of your home, you won't have rental or inventory storage costs.

As for taxes, you will need to get federal and state tax ID numbers, but the government doesn't charge for those (they get their reward later on, when you start paying taxes). Similarly, eBay doesn't charge for setting up a basic selling account. So the overall cost of setting up a basic eBay selling business is as close to absolute zero as it gets. The accountant who helps you prepare your Form 1040 each year will charge only a slight additional fee for filing Schedule C (the profit-and-loss schedule you will have to tack onto your 1040 to show how much your eBay business makes each year).

After that, it all depends on how much you wish to spend for your initial inventory. If you're selling items out of your own attic or merchandise you pick up at garage sales, your inventory cost won't be that great. Be aware, though, that if you treat eBay as a garage sale, you will only get garage sale prices.

If you wish to take your eBay business seriously, you should purchase one or more software tools to help you research and automate your eBay auctions, so you'll "know what the fish are biting on." For example, TeraPeak (www.terapeak.com) provides detailed coverage of eBay auction results for $16.95 per month.

The most commonly used automation tools for eBay sellers are Selling Manager Pro ($15.95 per month) and Turbo Lister II (free), both of which can be purchased directly from eBay. It takes time to create listings on eBay, and your time is probably the biggest cost of doing business on eBay. Anything that helps you save time is worth the cost.

Other significant start-up expenses are shipping materials, a photo studio and digital camera (estimated cost: $500 to $1,000), a photo tripod (about $20), and perhaps a mannequin if you're selling jewelry. Many large department stores trash their old mannequins in a back room and will give them to you for nothing as long as you don't mind that they're not anatomically perfect.

If you're thinking of setting up an eBay Store, the costs are likely to be greater than the $15.95 per month that eBay charges for a basic storefront. While eBay offers standard templates for store layouts, consider having a Web designer create a customized storefront and listing template for a professional presentation similar to a brick-and-mortar retail website. A basic storefront, custom pages, and customized template should cost about $1,000 to $2,000, depending on where you live and how many "bells and whistles" you want to add to your basic storefront design.

You should invest heavily in education. If you can't afford a consultant at $250 an hour, find an eBay Certified Education Specialist in your area, or a local group of eBay sellers. It's important to surround yourself with people who are doing the same thing, so you can make wise choices about where you're going to spend your money. A Certified Education Specialist is a local eBay seller who has been trained by eBay to teach classes or provide consulting services for other eBay sellers (to find one near you, go to www .poweru.net/ebay/student/searchIndex.asp). A basic library of eBay "how to" books (including this one) should cost less than $250.

Probably the best way to get a handle on eBay start-up costs is to get hold of a "chart of accounts" for an eBay selling business. This is a master checklist of income and expense items that accountants and bookkeepers use when setting up eBay businesses. Allegro Accounting of Portland, Oregon, offers several "charts of accounts" for sale on eBay beginning at $14.98 (go to eBay's home page, click on Advanced Search, then click on Search Items by Seller, then type in "Allegro-Accounting"). A comprehensive list of deductible eBay expenses can be found at Intuit's eBay Tax Center (www.taxcenter.turbotax.com).

One last thing: Every small business has surprise costs, especially at the beginning, so when you do figure out how much it will cost you to set up shop on eBay, add another 20 percent or 30 percent to the total. That way the only surprises you have will be pleasant ones.

COMMON QUESTIONS

Q. *What is the dollar point at which I need to file a tax return for eBay sales?*

A. Technically, it's one dollar ($1.00) for income taxes (sorry).

If you only sold a little bit on eBay in 2005, you are not required to treat it as a business. You can report your income as "miscellaneous income" on Form 1040 (as a "hobby"), but then you won't be able to take any business deductions. If you did have significant eBay sales in 2005, though, you should consider filling out Schedule C and treating your eBay sales as a "business."

Q. *I buy and sell stuff occasionally at flea markets, and I'm thinking of selling on eBay. If I am on Social Security disability and have no other income, would I just pay taxes as a business for what I sell on eBay?*

A. You're going to have to be careful here. I'm not an expert on Social Security disability rules, but I know that if you are collecting disability from the U.S. military, you cannot make more than a certain amount each year without losing your government benefits. You need to ask if the same rule applies to Social Security disability benefits, and if it does, what the income threshold is. I advise that you speak to an accountant, tax lawyer, or (preferably) an "elder lawyer" immediately. (I realize you're probably not that old, but elder lawyers tend to know the Social Security rules backwards and forwards.)

Q. *If I have different product lines and am willing to take the time to set them up as different businesses with different tax IDs, can I deduct the ones that didn't make money and report the ones that did, rather than have my successful lines have to pay for my failures?*

A. If I understand your question correctly, you are asking if you can create separate tax IDs for the businesses that make money, report the income from each business on a Schedule C, then treat the businesses that lose money as "hobbies" and lump the losses together with your 1040 personal filing.

If that's correct, the short answer is, "Sure, why not?" Just remember that losses from a hobby cannot be deducted from your day job income; if the items you sold at a loss on eBay qualify as "capital assets," you may be able to deduct those losses against other capital gains (say, from your stock portfolio).

Q. *How do you start being a business after having run as a "hobby" for several years? How does inventory already in-house/in-stock get reflected?*

A. Start filing a Schedule C this year. You can deduct the "cost of goods sold" of any inventory you sold on eBay during 2005, but the "cost of goods sold" of any inventory you had at the close of business on December 31 cannot be deducted in 2005. You can deduct it only when the inventory actually sells, presumably sometime during 2006.

Q. *I am fairly new to eBay and just started selling used items from around the house. I am making good money—nothing in comparison to what I paid retail, of course, but still good. Do I claim my earnings next year as income for selling these used items? What part of the 1040 form do I use? I don't consider this activity a business. Do I claim as a hobby, then?*

A. It depends on whether you made money. You sold used items on eBay for more than you paid for them. If you made money, you might want to consider filling out Schedule C to your 1040 and treating this money-making activity as a "business"—that way you can deduct expenses.

If you prefer to treat your eBay selling as a hobby, you should determine if the items you sold qualify as "capital assets" (your accountant can help you with that). If they do, you can take the loss as a capital loss on your 1040 and deduct the loss against other capital gains, such as income from a stock portfolio, but *not* against ordinary income (e.g., wages from your day job).

CHAPTER 2

Setting Up Your eBay Selling Business

So you're ready to start a business selling merchandise on eBay. This nine-step process will help you make key decisions on everything from picking a name for your business, to accounting for sales, to making sure you've set up your business legally (while getting the best tax advantages).

STEP 1: FIND THE RIGHT NAME

It used to be so simple to find a name for your business. All you had to do was travel to another part of the country, find a similar business with a name that you liked, and use the same name for your business. Not so long ago, "all business was local." If you ran an antiques or collectibles business, your customers came from within a twenty-mile radius of your store, and that was that. What were the odds that the other business would even find out you had "appropriated" its name, let alone care? After all, an antiques shop in Connecticut wasn't competing with an antiques shop in California.

But in the words of the old Monkees' song, "that was then, this is now." The Internet and online commerce has changed all that, and it's tougher than ever before to find a name for your eBay business that won't get you into trouble. Today, that California antiques shop probably has a website, an eBay Store, and heaven only knows what else. Its customers come from all over the globe. It has probably trademarked its name, which prohibits you from using it. If it finds out you have "ripped off" its name, no matter how innocently it happened, it will come after you with a baseball bat.

Now, let's say you do find a cool name for your eBay business. How do you go about checking it out to make sure it's available? Basically, there are several things you must do.

First Stop: U.S. Trademark Office

If someone else has registered a name as a federal trademark, you simply cannot use it, period. End of story. World without end, amen.

To find out if someone has trademarked the name you want, go to www.uspto.gov—the website of the U.S. Patent and Trademark Office—click on "trademarks," and follow the prompts. If someone else has trademarked the name you want, find another name.

If your search shows that the name has not been trademarked, should you go ahead and trademark it yourself? By trademarking the name, you can ensure that no one else anywhere in the United States can use it without your permission (see Chapter 15). But beware: The trademark office website gets pretty "user vicious" if you try to register a trademark online. The site will ask you several questions for which there are very precise legal answers, and unless you are intimately familiar with the U.S. Trademark Register and its rules and regulations, you will almost certainly get something wrong that will be very difficult to undo later on. Therefore, it's worthwhile to find a lawyer who specializes in trademark matters.

Second Stop: Network Solutions

If you have a really cool name for your business, you want to make sure it is available for use as an Internet domain name or URL.

• Picking the Right "Classification" •

When you register a trademark, you cannot use it for all categories of products and services. You can use it only for the products and services you specify in your registration. So an eBay seller and a funeral parlor in the same town could conceivably register the same name as a federal trademark, and each company would be granted the right to use the name for its own business.

When you register a trademark online at www.uspto.gov, at some point you will prompted to describe your "product classifications." These are listed by number in the U.S. Trademark Register (a publication you have never even heard about until this moment). What the trademark office site is looking for are those exact classification descriptions. If you use any other descriptions of the businesses you are engaged in, the site will assign you to several different classifications in an effort to make what you told it fit within the register's classifications, and you will be asked to pay a humongous fee for the privilege of registering your trademark in all of these classifications.

While the U.S. Trademark Office website is a great way to find out if someone else has a federally registered trademark, it isn't the best way for a newbie business owner to register a trademark. If you really must get a trademark for your business name, have an attorney handle the online registration for you. It won't be cheap—in fact, it will cost you somewhere between $500 and $1,500, depending on where you live and how extensively the lawyer has to "search" the trademark records to make sure the name you want is really available—but at least you will know it's been done the right way.

Go to the Network Solutions website (www.networksolutions.com) and follow the prompts to see if the dot-com (".com") address is available.

It is getting harder and harder to get dot-com domain names, as just about all of the good names have been snapped up (often by speculators who don't plan to set up a website themselves but will happily sell you the name for a few thousand dollars or so). If the .com address for your name has been taken, should you use one of the "lesser" domain registries such as .net, .biz, or .US? I would say no. When people search on the Internet for a business, they look for a dot-com address.

If the dot-com address is available for the name you want, grab it! If it isn't, consider using a different name for your website URL, one that is easy to remember. A good rule for naming a URL is to use the name of the merchandise you sell on eBay rather than the name of your company. For instance, FurryStuffedAnimals.com is a lot easier for folks to remember (and type) than Flibbertigibbet-AntiqueToys.com.

One more thing: EBay really hates it if you include the words "eBay" or "-Bay" as part of your Internet domain name. I know, I know, a lot of folks do that, but you really shouldn't. Legally it's "trademark infringement," and if eBay catches you, it has every right to make you shut down your domain name—not a good thing, especially years from now when you've built a huge "brand" on that website with thousands of customers worldwide that have gotten used to that name.

Third Stop: Secretary of State's Office

If no one has trademarked the name you want to use for your business, you must next find out if someone in your state is using it for his corporation or limited liability company (LLC). Your state secretary of state's office will not allow two corporations or LLCs to have the exact same name. To find your state secretary of state's website, type "[name of state] department of state" into your favorite search engine, or go to www.iaca.org (IACA—International Association of Commercial Administrators—is a trade association of state secretaries of state and their staffs). Click on the Members link, then click on IACA Directory. You should see a list of the URLs of the secretary of state offices in all fifty states, as well as U.S. territories and possessions.

Fourth Stop: Your County Clerk's or Town Clerk's Office

If your state secretary of state's office database shows that no one in your state is using the name you want for a corporation or LLC, you still have to make sure that no one in your county (or city or town) is using the same name for a sole proprietorship, partnership, or other unincorporated business. Generally, when you use a trade name or DBA (for "doing business as") for your business, you are required to file a registration form with your county clerk's office (or your town or city clerk's office if there is no county government where you live) so that no two businesses in the same geographic area will be using exactly the same name.

Most county clerk's offices have a website, but you probably will not be able to search for your name there. You will have to make a personal visit to the clerk's office and do your search manually.

Fifth and Last Stop: The Internet

Don't forget to type the name into all of the major search engines and see what shows up. Chances are somebody, somewhere is already using the same name, but there are "orders of magnitude" here.

If you are setting up an antiques shop in Connecticut and the only other person using the same name is a small business in Hong Kong, you are probably safe in using the name. If, however, your name has been selected by a Fortune 1000 corporation as the trade name for its latest product . . . well, I would pick another name if I were you.

Avoiding Names That Are Too "Cute"

It's tempting sometimes to pick a name that will resonate with your customers because it reminds them of another—much larger—company. So, for example, if you are selling teeny tiny rolls of toilet tissue (for people with boats or recreational vehicles who have trouble storing standard-size tissue), it may be very tempting to call your company "MicroSoft Tissues." I would resist this temptation at all costs. Even though you may not legally be infringing on the software giant's trademark (to my knowledge, they are not in the tissue business), I'm fairly certain Microsoft Corp. will not be happy about its name being used on toilet tissue and will do everything in its power (and that's a lot) to shut your little business down before it starts.

Naming Your eBay Store

If you are thinking about setting up an eBay Store, do not—I repeat *do not*—use your company name as the store "header." Why?

Example: Let's say you sell antique mechanical banks on eBay. You want to call your company "Flibbertigibbet Antiques." (That's a real word, by the way. It means "a silly, scatterbrained, habitually talkative person"—and, of course, it does not refer to any actual person, living or dead.)

Do you think anyone searching for mechanical banks on eBay, or on Google or Yahoo, is going to even think to type in the word *flibbertigibbet,* even assuming they can spell it properly? I think not.

• About Antique Mechanical Banks •

You will learn a lot about antique mechanical banks in this book. They will appear frequently in my examples. Why? Well, a number of reasons:

- I know a fair amount about them.
- Just about everyone knows a mechanical bank when they see one.
- They're fun to talk about.
- There's a lot to know about antique mechanical banks—entire books have been written about them—and you have to know a lot about them to sell them effectively on eBay.
- Mechanical banks are frustratingly difficult to describe accurately on eBay, because the vast majority of them have had "work done" to them— repainting, repairs, replaced parts, you name it.
- There is a very active and well-organized collecting community for mechanical banks, and at least one collectors' association—the Mechanical Bank Collectors of America (www.mbca.com)—with an annual convention and quarterly magazine.
- People who collect mechanical banks are generally fanatics who know a lot more about them than the average eBay seller. If you ever put one up for sale on eBay, prepare for some of the most interesting (and detailed) e-mail queries you will ever receive on eBay.

• Fictitious Names, Trade Names, and DBAs •

Any name you use in your business that does not appear on your birth certificate or Social Security card is a fictitious name—also known as a trade name or DBA (for "doing business as"). When you use a DBA, you introduce yourself to vendors, customers, and others as "Cliff Ennico, doing business as Flibbertigibbet Antiques."

In virtually all states, DBAs must be registered, either with your county clerk's office or with the secretary of state's office in your state. But be careful. Registering a DBA does not give you any legal right to use the name (only a federally registered trademark can do that). If someone else in town is using the name Flibbertigibbet Antiques and finds out you're using the same name, the other party has every right to complain about it.

So why register a DBA name at all? Because the law requires you to do so. The purpose of DBA registration laws is to prevent fraud. Otherwise, if you are sued, you could simply deny that Flibbertigibbet Antiques was your business name.

Even corporations, LLCs, and other entities can have DBAs. For example: Worldwide Widget Corporation dba Flibbertigibbet Antiques. When corporations and LLCs use DBAs, they are usually required to register the DBA with the state secretary of state's office.

Your eBay Store "header" should contain all of the important keywords (see Chapter 5) that will attract the major search engines and eBay's own search software. So, if you are selling antique mechanical banks on eBay, your header should read something like "Mechanical Banks Antique Toys Cast Iron Antiques." Your company name can, of course, appear on the "welcome" page of your eBay Store.

STEP 2: IF YOU NEED A LICENSE, GET ONE

Now that you have a name for your eBay selling business, you next need to figure out if you will need any sort of license or permit to sell the stuff you want to sell on eBay.

Typical Licenses eBay Sellers Will Need

The vast majority of merchandise you can sell on eBay will not require any sort of license. The most common licenses you will need to get are:

> ➢ A real estate broker's license, if you plan to sell other people's real estate on eBay and get paid a commission for doing so
> ➢ A motor vehicle dealer's license, if you plan to sell other people's motor vehicles (e.g., trucks, cars, vans, RVs, yachts, and sometimes motorcycles) on eBay and get paid a commission for doing so

• Getting a "Business License" •

Every once in a while someone in an eBay University program asks if it is necessary to get a "business license" before setting up an eBay selling business.

Strictly speaking, there is no such thing as a business license. I'm not aware of any state that requires a license or permit just for the privilege of setting up a business.

There are a number of things, though, that might be called a "business license" in casual conversation but are actually something else entirely. Here are some possibilities:

• In some states the fictitious name or DBA certificate you file with the county clerk's office to let the world know you are doing business under an "alias" is referred to informally (although inaccurately) as a business license.

• In some states your state sales and use tax permit (the document you get back from your state tax authority when you register for state sales and use taxes) is called a business permit or business license.

• In some counties, you may be required to get a license or permit from the local zoning authority to legally do business out of your home (see Chapter 10).

None of those situations may apply to you, so talk to your accountant or a local business lawyer before you presume that there's some sort of business license out there you need to get before you begin selling on eBay. Chances are there is no such license, and your accountant or lawyer will be able to clear things up.

State and local "license requirements" are all over the place, but here's a rule of thumb: Generally, state and local governments require licenses to sell a product or service if the product or service would injure someone—either personally or financially—if it were abused. For example, virtually all states require licenses to sell alcohol, tobacco, or firearms, or to engage in the professions of law, medicine, barbering, and stockbroking. Some states require licenses to sell used manufacturing or industrial equipment (a growing category on eBay, by the way). The idea, again, is that if you're selling large or complex equipment that could potentially hurt someone, you will need a license to sell it.

How do you find out about your particular state's requirements? Every state has set up an online licensing center where all of the state government agencies have combined forces and listed every type of license you need in that state. For example, the Connecticut Licensing Info Center is located at www.ct-clic.com. A list of all fifty state "licensing centers" is available at the website of the U.S. Small Business Administration, at www.sbaonline.sba.gov/hotlist/license.html.

Do You Need an Auctioneer's License to Sell on eBay?

It's no secret that Internet commerce—including eBay—has cost the states billions of dollars in lost sales tax revenue. Because the vast majority of e-commerce transactions are interstate or international in nature, states cannot legally collect sales taxes on them. And if there's one thing you can count on when it comes to taxes, it's that the tax authorities in just about every state are busting their brain cells looking for creative and legal ways to tax e-commerce, including eBay.

A couple of years ago a handful of states—mostly in the Midwest—passed laws requiring people to obtain "auctioneer's licenses" in order to sell goods in "online auctions" (these laws didn't mention eBay by name, but we all know who they had in mind). So, in order to sell on eBay in these states, you would have to fill out a detailed application form, pay a "license fee" (usually a couple of hundred bucks), and take an "auctioneer's course" at a local community college, where you would learn such incredibly useful e-commerce skills as hog calling, cattle brand identification, and tobacco leaf analysis.

Thanks to the unstinting efforts of the eBay Government Relations team, most of these laws have since been amended to specifically exclude eBay sellers, on the grounds that eBay sellers aren't really "auctioneers" in any meaningful sense.

But if you live in a state where the law hasn't been clarified, you may want to talk to an attorney before getting too deeply involved in an eBay selling business—especially if you plan to become an eBay Trading Assistant, run an eBay consignment shop, or otherwise take consignments of other people's goods (see Chapter 14). Those are the people the state licensing boards are most concerned about, because of the special relationship of trust—called a "fiduciary relationship"—that arises legally when you take possession of someone else's goods for sale on eBay.

To find out if your state is thinking about, or has adopted, a law that would require you to get an auctioneer's license to sell on eBay, go to www.ebaymainstreet.com, the website of eBay's Government Relations team, and click on Find Your State.

STEP 3: FORM A LEGAL ENTITY

Once you have picked a good name for your eBay selling business and obtained all of the licenses and permits you need to get going, you should at least think about whether it would be advantageous to form a legal entity for your business. Forming a corporation or limited liability company (LLC) for your business protects you against legal liability and may also give you tax advantages. It may also help you look like a "big" business, which isn't a bad thing.

The Big Trade-Off: Liability Protection vs. Ease of Operation

There is no one correct way to set up a business legally. Most states offer five or six different ways you can do it, and they all involve trade-offs of one sort or another. The biggest tradeoff is "protection against liability" versus "ease of operation." In plain English, the more protection against legal liability you need to have in your business, the more legal mumbo jumbo and paperwork you are going to have to put up with.

Let's take a simple example. If you're selling bobblehead dolls on eBay and somebody complains because the one you shipped isn't the one that appeared on the auction page, are you really going to get sued over that? Probably not. As a good member of the eBay community, you will promptly ship the correct item to the buyer and issue a refund if the correct item isn't available, or (worst case) the buyer will "flame" you by posting negative feedback on you. People rarely sue other people, especially in distant states, over a $10 bobblehead doll.

Now, let's pretend you're selling firearms on eBay. (Yes, yes, I know eBay rules don't allow that, but it's the clearest example I can think of, okay?) On a recent trip to Belgium, you dig up an unexploded artillery shell from World War I (farmers in Belgium, so I'm told, dig them up all the time). You bring it back to the United States and sell it on eBay. Unbeknownst to you, the ordnance is still "live." When the buyer opens the package, the shell goes off and destroys not only the buyer but the entire apartment building in which the buyer lives. The buyer's next of kin is almost certain to leave negative feedback in this situation, but—c'mon, people—this is certain to be a massive class-action lawsuit, if not a criminal investigation by the FBI and Homeland Security.

All kidding aside, the point here is simply that the amount of protection against liability you need when selling on eBay depends largely on what you're selling. If you're selling artillery shells (or classic cars or industrial machinery), you will need significantly more protection against liability than someone selling bobblehead dolls will need.

There are some wonderful legal entities, or ways to structure your company, that will protect you against just about any kind of legal liability as long as you're careful about how you use them.

The problem is that they're somewhat complicated and require lots of legal paperwork to keep them alive and kicking. If you are like most eBay sellers I know, you would rather cut off your right arm than get bogged down in legal paperwork.

There are also some wonderful legal entities that don't require lots of paperwork—you can operate them very informally, without a lot of fuss and bother. The problem is that they don't give you as much protection against liability. That's what I mean when I talk about trading ease of operation for protection against liability, and vice versa.

Let's now take a quick look at some of the ways you can set up your eBay selling business legally. In virtually all states I'm aware of, there are five basic choices (as well as some exotic species in some states that we won't be discussing in this book):

- ➢ The sole proprietorship
- ➢ The partnership
- ➢ The regular or "C" corporation
- ➢ The subchapter "S" corporation
- ➢ The limited liability company (LLC)

For a simple, easy-to-read chart comparing the different choices, see www.mycorporation.com/forms.htm. You can also download my own infamous "Demystifying the Business Organization," the five-page outline that has launched more than 10,000 small businesses, at www.cliffennico.com. (On the home page, go to the Click Here prompt that appears right below the question, "Not sure whether your business should be a sole proprietorship, limited liability company (LLC), or corporation?")

The Sole Proprietorship

If you are a human being over the age of twenty-one (or whatever the age of majority is in your state) and you have a pulse, you are a sole proprietorship—or, to use the IRS definition, "an individual engaged in a trade or business."

• Speaking of Insurance . . . •

Every small business should have at least an "umbrella" liability policy, for reasons that will become clear later. If you work out of your home, your homeowner's policy probably doesn't provide this coverage, so you will have to purchase a "home office rider" to your homeowner's policy, which is usually (but not always) the best deal.

As for the amount, I always recommend that you purchase at least $1MM/$2MM—that means $1 million per occurrence and $2 million overall. (Whenever anyone gets hurt, they never sue for less than $1 million.) Be sure to shop around, and get the most coverage you can afford.

Also, you should seriously consider taking out disability insurance. Yes, it's expensive, but it can save your life if an accident puts you out of commission for several months. By definition, when you're a sole proprietorship, you're "performing without a net" because there's no one to back you up if something bad happens, like if your motorcycle hits a tree or if you drop a thirty-five-pound rock on your foot while gardening—don't laugh, these actual events have happened to my law clients.

What's good about a sole proprietorship? Well, you don't have to pay a lawyer to set you up—your mom and dad did that a long time ago.

The paperwork for a sole proprietorship is also very simple. Each year you will have to file Schedule C (income or loss from a trade or business) on your Form 1040.

Also, if you are using a trade name for your business (such as "Cliff's Antiques" or any name that doesn't appear on your birth certificate), you will be required to file a "trade name certificate" (sometimes called a DBA, for "doing business as") with your town or county clerk's office. This is a very simple form, however, and you won't have to pay an attorney to help you prepare it. Just go to your town or county clerk's office, get the printed form, fill it out and sign it before a notary, and pay a $5 to $10 filing fee. That's it.

Keep in mind that filing a trade name certificate doesn't give you any legal right to use that name for your business—to get that, you have to register your name (if you can) with the U.S. Patent and Trademark Office in Washington, DC (www.uspto.gov). The trade name certificate is just a notice to the world that if anyone is ever hurt by "Cliff's Antiques" at your home address, you are the person to be sued.

Sole proprietorships are really simple to operate, and the vast majority of eBay sellers are sole proprietorships. The problem? Remember the big trade-off? Sole proprietorships are easy to operate, but they give you absolutely no protection against liability. If someone sues you and you are a sole proprietor, they can grab not only your business assets, but everything you own (your house, your car, your stamp collection, etc.). With a sole proprietorship, there is no legal separation between you and your business—you stand naked to the world (although you can purchase liability insurance to manage that risk).

The Partnership

Now let's talk about partnerships. If you are in business with someone else (including a family member or spouse) and are sharing profits and losses with that someone, congratulations! You have a partnership! Believe it or not, the law does not require you to have a written partnership agreement in order to create a partnership (although you are a fool if you don't have one). Partnerships are so easy to form that you can actually create one by accident.

The Accidental Partnership. Here's how it happens. You go into business and hire a family member to work for you. Instead of paying him a regular salary, you pay him a variable amount each week, depending on how well the business does. Later on, you and the family member have a falling out (say, it's your spouse, and you get divorced), and the family member's lawyer sues you, claiming a percentage of all profits from the business going forward because you were partners. Without solid paperwork (such as W-2s and 1099s you file with the IRS showing the amounts you paid the family member), this will be a tough case to defend.

The moral of the story: Whenever you are in business with someone and are sharing in the profits with that someone, make sure to get something in writing with that someone that says you are not partners! Otherwise you risk getting involved in what lawyers call an "inadvertent partnership."

Partnership Taxes and "Phantom Income." Partnerships are easy to form—you can legally form a partnership with a handshake. What's more, taxes are easy to figure out for partnerships. Partnerships are not taxable entities, meaning that they don't pay taxes. Everything the partnership makes "passes through" the partners and is divided according to the partnership shares each partner owns. For example, let's say you and I are 50/50 partners. The partnership makes $100 in net income (basically, sales less operating expenses) at the end of the year. You have to report $50 as income on your tax return (Form 1040) come April 15, and I have to report the other $50 on my tax return (Form 1040). It's that simple.

Well, not quite—there is one little wrinkle here. Let's say you and I decide to keep that $100 in the partnership checking account, because we need to buy something expensive right after January 1. Come April 15, you and I still have to report $50 each as income on our tax returns and pay the taxes on that $50. Lawyers call this "phantom income," meaning we have to pay taxes on income we never actually saw in the form of cash money. If the phantom income is only $100, of course, it's not a big deal. But add a couple of zeroes at the end . . . you see what I mean.

All legal entities that "pass through" income to the owners, like partnerships do, have the phantom income problem. With a pass-through, you can't retain earnings from one year to the next without paying taxes on the earnings.

Other than the phantom income problem (which may not be a problem at all, if you distribute all the cash in your partnership checking account to the partners at the end of each year, as many partnerships do), what's bad about a partnership? Plenty. Partners in a partnership have no protection against legal liability, and it's actually worse than it is for sole proprietors. "Wait a minute!" I can hear some of you saying. "You just said a couple of paragraphs ago that sole proprietors are 'naked to the world.' How can you be more naked than totally naked?"

Joint and Several Liability. Simple. When you're a sole proprietor, you are legally liable only for the things you yourself screw up. When you're in a partnership, you are liable not only for your own screw-ups, but for all your partners' screw-ups as well. If one partner makes a mistake and the partnership gets sued, all partners go down together and lose their houses. Lawyers call this "joint and several liability."

Knowing what you now know, how many of you out there in a partnership still want to be partners with your partners? Partnerships are generally not a good way to organize an eBay selling business, especially if your partner is someone you don't know intimately well.

The Corporation

That brings us to the corporation—specifically, the "regular" or "subchapter C" corporation. It's called that because corporations are taxed under Subchapter C of the U.S. Internal Revenue Code of 1986, just in case anyone ever asks you at a cocktail party and you want to show off.

Unlike a partnership, a corporation is a "legal entity," meaning it has a life separate from the people that own shares in the corporation. If you and I form a corporation, we are having a baby, although a baby that pays taxes from the day it's born.

If you're careful and treat your corporation with the respect it deserves, it should protect you from personal liability if someone sues you.

Limited Liability. What's good about a corporation? In two words (cue the neon lights): LIMITED LIABILITY. When you form a corporation and put money into it, only that money is at risk. So if you screw something up and the corporation gets sued, the bad guys can get at the corporation's money, but they can't get to any of your personal assets (such as your house, jewelry, etc.).

There are some exceptions, of course. While forming a corporation will protect you legally against your business partners' screw-ups, you are still liable for your own negligence or intentional acts. So if I'm negotiating aggressively with a vendor and push him down a flight of stairs in an effort to get him to lower his price a few bucks, I won't be able to avoid personal liability because I was acting on behalf of my corporation. This is why you still need liability insurance to cover your own "acts and omissions," even if you have a corporation.

"Piercing the Corporate Veil." There's another loophole when it comes to a corporation's limiting your legal liability. If you form a corporation but continue doing business in your personal name, the government takes your corporation away at some point and leaves you exposed to personal liability as if you never formed it in the first place. When you have a corporation, you have to make sure and "stick it in people's faces" so they *know* they are dealing with a corporation and not you personally. If I think I'm dealing with "Joe Blow," then all my checks are payable to Joe Blow and are processed through Joe Blow's personal checking account, and all invoices come from Joe Blow. That means Joe Blow will not be able to claim at a later point that I was really dealing with "Joseph M. Blow Incorporated." If you don't use your corporation status every day you're in business, you lose it sooner or later.

Lawyers have a lovely name for when somebody is able to shove your corporation to one side and grab all your personal assets in a lawsuit because you didn't treat the corporation with enough respect. They call it "piercing the corporate veil."

How do you avoid getting your "veil pierced" if you have a corporation? Here are the basics:

➤ Make sure you do all of the paperwork that a corporation requires (which I'll get to in a moment).

➤ Make sure your corporation name appears on all business cards, office stationery, flat mailing labels, and other documents you send to your customers, suppliers, and others.

➤ Make sure the corporation has its own checking account, that all checks are made out to your corporation (not to you personally), and that all checks are processed through your corporation's checking account.

➤ Make sure to sign all documents as an agent of the corporation, as follows:

Cliff Ennico, The LLC Guy, Inc.
By: _____ [your signature goes here]
Cliff Ennico, President

Legal Paperwork. So what's bad about having a corporation? In six words: "expensive to operate; tons of paperwork." Like a human baby, a corporation needs food to survive, and what corporations love to eat is paper—tons of paper. When you have a corporation, you have to be very disciplined about doing the paperwork necessary to keep your corporation alive. If you fail to do the necessary paperwork, you risk getting your "veil pierced" if someone sues you.

So how can you get help keeping in compliance—without having to manage the paper mound? And what kinds of paperwork do you have to do when you have a corporation? Here are some key points:

➤ You'll need an attorney to do the paperwork for you. Most attorneys will charge anywhere from $800 to $2,000 to form a corporation (when you see the stack of papers your attorney will ask you to sign, you will understand why it's so expensive).

➤ Since the corporation is a legal entity separate from its owners, it gets to file its own income tax return (Form 1120) by March 15 each year.

➤ Whenever the corporation makes a decision, you have to fill out forms (called "minutes" or "resolutions") authorizing the corporation to do it.

➤ You usually have to file an annual report with your state secretary of state's office each year, and pay a filing fee ranging from $25 to $150.

➤ Some states (e.g., Connecticut) have an annual tax on corporations that must be paid regardless of whether you made money that year.

"Incorporate for Only $100" Scams. "But Cliff, I see ads on the Internet from folks who say they will form a corporation for me and charge me only $100." Don't believe it. While some do-it-yourself incorporation services are extremely reputable (as will be discussed later), there are a lot of fly-by-night outfits on the Internet that will charge you $100 just to file a one-page Certificate of Incorporation (a corporation's "birth certificate") with the appropriate government agency, and then conveniently forget to tell you about all of the other paperwork (such as tax registrations and follow-up state filings) you must do to get the corporation set up properly. So years later you get a nasty letter from your state attorney general's office (or the IRS, or your state tax authority) accusing you of operating an illegal business, and you wonder why . . .

Corporation Taxes. How is a corporation taxed? Because a corporation is a legal entity separate from its owners, it has to pay taxes on the income it earns—although, under current tax law (subject to change at any moment), it pays taxes at a much lower rate than you probably do. So, for example, the first $100,000 of a corporation's net income is taxed at only 15 percent by the IRS.

There is no "phantom income" problem with corporations. Once you pay the corporation tax on the income it earns, it doesn't "pass through" to your personal return as long as it sits in your corporation's checking account. If you don't need your eBay selling income to live on, forming a corporation and leaving all of your income in the corporation checking account is a good way to shelter 20 percent or more of your income from taxes if the corporation is set up properly.

Here's the catch, though. Let's say you *do* need the income from your eBay selling business to live on, and you withdraw money periodically from the corporation checking account to pay your personal bills. The IRS views those withdrawals as "wages" or a "dividend" and taxes you again on the amounts you withdraw, this time at your personal tax rate. This is why some experts refer to corporations as having a "double taxation" problem: A corporation's income is taxed once when it is earned, and again (usually at a higher rate) when it is distributed to the corporation's owners. This can get expensive, especially when you factor state and local income taxes into the equation. In some states, the "tax bite" can be as much as 50 percent.

There are a number of ways to reduce the tax bite on corporation income, but you will need a clever accountant to do the necessary paperwork. For example, you can put yourself on the corporation's payroll as an employee and pay yourself a regular salary. In this case, you still pay taxes on the money you draw out of the corporation, but the corporation gets a deduction for your wages, which offsets the corporation's net income and may "zero out" the corporation so it shows no income for the year.

To sum things up, with a corporation you get some protection against legal liability, but you pay a price for it in the form of high start-up and operating expenses, income that is taxed twice, and lots of legal paperwork to deal with. Still, if you're making tons of money selling on eBay, it may be worth your while to set up a corporation for the business, because you can offset the corporation's income with literally hundreds of business deductions that are a lot easier for corporations to take than individual business owners.

The Subchapter S Corporation

In 1953, Congress passed Subchapter S of the Internal Revenue Code creating a new type of legal entity—usually referred to simply as the "S corporation."

An S corporation is a regular corporation that elects to be taxed as if it were a partnership. Any regular or C corporation can become an S corporation by filing IRS Form 2553 during the first three months of the calendar year in which S corporation status is desired (in some states, including New York, you may also have to file a similar form with your state tax authority to claim subchapter S status from state income taxes). Once you elect to be an S corporation, you can revert to a regular or C corporation at any time, but if you do, you are prohibited from electing subchapter S status again for three years.

Advantages and Disadvantages. An S corporation offers exactly the same protection against legal liability that a regular or C corporation does, with the added benefit of a simplified tax structure.

What's good about an S corporation? Two things: limited liability and a "pass-through" tax structure. Because S corporations pay no taxes (in this respect they are just like partnerships), there is no double taxation of income as there is with a C corporation.

S corporations do have their problems, though. Because they are corporations, they are expensive to form and operate, and there is a ton of paperwork you will have to deal with on an ongoing basis. While S corporations do not pay taxes, they must file Form 1120-S with the IRS each March 15 on the preceding calendar year's income. And because S corporation income passes through to the corporation's owners, you have the phantom income problem.

Some "Icky Rules." What's more, because Congress decided a long time ago that only small businesses could take advantage of the S corporation structure, there are a number of "icky rules" you have to keep in mind when you own an S corporation. Violate one of them and you lose your subchapter S status. You're still a corporation, and you don't lose your limited liability protection, but now you have to go back, redo all of your corporation tax returns from the time you violated the particular rule to the present time, and pay all the additional taxes you should have paid all those years, along with interest and penalties—not a good thing.

Some of the "icky rules" for S corporations are pretty easy to deal with. For example, S corporations cannot have more than 100 owners (you would love to have that problem, wouldn't you?). And S corporations cannot issue preferred stock (unless you're a high-flying technology start-up looking for venture capital, there's no reason for you to issue preferred stock).

But here's a tough one: All S corporation owners must be natural human beings (no corporations or other entities allowed, with a few minor exceptions) and must be either U.S. citizens or green-card holders. The government does not want any "foreigners" owning any piece of our S corporations.

So let's say you're selling a ton of stuff in France through a French distributor. You want to make the distributor a part of your company so she can grow as your company grows. With an S corporation, you can pay your French distributor tons of money in salary, commissions, or bonuses, but you can't give her stock in your company. If you do, you blow your "S corporation election" and revert to being a regular or C corporation.

To sum up, with an S corporation you get limited liability plus a simplified pass-through tax structure. The price you pay for those benefits: expense, lots of paperwork to deal with, the "phantom income" problem, and lots of "icky rules" to have to keep in the back of your head.

The Limited Liability Company (LLC)

That brings us, at last, to the limited liability company, or LLC.

PLEASE DO NOT REFER TO THIS ENTITY AS A "LIMITED LIABILITY CORPORATION," AS MANY PEOPLE DO. THERE IS NO SUCH THING AS A "LIMITED LIABILITY CORPORATION." YOU ARE EITHER A "LIMITED LIABILITY COMPANY" OR A "CORPORATION." YOU CANNOT BE BOTH.

There—I'm glad I got that off my chest. Think of an LLC as an S corporation, but without all of the "icky rules" you have to remember with S corporations. An LLC, like an S corporation, gives you limited liability and a simplified pass-through tax structure. Unlike an S corporation, though (but like a partnership), an LLC is relatively inexpensive to form (most attorneys I know charge $500 or less), and if you have partners you can operate an LLC informally, without having to fill out all the legal paperwork that corporations require.

LLCs vs. Corporations

"So, Cliff," you ask, "why didn't you tell us about the LLC about ten pages ago?" You are thinking, no doubt, that this clearly is the way to set up your eBay selling business. You don't want to have to deal with legal paperwork, you don't want to pay a huge fee for lawyers to set the thing up, and you want some protection against liability. Sounds like the LLC is the perfect "trifecta," giving you all three of the things you want in a legal entity. Why would you want to know about any of the other options?

Well, not so fast, folks. The LLC is a pretty decent way to set up a small business, especially a simple retail or service business such as eBay selling. But it's not perfect. Remember that there are no "perfect" ways to set up any business. They all involve tradeoffs of one sort or another.

Disadvantages of LLCs. Like all legal entities that offer pass-through tax treatment, LLCs have the phantom income problem. Also, a growing number of states require LLC owners to pay an annual tax for the privilege of doing business as an LLC (in Connecticut, for example, it's a "flat tax" of $250 a year), whether or not your LLC actually made any money during the year.

For most eBay sellers, the choice will be between forming an LLC or a corporation (either a regular or subchapter S corporation). While the LLC is a "perfect fit" for many eBay sellers, there are certain circumstances in which a corporation may be preferable.

"Small Business" Stereotype. For one thing, LLCs often convey a "mom and pop" or "small potatoes" image. This has nothing to do with the law, but with the way some people (especially investors) look at them. If you have a fast-growing eBay business and are looking at possibly bringing on some professional investors down the road, forming an LLC may actually put you at a

disadvantage because professional investors won't take it seriously. A corporation (either regular or subchapter S) is preferable in this situation.

Expensive in Some States. In some states, including New York and California, LLCs are actually more expensive to form than corporations. When forming a New York LLC, you have to publish a "legal notice" (similar to a classified ad) in two newspapers of general circulation in each county where the LLC has a physical place of business—that can get really expensive, especially in New York City. In California, LLCs are subject to an annual flat tax of $800, which must be paid whether or not the LLC makes money each year.

Not-So-Same Level of Protection Against Liability. You will also hear some accountants and lawyers tell you that an LLC does not give you the same level of protection against legal liability that corporations do. This isn't true, strictly speaking, but because the LLC is a relatively new entity and we lawyers don't have hundreds of years of case law telling us exactly when a court will "pierce the veil" and allow someone to sue LLC owners personally, you should take any such advice seriously.

Payment of Self-Employment Taxes. Also, the owners of an LLC (as with any legal structure where taxes pass through to the owners) have to withhold income taxes and pay "self-employment taxes" on the income they earn. Self-employment taxes are the Social Security and Medicare taxes that used to be withheld from your paycheck when you worked for someone else and that you now have to withhold and pay yourself, usually in "estimated tax" payments four times a year. (See Chapter 12 for a more detailed discussion of how to pay yourself when you own an LLC.)

If you have a regular or subchapter S corporation, you can reduce your self-employment tax burden by putting yourself on the corporation's payroll and paying yourself a regular salary, withholding taxes from each paycheck as you go. This way, you are shifting 50 percent of the self-employment tax burden onto your corporation, leading to a reduced tax bill. If you pay yourself a sufficiently large salary, you may also be able to avoid having to pay quarterly estimated tax payments—one of the biggest headaches any self-employed person has to face.

The owners of an LLC, on the other hand, are not legally allowed to take regular salaries and withhold taxes from their paychecks (although many LLC owners do so in practice, as a way of avoiding having to deal with quarterly estimated tax payments), and so they are subject to the full self-employment tax load, which can be as much as 15.3 percent of your eBay selling income.

What should you do? Still can't decide between a corporation and an LLC? You should talk to a lawyer or accountant and get some one-on-one advice. But here are some rules of thumb to guide you if the decision really comes down to a 50/50 call:

➤ If you are in New York, California, or another state where it is more generally expensive to form an LLC than a corporation, set your eBay business up as a corporation to save on the start-up costs.

➤ If you expect to make tons of money right away on eBay, you will probably need the tax advantages that corporations give you and should set up as a corporation from "day one" to get them.

➤ In all other cases, set it up as an LLC. Why? Because if you form an LLC and realize later you made a mistake, it's fairly easy and inexpensive to convert your LLC into a corporation. Going the other way (from corporation to LLC) is much more expensive, since you have to dissolve your corporation, distribute all of your assets to yourself personally, form the new LLC, and then contribute your business assets to the LLC, incurring taxes at a couple of points along the way.

Using a "Do-It-Yourself" Incorporation Service

If you're thinking of setting up a corporation or limited liability company (LLC) for a small retail business, you probably already know that attorneys charge a bloody fortune to do the paperwork. If you surf the Web a lot, you'll see countless websites that offer to set up a corporation (usually in Delaware or Nevada) for under $200. Seems too good a deal to be true, right? How do you know if these services are legitimate and, if they are, why not use one of them instead of an attorney?

There is nothing wrong with using a do-it-yourself service to set up a corporation or LLC, but be careful. An online service may give you a brochure or DVD illustrating the differences between corporations and LLCs generally, but they won't give you one-on-

one advice. That's considered "practicing law" or "practicing accountancy," and only a licensed professional can do that.

When looking to set up a corporation or LLC for your small business, it's best to consult with a lawyer *and* an accountant to determine the type of entity (corporation, S corporation, or LLC) that will give you the most legal and tax advantages. Once you've settled on a particular entity, though, you can (if you wish) go to the online service and save some money getting the paperwork done. Just remember that if they make a mistake, you can't sue them for malpractice.

There are some pretty reputable online incorporation services now that are giving the legal profession a run for its money. Intuit Corp. (which publishes the QuickBooks, Quicken, and TurboTax software products) recently acquired MyCorporation Business Services, Inc. (www.mycorporation.com), a Calabasas, California–based incorporation service. Other major players online are LegalZoom (www.legalzoom.com) and BizFilings (www.bizfilings.com). There's even a franchise called We the People (www.wethepeopleusa.com) that prepares incorporation and other simple legal documents, with 166 brick-and-mortar locations in twenty-nine states.

But beware. There are a lot of fly-by-night incorporation services that will take your money, file a generic incorporation form with the secretary of state's office in your state, and leave you to figure out the rest. When looking at a do-it-yourself incorporation service, you should ask six questions:

1. *Will they register your entity with the secretary of state's office in your home state?* Virtually all online services will, but if they're charging less than $200, that's probably all they're doing.

2. *If you're incorporating in a state other than your own, will they help you find a "registered agent" to act as your local mailing address in that state?* Most online services do this, but will send you the bill for the registered agent's service fee (usually $150 to $250 a year).

3. *Will they provide you with the internal corporate documents (e.g., bylaws, minute book, corporate resolutions, and share certificates) you need to run your business day to day?* Some services will, but most do not.

4. *Will they give you notice of filing deadlines on an ongoing basis?* Only the better services will provide you with regular filing deadline notices.

5. *Will they register your entity with the IRS and get you a taxpayer ID number?* Again, only the better services do this type of registration for you.

6. *Will they help you register your entity for state and local taxes (including sales taxes, since you are a retailer)?* I'm not aware of any online service that will do the actual registration for you, but some will tell you that this is a necessary step, and the better ones will offer you some assistance (such as a link to your state tax authority's website) to make sure the job gets done.

Until steps number 1, 5, and 6 have been performed, you are not legally incorporated, and it will be only a matter of time before you receive a nasty letter from a government agency saying you owe them something. Even using one of the very best do-it-yourself incorporation services, you will probably have to hire an accountant or attorney to help you register your entity for state and local taxes.

STEP 4: REGISTER IN ALL STATES WHERE YOU ARE "DOING BUSINESS"

The next issue you have to confront is whether you must register the business you've just set up in another state, and how you do so.

Where Are You Legally "Doing Business"?

There are a number of situations where you are legally "doing business" in more than one state. Here are the most common situations for eBay sellers:

> ➢ You live in Texas and are selling on eBay in a "partnership" with your sister, who lives in New Jersey. In this situation, your partnership is legally doing business in both Texas and New Jersey and should be registered in both states.

> ➢ You live in Maine most of the year, but spend the cold winter months at your "retreat" in Florida, where you continue selling merchandise

on eBay. Your business would have to be registered in both Maine and Florida.

➢ You live in California and have an exclusive drop-shipping arrangement with a manufacturer in Georgia (in other words, you are their only eBay seller). In this case, you and the Georgia manufacturer look a lot like "partners," whatever your actual contract might say, and I would recommend registering your California business in Georgia, just to be safe.

Generally, if you have a business incorporated in State X, you must register it as a "foreign entity" in State Y (by registering with State Y's tax authority and secretary of state's office) if:

➢ You have an office, warehouse, or other physical location or address (e.g., a PO box or UPS Store "private mailbox") in State Y.

➢ You have an employee or partner who lives in State Y and uses his home or business address in State Y to help you conduct your eBay selling business.

➢ State X and State Y have entered into an "interstate compact" requiring sellers in each state to charge the other state's sales and other taxes when selling to people living in the other state. (These "compacts" are discussed further in Chapter 8.)

Should You Incorporate in Delaware or Nevada?

Delaware and Nevada are popular places to form corporations and LLCs, for a number of reasons. Delaware is popular because almost all of the Fortune 1000 corporations are incorporated there, so there're tons of things we lawyers know about Delaware corporations that we don't know about corporations in other states. Nevada is popular because of its extremely low taxes and its "secrecy" laws (which make it extremely difficult for bad people—such as creditors, lawyers, and ex-spouses—to find out exactly who runs a Nevada corporation or LLC), and—Vegas, baby!

Here are Cliff's Rules to determine if you should incorporate in Delaware or Nevada:

➢ If your business is physically located in Delaware, you should be a Delaware corporation or LLC.

➢ If you are starting up a high-technology venture (such as a software company) and plan to raise venture capital in your first two to three years in business, you should be a Delaware corporation or LLC.

➢ If your business is physically located in Nevada, you should be a Nevada corporation or LLC.

➢ If your business does not fall into any of the first three categories, there is absolutely no reason in the world to incorporate in Delaware or Nevada!

A lot of people believe—*and they're wrong!*—that they can incorporate in Delaware or Nevada and not have to do anything in the state where they are actually located and doing business. A lot of eBay sellers especially fall victim to sites on the Internet that say "Form your own Nevada corporation for under $50." If you form a Delaware or Nevada entity for your eBay business but fail to register it with your home state's tax authorities and secretary of state's office, you can get into a heap of legal and tax trouble that the "do it yourself in Nevada" sites won't help you get out of.

I've said it before, and I'll say it again: Forming a Delaware or Nevada corporation or LLC when you're actually doing business in Wisconsin will not protect you one bit from Wisconsin state and local taxes, and you shouldn't believe anyone who tells you otherwise. Since you're going to have to pay taxes in Wisconsin anyway, why bother learning about the laws in a remote and faraway state that has absolutely no connection to your business beyond a "PO box"?

How to Register in Another State

If you must register your business in another state, it's a three-step process:

1. Begin by filing an Application for a Certificate of Authority with the other state's office of the secretary of state. There will be a fairly hefty filing fee

(usually $200 to $300), and you will have to attach a Certificate of Good Standing from your own secretary of state's office (which costs about $25) showing that your corporation or LLC does in fact exist.

2. Register for the other state's sales, use, and other business taxes by filing the appropriate registration form with the state tax authority in that state.

3. Visit the tax assessor's office in the county, city, or town where your business office is located (or have your partner or employee in the other state do this step for you) and find out if you have to sign up for any local taxes in the other state.

STEP 5: REGISTER FOR FEDERAL TAXES

If you are a sole proprietor, you can use your Social Security number as your federal tax ID number. I generally recommend against this, though, and strongly advise all of my new small business clients to get a separate federal tax ID number (sometimes called an EIN, for Employer Identification Number, even though you don't have any employees). The reason? You will have to give this number to a lot of people, and many of them should not be entitled to know your Social Security number, since that can lead to identity theft.

If you are anything other than a sole proprietorship (i.e., you are a partnership, corporation, subchapter S corporation, or LLC), you *must* have a separate federal tax ID number.

To get a tax ID number, you have to fill out Internal Revenue Service Form SS-4 (available as a free download from the IRS website). Once you have filled out and signed the form, you can get your federal ID number over the telephone (1-800-829-4933) or through the Web (www.irs.gov).

One last thing about federal tax ID numbers: If you change status (from partnership to sole proprietor, for example), you must get a new tax ID number. So if you and your wife start a partnership together to sell on eBay, and your spouse has to leave the partnership at some point (say, because she's found a day job or you got divorced), you have to remember to notify the IRS and get a new federal tax ID number. You do this by checking the Changed Type of Organization box on line 9 of Form SS-4 (instead of the Starting New Business line).

• Some Tips for Filling Out IRS Form SS-4 •

Filling out your own SS-4? You are an extremely brave person . . .

Actually, it's quite easy, but there are a couple of "tricks" you need to be aware of.

If you have a corporation or LLC, the "applicant" (line 1) is your corporation or LLC, not you individually. On line 2, your "trade name" is your DBA, if you have one. If you have a website, consider putting your URL in this box as a trade name.

If you are a sole proprietor, or you are in partnership with a spouse or friend and the two of you are the only people who will be working in the business, you *do not have any employees*. When Form SS-4 asks you if you have any employees (such as on lines 12 and 13), you should fill in "zero" or "not applicable (N/A)." In a sole proprietorship or partnership, the owners are not considered employees for tax purposes; they are "owners." If you tell the IRS you have employees, be prepared for a deluge of paperwork: The IRS will assume you will be withholding taxes from each employee's paycheck (see Chapter 12) and will send you all of the information about Form 940, Form 941, and other payroll tax forms that you are *not required* to submit when it's just you and your partners.

Fill in line 15 as follows: "Retail sale of goods on eBay and other online venues."

On line 16a, keep in mind that the "applicant" is the corporation, LLC, or other entity listed on line 1. If you have other federal tax ID numbers but this is the first time your "entity" has applied for a federal tax ID number, put "zero" on this line.

Finally, if you are filling out the form yourself, without the assistance of a lawyer or accountant, do not fill out the "third-party designee" box.

Other than that, Form SS-4 is pretty intuitive. If you're not sure how to fill in any of the line items, call the IRS toll-free number (1-800-829-4933) and someone will walk you through the form.

STEP 6: REGISTER FOR STATE AND LOCAL TAXES

Once you've gotten a federal tax ID number for your business, you need to register for a state tax ID number as well. This number is sometimes referred to as a "resale" number, since it is the number you will provide to your vendors when you buy merchandise from them for resale on eBay and claim exemption from state sales taxes.

Your state tax ID number will be issued by your state tax authority. To find the website for your state's tax authority, go to www .natptax.com/state_information.html and click on your state when the map of the United States pops up. Once you're there, click on "sales tax forms," then click on "registration form."

Your state tax registration form will give you a laundry list of all state taxes you have to sign up for in your state. As an eBay seller, you should definitely sign up for "sales" and "use" taxes (see Chapter 8). If you have employees (other than yourself and your spouse), you should also sign up for "withholding taxes" (see Chapter 12).

Any questions you may have about filling out your state tax registration form should be directed to your accountant; presumably, she fills them out for her clients every day.

What should you do about local government taxes? Each county, town, or city in the United States probably has at least one local tax that businesses have to deal with, and the wonderful person who administers these taxes is known as the tax assessor. Go and visit your local tax assessor's office—preferably when they're not too busy—and simply ask what local taxes you need to pay for an eBay selling business. They will probably be delighted that someone actually had the foresight to ask for advice and will do what they can to make your life (and their own) easier. If your town, city, or county has any special requirements about working out of a home office (see Chapter 10), you will find out about those as well.

STEP 7: HIRE PROFESSIONALS AND MENTORS TO HELP YOU

You do not have to have partners or employees to be successful in business. Many of my most successful law clients over the years have been sole proprietors in the legal sense.

Having said that, though, "loners" seldom succeed in business. When you're running a business, whether on or off of eBay, there's no way you can figure out all of the answers to all of the questions that will come up on a daily basis.

When setting up a business on eBay, you need to build a "support team" of professionals to help you solve problems when you don't have the time or patience to figure it all out yourself. Every small business needs at least five different types of adviser:

- ➢ A good lawyer
- ➢ A good accountant or tax adviser
- ➢ A good insurance agent
- ➢ A "mentor" or industry expert
- ➢ A spouse, significant other, or "personal adviser"

Finding the Right Lawyer

People complain all the time that lawyers are too expensive. Yet, in the same breath, they tell me they think there are "far too many lawyers" around.

Do you see the contradiction in that? Here's a question from Economics 101: In a market where there are many sellers (lawyers) and relatively few buyers (clients), what should happen to prices? They should fall, shouldn't they?

Lawyers today are extremely competitive, and no matter what they might say, you *can* negotiate their fees. But if you don't negotiate, they won't have an incentive to cut their prices. Hey, you're an eBay seller! You negotiate *everything* with your vendors, don't you? You don't put up with nonsense from your buyers, right? So why should you treat professionals any differently?

Picking a lawyer is like dealing with any other vendor: Shop around, and try to get the best deal you can.

Here are some tips when looking for a lawyer:

➢ Avoid litigators. A lawyer who specializes in lawsuits (what we call a "litigator") is the wrong type of lawyer. Litigators only make money *after* you've been sued, and that's far too late to do you any good.

➢ Seek a good *business* lawyer—someone who deals in contracts and other ways of keeping you and your business out of court.

➢ Seek a "small business generalist"—somebody who not only can form your LLC or corporation, but can advise you on employment, tax, and other questions that will arise on a daily basis. If the lawyer has to refer you to a "specialist" each time you call him, he's not the lawyer for you.

➢ Be candid about your budget. Tell the lawyer what you are prepared to spend for legal services and then let him tell you what he can and cannot do for that amount.

➢ Ask for "flat fees" whenever possible. A good small business lawyer forms LLCs and corporations every day of his working life and should not have to bill something like that "by the hour."

➢ Last but not least, always ask for a "detailed billing statement" each month. That's a bill where the lawyer details every minute he spent working on your legal issues and justifies every penny of his bill. That way, if the lawyer has been "padding the account," you will be able to spot it right away and call him on the carpet.

Finding the Right Accountant

Your accountant is the most important professional you will deal with when starting a small business of any kind (more important than a lawyer, believe it or not).

The right accountant is not just someone who can fill out your tax forms each year (heck, you can go to H&R Block and get that done). She is someone who has business savvy—someone who can tear apart your books and records (okay, your shoebox full of receipts) and tell you what is actually going on in your business; she can piece together the "stories" behind the "numbers," which are every bit as important as the numbers themselves.

Here are some questions for any accountants you are thinking of hiring:

> Do they just fill out tax returns, or are they willing to meet with you once every three months (at your expense, of course) to go over your books and tell you what you might be doing wrong?

> Do they work with other online retailers?

> Do they "get" eBay? Have they ever bought or sold anything on eBay?

> Do they work online (is the office fully equipped with computers, and are they turned on)? Or are they still using number-two pencils and green analysis pads?

Finding the Right Insurance Agent

A good insurance agent/broker can save your life when you're starting your own business. Most first-time small business owners call their insurance agent when they need liability insurance, and that's certainly important. But a good insurance agent will point out other types of insurance your business will need as well (see the sidebar).

Finding the Right "Mentor"

A mentor is someone who understands your business—someone who's "been there, done that" and can point out to you where all of the land mines are buried.

When you're in business for yourself, you will make mistakes. Count on it! But with a good mentor, you should be able to avoid the most common mistakes—the ones everybody makes when they're first starting out.

So where do you find a mentor for an eBay selling business? Here are some ideas:

> Contact your local chapter of the Service Corps of Retired Executives (SCORE). This is a volunteer organization of retired business people who

• How My Insurance Agent Saved My Life •

When I first started practicing law out of my home office, I made an appointment with my insurance agent to talk about professional liability insurance (otherwise known as malpractice insurance); my wife wouldn't let me practice without it.

After meeting with my agent and going over some malpractice insurance quotes, we decided on a carrier. Just as I was standing up to leave, she said, "Sit back down, Cliff. We've taken care of your malpractice coverage, but you're not leaving this office until you sign up for disability coverage."

"Disability coverage?" I said. "That's very expensive coverage, and what's the likelihood I'm really going to be disabled? I mean, I'm a lawyer; I work with my head. As long as I have brain cells and a personal computer, I can function as a lawyer."

"Oh, yeah?" she responded. "Tell me, Cliff, you will be practicing law out of your home, but you won't be seeing clients there, right?"

"Right."

"So, when you have to see clients, where will you see them?"

"In their offices, most often, or perhaps in a local restaurant or diner."

"Okay, and how are you going to get there?"

"By car, of course."

"Okay, so let's say you're skiing in New Hampshire and you fall and break your right leg. What then?"

"No problem. My brain isn't affected, so I can still practice law."

"Oh, really? How can you drive a car without a right leg?"

There's profound silence on my part, then: "Oh, I see what you mean."

"Exactly!" she said. "So let's look at some disability coverage you may be able to afford."

At the time, I thought disability coverage was an outrageous luxury. But five years later, while doing some gardening in my backyard, I managed to drop a thirty-five-pound rock—from about five feet up—on my bare right foot, smashing it (the foot, not the rock) to smithereens.

Do you know you can't drive a car without a right foot?

Thank goodness for that disability policy, which kept me going for the six months I was in a cast, unable to walk except for short distances.

give free advice and counseling to people starting up businesses "from scratch."

➤ Join every trade association you can, including the Professional eBay Sellers Association (PESA), and be sure to attend their conventions and annual meetings. There are always retired or "between jobs" people at these functions, and they're itching for something to do with their spare time.

➤ Find an eBay Certified Education Specialist near you. These folks are usually PowerSellers who have been trained by eBay to help newbies get their selling business off the ground. You can find them at www .poweru.net/ebay.

➤ Post an entry on eBay's Community Help boards and ask local Power-Sellers or eBay Trading Assistants to contact you for some "paid counseling."

➤ Search eBay and look for sellers in your area with more than 1,000 positive feedback ratings. They may not be "experts," but heck, they must be doing something right!

Finding the Right "Personal Adviser"

Please don't get me wrong—I am not suggesting you should make your spouse your business partner. I could easily write an entire book on that subject (and probably won't, because I would likely be shot by someone)!

I do think, however, that even if your spouse is not part of your eBay selling experience, this person should know enough about what you're doing to be able to help you manage the impact of your new "entrepreneurial venture" on your personal life.

Here's a simple but easy-to-understand example of what I'm talking about. Let's say you are an avid golfer. Your Saturday "foursome" with three buddies is the highlight of your week. You have been meeting with these guys every Saturday for more than ten years.

You get an idea for a wonderful retail store in your town. The idea's solid: There's nothing like it anywhere in your community, and there's huge demand for the merchandise you would be selling. The inventory's affordable, and there's even some cheap retail space available on Main Street in your town—the perfect location! Your lawyer loves it. Your accountant loves it. All of the arrows point to "success" for this business.

Yeah, right. But what about your Saturday "golf foursome"?

As everyone knows, Saturday is the busiest day for brick-and-mortar retailers. Now maybe the other three guys in your foursome can play golf with you on Wednesday when you're free—but probably not. You will be giving up your foursome. This may be the end of three wonderful friendships you have cultivated over the last ten years. Heck, you may even have to give up the game of golf for a while—or maybe forever.

Now, don't get me wrong—I'm not saying you should pass on the retail business because golf is more important. What I am saying is that starting your own business has a nasty way of turning your personal life around. You won't be the same person five years from now that you are today. Your lawyer, your accountant, your insurance agent, your mentor—none of them will help you through the personal agony you'll have to go through as you metamorphose from a "weekend golfer" into a workaholic entrepreneur. Only someone who knows you as a human being and loves you for who you are (such as a spouse or significant other) will be able to help you with this one.

STEP 8: MAKE SURE YOUR CUSTOMERS AND SUPPLIERS KNOW YOU HAVE A BUSINESS!

Once you have started your own business—on eBay or anywhere else—it isn't enough to create a corporation or LLC. You have to let people know they are no longer dealing with you—they are dealing with a "soulless entity." And while they are free to sue your "legal entity" if anything goes wrong, they cannot sue you personally, because you are no longer legally responsible for what the "business" does.

As pointed out earlier, if you are not careful in how you set up your corporation or LLC, a judge will allow an injured person to "pierce the corporate veil" and get to your personal assets. This is not a good thing. It's why you formed the corporation or LLC in the first place.

And yet the biggest mistake people make when they set up corporations and LLCs is . . . they forget they set them up! If you create a corporation or LLC for your business, but then continue to do business in your personal name, your corporation or LLC won't protect you when the you-know-what hits the fan.

Here are three tips for making sure people know they are doing business with your corporation or LLC, not you personally:

> ➤ Make sure your corporation or LLC name appears prominently on your business cards, stationery, website, eBay auction pages, eBay Store, and every document (paper or electronic) your customers and suppliers come into contact with.

> ➤ Open a separate checking account for your corporation or LLC, and make sure when people make checks out to you they make them out to your corporation or LLC, *never* to you personally. Likewise, when checks are delivered to you, deposit them in your corporate or LLC account, and *never* in your personal account.

> ➤ Be sure to use the "signature block" whenever you sign anything. For example:
> Cliff's Antiques, LLC
> By: _____ [signature]
> Cliff Ennico, Managing Member

STEP 9: CHOOSE THE RIGHT WAY TO ACCOUNT FOR SALES

So you started a business selling on eBay last year, and now you're doing your taxes. Your accountant says you have to choose between the "cash" and "accrual" methods of accounting. Problem is, you haven't been doing any accounting as such. When people pay you, you just deposit their checks or money orders into your business checking account. You're not even using PayPal yet (though you plan to, next year). If that's your situation, you are asking about now, "Could someone please explain the difference between these two accounting methods in language I can understand?"

As Curly Joe Howard of the Three Stooges used to say, "Soitenly."

The IRS allows small businesses to use two different accounting methods—the cash method and the accrual method.

Under the cash method of accounting, you report sales when, and only when, you actually receive the "cash" from your winning bidder. So, if someone buys something from you on eBay and pays with a check or money order, you do not report the sale until the check or money order has arrived. If you hold onto the check for a few days before depositing it in your account (as many folks do, especially in late December, when they're trying to push income into the next tax year), it doesn't matter—you record the sale when the buyer's check hits your mailbox.

> Example: Joe sells laptop computers on eBay. He puts a laptop computer up for sale on eBay using a seven-day "traditional" auction format, closing on Sunday night. At the end of the auction, Mary is the winning bidder at $500. Mary elects to pay by personal check and mails the check to Joe on Monday morning. Joe receives Mary's check on Thursday, deposits it in his business checking account on Friday, and the check clears the same day. Using the cash method of accounting, Joe records the $500 sale on Thursday, when he receives the check from Mary.

Under the accrual method of accounting, you report sales when you have the legal right to payment, even if you haven't received the cash yet. So, if someone buys something from you on eBay and pays with a check or money order, you can report the sale as having occurred the moment the auction ended, even though it will be a few days before you receive the buyer's check or money order.

Example: Mary sells Barbie dolls on eBay. On Monday, Mary puts a genuine 1971 Malibu Barbie (the one with the sunglasses sewn to her head) up for sale on eBay for a fixed price of $1,000 using eBay's Buy It Now! feature. On Wednesday, Alphonse clicks the Buy It Now! button and buys the Malibu Barbie doll for $1,000. Alphonse chooses to pay for the doll by personal check and mails the check to Mary on Thursday morning. Mary receives the check on Monday and waits until Tuesday to deposit the check to her business checking account, which means the check doesn't clear the bank until the following Friday. Because Mary uses the accrual method of accounting, Mary must record the $1,000 sale on Wednesday—the day Alphonse buys the doll on eBay and becomes legally obligated to purchase the doll—even though Mary doesn't actually receive "good funds" until the following Friday, when Alphonse's personal check clears her bank.

Under either the cash or the accrual method of accounting, holding onto a check or money order for several days before depositing it does not affect in any way the recording of the sale. You record the sale either when the check or money order arrives in your mailbox (cash method) or when the eBay auction closes and the winning bidder has been identified (accrual method). If you have a PayPal account and use the cash method of accounting, you record a sale when the buyer's payment hits your PayPal account.

Still not sure what to do? When in doubt, select the accrual method of accounting. Just about all eBay selling businesses have inventory, and the accrual method of accounting gives a more accurate picture of sales and income for a business that has inventory. Besides, when you find yourself selling more than $1 million worth of merchandise on eBay each year (you should be so lucky, right?), the IRS is going to require you to use the accrual method of accounting anyway, so you might as well get familiar with accrual accounting now. Hey, you never know . . .

COMMON QUESTIONS

Q. *I run several businesses on eBay. Do I have to prepare a Schedule C for each one?*

A. Assuming that your businesses are all sole proprietorships (meaning you are the only owner), and you use only one tax ID number (or your Social Security number) for all of these businesses, the short answer is "no." You can lump all of your income and expenses together on one Schedule C.

If you have separate tax ID numbers for each of these businesses, you should file a separate Schedule C for each business, because the IRS will expect to see a tax return (Schedule C) for each tax ID number you have registered in your name.

If you are selling radically different types of things (for example, Barbie dolls and motor vehicles), it may make sense for you to have two or more separate tax ID numbers and checking accounts for these businesses and file a Schedule C for each one, just so it's easier for you to track your expenses. But it isn't required.

Q. *I've had a tax ID number for three years that I've used on tax returns and financials. Problem is, it's a partnership . . . or it was. It isn't a partnership any longer. It's just me now. The IRS says you can't be one person and be a partnership. They say I have to apply for a new tax ID. No way. I have all my records under this tax ID. I don't want to change it. What should I do? Help!*

A. Okay, so you had a business partner, but you bought him out last year. Under IRS rules, this is a "change of status" that requires you to get a new federal tax ID number. If there is still time (i.e., if you bought your partner out after December 31, 2005), you may want to consider making your spouse or significant other a partner with a one percent partnership interest. That way you will preserve your status as a "partnership" and can keep your current tax ID number. Just don't backdate any documents, because that will get you in serious legal trouble if you're found out.

Q. *I was thinking about setting up an LLC last year with two friends and got a federal tax ID number. No sooner did I do that than my two friends got* *full-time jobs, so we never ended up forming the LLC. Do I have to file a tax return for an LLC that never existed?*

A.   I would if I were you. If you have a federal tax ID number and fail to file a tax return with that number on it, the IRS will charge you a nonfiling penalty—in your case $600 per partner, or $1,800 total. Not a good thing.

You should download Form 1065 (partnership tax return) from the IRS website (www.irs.gov) and fill in all the blanks with zeroes. On the line reading "date business commenced," write in "n/a—never commenced business," and be sure to check the "final return" box on page 1 of the form. That should be enough to put the IRS on notice that you are not planning to use your tax ID number in the future. You're telling them, "There's nothing to see here."

Q.   *If I carry inventory in my business, do I need to file as an "accrual" tax-payer or can I be "cash basis"?*

A.   If you have more than $1 million in sales each year, the IRS requires you to use the accrual method of accounting, where you record sales when your customers have a legal obligation to pay (not when you actually receive the cash). The IRS is more flexible when it comes to smaller businesses, but I would get into the habit of using the accrual method, because it more accurately reflects the operating results of a business that maintains inventory.

Q.   *In 2004, I had the opportunity to buy a large inventory that I started to sell on eBay in 2005 under my seller ID. It was paid for with my husband's credit card account and a credit card of my own. Last year, my husband paid off both credit card bills. Should we file Form 1065 and make it a partnership, or should it be treated as an investment in the business by him? Is there a difference between an investor and a partner?*

A.   First of all, your paying the credit card bills does not affect your cost of goods sold, for tax purposes. Your COGS is the cost you paid for each item (as shown on your initial credit card statements). When you sell each item on eBay, you report the difference between the selling price and the COGS as income on your tax return. The fact that you paid off the credit card bills in between buying and selling the goods doesn't affect the calculation of COGS.

As to the items your husband purchased, you have a number of options here. You can treat them as a "consignment" of goods from your husband to you, and pay him back (after deducting a reasonable consignment fee, of course). Since this was your first year in business, you can treat it as a partnership and file Form 1065. Or you can "purchase" the goods from him and pay him back over time with interest at the applicable federal rate or AFR (that's the lowest rate of interest the IRS will allow on interpersonal loans). If you take the last option, be sure to have a lawyer draft a legal promissory note, since the IRS will require one if you are ever audited.

It really boils down to how much of your eBay selling business you want your husband to have. If this is truly "your thing," then keep the relationship at arm's length.

Q. *If I send my wife to ship a package for me a couple of times a year and she obviously shares my eBay income with me because she is my wife, is it necessary to file a Form 1065? If so, are all of the IRS guidelines as explicitly black-and-white, or are there exceptions?*

A. First of all, there's no law that says your wife has to be your business partner. If the amounts are small, you might be able to argue that this is just your business and you pay your wife some 1099 income every once in a while as a "thank you" for her services. Just don't pay her more than $600 a year, or else you have to include her among the rest of your "contractors" and send her a Form 1099 next January 31 (see Chapter 12).

There are some accountants who take the view that a partnership consisting solely of a husband and wife does not have to file Form 1065 each year, but I can't find a basis in the IRS literature for that position. Since you are doing the bulk of the work in this business, and there is no tax advantage in "hiring" your spouse as an employee, I would talk to your accountant about paying your wife for her services on an arm's-length basis.

Selling on eBay

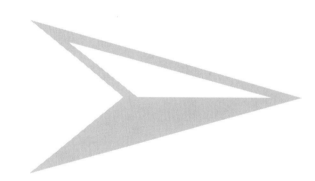

CHAPTER 3

Setting Up Your eBay Auction Pages

The first step in any eBay auction or Buy It Now! sale is setting up the auction or sale page. (Throughout this book, the term *auction page* will refer to both traditional auctions and fixed-price Buy It Now! sales, since the process is basically the same for both transactions.)

Most of the legal mistakes a seller will make on eBay occur at this stage, so it's important to pay close attention to what you are doing.

SELLING ONLY "LEGAL" STUFF

Generally, if it is illegal to sell something anywhere in the United States, you cannot sell it on eBay. Before putting anything up for sale on eBay, you should check eBay's Prohibited and Restricted Items overview (pages.ebay.com/help/policies/items-ov.html), which is pretty comprehensive. If eBay sees you selling something illegal on its network, it will pull your auction and send you a polite note saying "Don't do this again." In extreme cases you may be barred from eBay altogether.

• What About Other Countries' Laws? •

When you sell globally on eBay, you cannot possibly know, or be expected to know, the laws of every country on earth.

Back in the 1980s, the British government for a brief time banned the publication and sale of Peter Wright's book *Spy Catcher: The Candid Autobiography of a Senior Intelligence Officer* because of allegedly confidential information the author disclosed about the internal operations of the British secret service. If eBay had existed back then and you had put a copy of *Spy Catcher* up for sale on the network (the book was, after all, perfectly legal in the United States, Canada, and other countries), what would you have done if a U.K. national bid on the item?

As a U.S. citizen, you are not bound by any U.K. laws (you may recall a revolution was once fought over that), yet as a member of the eBay community, you are duty-bound to make sure nobody's breaking any laws if you can at all help it.

Because the British government's ban on *Spy Catcher* was widely publicized, and it would have been difficult *not* to know about it, your best course of action would have been to include a sentence in the item description that "due to legal difficulties, residents of the United Kingdom are not allowed to bid on this item." And, of course, you should not have listed the item on eBay U.K. or any other website "targeting" British nationals.

In situations where it is not well known that certain countries ban certain goods, you should include a clause in your General Terms and Conditions (see Appendix B) that "the laws of your country may not allow you to purchase or import this item."

Don't forget to use common sense. If the goods you are selling on eBay are likely to offend people in certain parts of the world, use extreme discretion before deciding to deal in that merchandise. If someone offers to sell you some "genuine cartoons featuring the adventures of the Prophet Muhammad," for example, beware.

But you shouldn't rely solely on eBay's own list of prohibited and restricted items. Check out your state's licensing center (see Chapter 2) and make sure you don't need a license to sell whatever it is you are planning to sell. Checking out the website of your state's consumer protection department is probably also a good idea (type "[name of state] consumer protection" into your favorite search engine), since it will tell you about other things you may not be able to sell to residents of your state.

AVOIDING "KNOCKOFFS"

It is illegal to sell counterfeit goods on eBay. That "genuine Rolex watch" you bought from a street vendor for $5 is probably a knock-off from somewhere in deepest Asia, and by selling it under the Rolex name, you are infringing upon Rolex's trademark.

If the watch has the Rolex name stamped on it and is not a genuine Rolex, it is counterfeit and should not be sold at all. If the watch itself does not have the Rolex name stamped on it anywhere (it just looks like a Rolex-type watch), you can sell it on eBay as a plain old watch, but you can't use the name Rolex in any manner, shape, or form on your auction page. Calling it a "watch that resembles a Rolex" won't get you out of hot water. If the Rolex people find out about what you are doing—and eBay makes it very easy for them to do so through eBay's Verified Rights Owner (VeRO) program—they will complain to eBay and eBay will pull your auction.

The best approach when selling name-brand merchandise is to contact the manufacturer directly and find out if the merchandise is truly genuine. Most manufacturers post information on their websites about how to recognize knockoffs, and with a little effort you can find someone in their "rights" department who can help you evaluate the merchandise that has landed (somehow) on your doorstep.

Again, use common sense. If the stuff you bought is "too good to be true," it probably is. Stay away from name-brand merchandise unless you are thoroughly familiar with it and can spot a "genuine replica" a mile away.

RIPPING OFF OTHER PEOPLE'S PHOTOS

It's a pain in the neck to have to take digital photos of every single item you sell on eBay. If you are selling generic merchandise—

• Using Images of Someone Else's Artwork •

Bill Graham was one of the legendary rock-and-roll concert promoters of all time. The owner and operator of the Fillmore Auditorium in San Francisco (and later the Fillmore East in New York City), Graham booked virtually every major rock band and solo artist in a career that spanned from the early 1960s to the late 1980s. The posters that Graham commissioned to promote his concerts—produced by such amazing artists as Victor Moscoso, Stanley Mouse, Alton Kelley, and the late Rick Griffin—are icons of the 1960s psychedelic era in America and are highly prized as collectibles by "rock art" collectors worldwide.

The problem is, when Bill Graham commissioned an artist to produce a concert poster, he also made darn sure the copyright to the poster design was in his name, not the artist's or anyone else's.

Flash forward to just a few years ago. The Bill Graham Archives—which owns the copyright to Bill Graham concert posters since Graham's death in 1991—discovered that eBay sellers were taking and sharing high-quality digital photos of the Bill Graham concert posters they were selling on eBay. By doing so, the Archives alleged, eBay sellers were allowing people to "cut and paste" images of posters onto their computers and make unauthorized copies without paying royalties to the Graham estate. The Archives sent very polite letters to eBay rock-art dealers warning them to "cease and desist" their use of photos without the Archives' permission if they wanted to avoid legal action for copyright infringement.

To get the Archives' permission to use photographic images of Bill Graham concert posters in eBay auctions, you are now required to pay a one-time fee of $1,000 to the Archives, and you must insert an encryption at the bottom of each photo to prevent unauthorized duplication.

such as laptops or handbags—it is very tempting to search out other eBay sellers who specialize in the same goods and "cut and paste" their photos to your own auction page.

There are two problems with copying photos from someone else's pages.

First, there is always the risk (especially if you are not an expert in the merchandise) that you may "cut and paste" the wrong photo. Laptop models look a lot alike after a while, and if you make even a small mistake (you copy the photo for Model XYZ34791B-2 rather than Model XYZ34791B-3), you will be committing that gravest of all eBay selling sins—offering one product and selling another (see Chapter 6).

Second, even if the photo is accurate, you may be violating the copyright of whoever took the photo. Whenever you use someone else's photo, you should give that person a photo credit beneath the photo. For an example, see the credit line accompanying the photo of "Duffy" on the Dedication page of this book.

Oh, and one more thing. If you are selling "unique" merchandise (such as any sort of antique), where no two items are exactly alike and where the condition of the item has a dramatic impact on the item's price, you should never, ever, ever display a photo of anything that isn't the actual item you have for sale. If you post a photo of an antique mechanical bank in "pristine condition" and what arrives in the mail is a bank that's half rusted away, with missing pieces and replaced parts, you can only imagine what a fussy mechanical bank collector like me (and a lawyer, to boot) is going to do to your reputation on eBay.

"I DON'T KNOW NUTHIN' ABOUT THIS STUFF"—AVOIDING LEGAL WARRANTIES

A warranty is a promise, of sorts, about the quality of the material you are selling on eBay. Warranties can be express (in writing) or implied. There are problems with warranties. Here's what you need to know to avoid them.

Express Warranties

Everything that you say about the items you sell on eBay—whether in your item description or in your e-mail response to buyers' questions—is what we lawyers call an "express warranty," and buyers are entitled to rely on it when deciding whether to bid on your items.

Let's say you are putting up for sale a mechanical bank that was originally made in 1885. Your item description says, "This is a 100 percent original, genuine 1885 mechanical bank." What you've just said is that *everything* about this bank is original: There are no replaced parts, no repairs, no rust spots, and every speck of paint that went onto this bank in 1885 is still present and accounted for, even though this is a children's toy that has been played with by six generations of American youngsters. Do you want to think again about that item description? I think you should, because with an item description like that, if I can find even one thing about that bank that isn't 100 percent original, I can return it to you and get my money back.

Implied Warranties

Even if you don't make any express warranties to your buyers, the law imposes several "implied" warranties on every one of your eBay auction pages. If you don't specifically "disclaim" these, you are deemed to have made them.

The two most common implied warranties are merchantability and fitness for a particular purpose.

➤ *Merchantability.* It's a big word, but it simply means that the item is of a type that may legally be sold. Items that are listed on eBay's Prohibited and Restricted Items list are by definition not merchantable, but the concept is a bit broader than that.

Let's say you are looking in the Totally Weird section of eBay and come across an auction called Chickens Infected with Salmonella. Intrigued, you open the auction, and there are several digital photos of dead chickens with large red blotches all over them. The item description reads as follows: "We guarantee that these chickens are infected with the salmonella virus. Anyone who eats these chickens is almost certain to contract salmonella poisoning, will become violently ill, and may possibly die."

Well, I guess "full disclosure" isn't a problem here; the seller isn't making any express warranties that these chickens are edible in any way. And—let's face it—there's a market for just about everything in life. Think about it. If you are having your ex-boss over for dinner—you know, the guy who fired you, downsized your entire department, and put you in a position where you have to sell on eBay to make a living . . .

C'mon, folks! There are some *serious* problems with this auction:

It violates just about every health and safety law known to humankind.

It is a threat to public health.

It may be an act of terrorism.

Get it? It is not legal to sell sick chickens, on eBay or anywhere else! Period. That's one example of what merchantability means.

➢ *Fitness for a Particular Purpose.* The other important warranty the law "implies" in your auction pages is fitness for a particular purpose. If you know that people normally use an item for a certain purpose, and you don't state clearly that the item you're selling *can't* be used for that purpose, then you are saying that the item *can be* used for that purpose.

Example: You are selling a vintage 1920s box of Arm & Hammer Baking Soda. The item sells on eBay for $30. Two weeks later the buyer calls you and says, "You know, that box of Arm & Hammer Baking Soda you sold me doesn't work at all the way it's supposed to. I put that thing in my refrigerator last week, and today it stinks to high heaven!" Believe it or not, you may be obligated to refund the buyer's money. I mean, everyone knows you put Arm & Hammer Baking Soda in your refrigerator to kill odors, right?

Warranty Disclaimers

You can't really disclaim an express warranty—once you make a statement about an item, it's out there for public consumption, and you really can't take it back. The goal is to disclaim all warranties *other than* those you have expressly made in your item description.

There are two parts to a standard warranty disclaimer:

First, you have to state clearly that the item is being sold "as is" and "with all faults." These phrases carry a lot of legal meaning with them. They basically say, "What you see is what you get."

Second, you have to make the following statement:

"Except as set forth in this description, Seller disclaims any and all warranties about this item, express or implied."

Or, if you want to make it more user-friendly, you can just state: "Look, we're not experts on these things, so we are not responsible for any defects or problems we haven't pointed out to you either in this description or in the auction photos."

By disclaiming all warranties, you are telling buyers that you will not permit them to return the merchandise if after delivery they see additional defects, damage, or problems you didn't spot and disclose in your auction description. If they have specific questions about an item's description, they are free to e-mail you and you will answer the questions to the best of your ability. Otherwise, the sale is final. (See Appendix B, "Sample 'Terms and Conditions' for eBay Auction Pages," for the language you will need.)

YOU KNOW YOU'VE COMMITTED FRAUD WHEN . . .

When you make a warranty about an item and it turns out to be something other than you thought it was, that's called *breach of warranty* or *breach of contract*. It's not a happy place to be, certainly, but you can usually deal with it by apologizing, admitting your ignorance of the defect, giving the buyer his money back, and chalking it up to experience.

Fraud is a lot uglier. You can get kicked off of eBay for fraud. You can go to jail for fraud.

You have committed fraud if you know something is wrong with an item, but you look the buyer in the face (figuratively speaking) and tell her it's okay. You also commit fraud if you know something is wrong with an item and you keep silent about it, or tell only part of the truth.

The key to fraud is "knowledge." If you honestly and sincerely do not know something is wrong with the item, that can never be fraud (although it may be breach of warranty if you innocently claim it to be okay and it's not). Fraud involves "intent" to cheat the buyer out of money, and that's a tough thing to prove, although not impossible, as the thousands of consumer fraud cases pending in courtrooms around the country prove.

• It's Not What You Say, It's What You Don't Say •

There are four things collectors of nineteenth-century mechanical banks care about more than just about anything else:

- Is all of the paint on the bank original, or have there been "touch-ups"?
- Are all of the parts original, or have there been replacements over the years?
- Is the bank in good working condition?
- Are there any parts missing?

So, if you put a bank up for the sale with the description "Bank is in good working order, with all original parts and no obvious repairs or replaced parts," that's all very helpful, but you have left out some very important information—you have said nothing about the bank's paint!

If I am a sophisticated mechanical bank collector and I see you are an "amateur seller" who doesn't offer banks on a regular basis, I will be a gentleman and send you an e-mail asking for clarification about the "paint status." But, if I see that you deal frequently in banks and claim expertise on them, I am not going to give you the benefit of the doubt and assume it was an innocent oversight. Instead, I am going to assume that there is a problem with the paint (either there's not much original paint left or the bank has been repainted) and that you are deliberately withholding this information because you want to "sucker in" a less sophisticated collector. I will be thinking "fraud," and you can bet that will get around the community of mechanical bank collectors in no time. (We all talk to each other, you should know.)

Should you disclose every defect, problem, fault, and flaw in your merchandise that you know about? That's probably the single most difficult question you will face as an eBay seller, and you will face it in virtually every auction.

My short answer is "yes," if only because if you disclose everything, it will be difficult or impossible for any buyer to argue with a straight face that you committed fraud on eBay. It is the buyer's own fault, after all, if she doesn't read all of the "disclosures" in your item description.

The law in many parts of the country is still *caveat emptor*—"let the buyer beware"—but as a member of the eBay community, I think you have an obligation to your buyers, at the very least, to:

➤ Make a reasonable inspection of each item you sell and point out defects that you see.

➤ Post as many photos of each item as you can afford, from every angle and in sufficient detail that I can see chips, gouges, missing pieces, and other defects that you can see with the naked eye.

➤ Have someone who is knowledgeable about the item (especially expensive or one-of-a-kind items such as antiques) give it a "once-over" and tell you if there are any defects that would make a reasonable and knowledgeable buyer want to reject the item.

Finally, if you still think there might be hidden defects in the item you couldn't spot without tearing the item apart, warn the buyer:

"We have not conducted a thorough investigation of this item; in the event there are additional defects, faults, or flaws that impair the value of this item to you, your Sole Recourse is to return the item to us within X days of the auction closing for a full refund. We will not accept returns after that time."

THE "TERMS AND CONDITIONS" SECTION OF YOUR AUCTION PAGE

Now it's time to fill out the "terms and conditions of sale" section of the eBay auction page template. There are a number of blanks to fill in here, but in my opinion most eBay sellers need to go a step further. If you are planning to sell regularly and professionally on eBay, you should draw up a General Terms and Conditions document and make sure it appears in a fairly prominent place on *all* of your eBay auction pages.

Appendix B is a sample General Terms and Conditions section, which I have assembled after looking at more than a hundred top eBay sellers' auction pages. Having said that, you should not simply copy this example and start using it blindly. You should show Appendix B to a lawyer and ask him to "custom tailor" it to the type of merchandise you are selling. Depending on what you are selling, you may need additional terms and conditions, or maybe some of the terms and conditions in Appendix B don't apply to you.

Whatever Terms and Conditions you decide to adopt for your own eBay auctions, *make sure you read and follow them when selling on eBay*. I am amazed at the number of eBay sellers who, in conversations with disgruntled buyers, claim that "all sales are final" when their Terms and Conditions state clearly that "items may be returned within five days after an auction closing for any reason."

Here are some of the things you should consider including in your Terms and Conditions section:

1. *Disclaim all warranties.* You absolutely must disclaim any express or implied warranties, except for things that you specifically say in your item descriptions or that are "readily apparent" from an examination of your auction photos.

2. *Spell out your refund and return policy.* State clearly when you will accept (and not accept) returns. I always advise eBay sellers to be flexible in their return policies. If you want your return and refund policy to be "all sales are final," that's fine, but you must spell out this policy (in CAPITAL LETTERS AND BOLDFACE TYPE) so your buyer will see it before bidding. If it were me, I would also include the boldfaced statement as part of the item description, so the buyer can't complain later on that you "buried it in the fine print."

3. *Apply sales tax.* Believe it or not, in most states you are not allowed to add sales tax to a buyer's winning bid unless you tell them in advance that you will do so. Failing to include an advance warning in your Terms and Conditions policy will force you to "eat" the sales tax if a smart buyer complains. Include a statement as follows: "Note to Residents of [your state]: Sales tax will be added to your winning bid."

4. *Tell buyers they may have to pay use taxes.* Even though they are a buyer's responsibility and generally "not your problem," buyers really hate it when they have nasty tax surprises you didn't warn them about. I always recommend that eBay sellers include this short statement in their Terms and Con-

ditions: "Your purchase may be subject to use tax in your state; check with your accountant or tax adviser before bidding on this item." That way, if buyers get nailed by their state tax authority, they can't complain that you didn't warn them. Use taxes are covered further in Chapter 8.

5. *Advise foreign buyers.* If you are open to selling to foreign buyers (and you should be—as discussed in Chapter 13), you should warn them up-front that:

> ➢ Their shipping costs may be different from the auction terms disclosed for U.S. buyers.

> ➢ You retain the right to use whatever shipping carrier you like, based on your experience with similar goods.

> ➢ All prices are in U.S. dollars, and you will not accept foreign currency.

> ➢ You are not responsible for taxes (such as value-added tax or VAT, imposed by Canada and most European nations) and regulations imposed by the buyer's country.

• One Final Word About Your Auction Terms and Conditions •

Don't follow them "to the letter."

General terms and conditions are just that—they are "general" and do not necessarily apply in all situations. Whenever you draft Terms and Conditions for your eBay auctions, always give yourself the flexibility of doing something a little differently if a specific auction calls for it.

Situations that may cause you to "bend" your sales policies include the following:

*   *A buyer yells and screams so loud you begin to fear for your family's safety.* In such a situation (especially if the amount involved is small), you should let this buyer return the item and give him his money back, no matter what your policy says, both to achieve peace of mind and to avoid negative feedback.
*   *One of your best customers has a problem with a purchase.* Like everywhere else, 80 percent of your eBay business is going to come from 20 percent of your customers, and if this buyer is one of the 20 percent, she is to be treated with kid gloves and given the best service you can possibly deliver.
*   *The buyer convinces you that you didn't look hard and long enough at this item before you put it up for sale on eBay.* In this instance, perhaps you might—just might—have some legal exposure if you press the matter too hard.

6. _Detail interest charges on overdue payments._ Believe it or not, you are not allowed in most states to charge interest on overdue payments unless you tell the buyer in advance that you will do so. Add a provision to your Terms and Conditions that "interest at the rate of 18 percent per annum, or the highest rate allowed by law if less, will be charged on all payments that are more than X days overdue." This precise language protects you in case 18 percent per annum is higher than your state's highest allowed rate of interest (called a "usury ceiling").

7. _Detail any restrictions on buyers._ eBay allows you some flexibility in telling the world you will not deal with certain types of buyers. Common "buyer restrictions" include:

   ➤ Buyers with a feedback rating of X or less.

   ➤ Buyers with less than Y percent positive feedback rating.

   ➤ Buyers from certain specified countries. (But use common sense—a statement excluding buyers from just one country, say, "France," may send buyers a signal you've got problems that go beyond international trade issues.)

   ➤ "Nonpaying buyers" in your previous auctions.

   WARNING: Do not let your prejudices and biases creep in. I would hate to be the eBay seller who gets caught discriminating against people of a certain race, religion, ethnic group, or national origin in a "restricted buyers" policy.

8. _Don't overdo it—you will scare buyers away._ In drafting Appendix B, I have tried to make it short and sweet and as user-friendly as possible while still doing the job it's intended to do—protect you against crazy buyers.

   I have seen eBay sellers whose Terms and Conditions section goes on for pages and pages of closely spaced, dense text that was obviously prepared by an attorney. Lawyers refer to documents like that as "killer forms"—they protect you extremely well, because they kill so much business (by scaring away buyers) that you will never have to worry about being sued! If your Terms and Conditions section is too long, or is written in legalese, I guarantee your buyers will be thinking that:

   ➤ You are a neurotic loser who looks at every eBay buyer (if not all of humanity) as a potential lawsuit.

   ➤ You are trying to cheat them out of their hard-earned money because "in all of this legal language, there's bound to be some 'gotcha' that's going to bite me."

➢ "I don't have the time to read all this garbage, so I'm just not going to bid on this guy's stuff."

YOUR "SHIPPING AND HANDLING" CHARGES

eBay policies specifically permit sellers to charge a shipping and handling fee to cover the seller's reasonable costs for mailing, packaging, and handling the item. (For details, see pages.ebay.com/ help/policies/listing-shipping.html.) The question is, should you charge such fees, and if so, how do you report them on your tax return?

Should You Charge a Handling Fee?

While shipping fees should clearly cover the actual cost of postage, shipping and packaging materials, and other reasonable and legitimate out-of-pocket costs an eBay seller incurs, there are a few rules about what can and cannot be included in a handling fee.

One rule, which eBay enforces strictly, is that a handling fee cannot include the seller's merchant card fees, eBay fees, or PayPal fees. Such costs should be built into the price of the item. Also, eBay sellers are prohibited from charging different handling fees to bidders depending on the method they use to pay for their items.

eBay's policies also prohibit shipping and handling fees that are calculated as a fixed percentage of the final sale price regardless of the seller's actual out-of-pocket costs. Beyond that, eBay's policies offer little clear guidance on the question of whether labor and other overhead costs can be included in a seller's handling fee, other than suggesting that a seller's handling fees must be reasonable.

To avoid receiving negative feedback on the Feedback Forum, you should develop a uniform policy about what is and isn't included in your handling fee, and you must disclose that policy to potential bidders on your Terms and Conditions page. If you decide to include your own labor, be sure to value it fairly—shipping clerks don't normally get paid $500 an hour.

Reporting Your "Shipping and Handling Fee" on Your Tax Return

There are two ways you can handle your shipping and handling fees on eBay when preparing your tax return. The better approach, and what the IRS would prefer you to do, is total up all the shipping and handling fees you collect from your winning bidders on eBay and report them as income on Schedule C. Then total up all the amounts you paid for shipping and packaging materials, postage, and other reasonable and legitimate shipping charges and report that total as deductible Materials and Supplies on Schedule C.

If you do it right, the two amounts should net out to zero. If they net out to a positive number, then you are padding your fees (also known as "gouging your customers") and should report the excess fees as taxable income. If they net out to a negative number, then you lost money on your shipping and handling fees, which should reduce the total income from your eBay selling activities as a business loss.

You probably won't get into too much hot water with the IRS, however, if you subtract your total shipping and handling costs from the shipping and handling fees you collected from buyers and do not report anything on Schedule C (since presumably the math will net out to zero).

Just be sure you keep accurate records of both your total shipping and handling fees and your actual shipping and handling costs, because you may have to defend your calculation if the IRS audits you.

COMMON QUESTIONS

Q. *I just began selling on eBay last year, and I am in the process of filling out my first tax return (ugh). Can I deduct the cost of postage, duct tape, materials such as plastic peanuts and bubble packaging, and other supplies? I pay for these items out of my own pocket, but I don't pass the actual costs on to the buyer because they're too difficult to track. Instead, I charge each buyer a shipping and handling fee of $10 for each auction, regardless of* *the amount involved. Does the $10 shipping and handling fee wipe out any deduction I might have for my packaging and shipping materials?*

A.   When selling on eBay, it's often difficult to come up with deductible business expenses when tax time rolls around. You probably have a computer or laptop that you use in your business, a couple of eBay "how to" books, and maybe some paper clips. But that's about it. Unless you are selling so much on eBay that you need to rent a warehouse, buy forklifts, and hire guys with tattoos to run them, you really don't have a lot of expenses running a selling business on eBay.

The one exception, of course, is "postage, packing, and shipping." Whenever someone buys something from you on eBay, you've got to get it into their hands somehow. How should you deal with these costs on your tax return?

Well, believe it or not, there are two ways.

The first (and better) method—and what the IRS really wants you to do—is to inventory your postage, packing, and shipping costs by adding them to your "cost of goods sold," or COGS for short. That's basically the total of everything you spent to acquire your inventory—the stuff you sell on eBay. Whatever you paid for your inventory is part of the COGS of your inventory. However, COGS also includes such things as postage and packaging materials. The COGS method requires you to keep track of the COGS of each item of inventory you sell on eBay, because you cannot deduct your COGS for inventory until it is actually sold. When you sell an item on eBay, you record the winning bid amount as income and deduct the COGS for that item to offset the income.

The COGS method works well when you are selling only a relatively few high-priced items on eBay. But what if you are like the vast majority of eBay sellers and are selling lots and lots of low-priced items? In that situation, it is difficult, if not impossible, to track the COGS of each item you sell unless you have lots of discipline and patience, too much time on your hands, and some sophisticated accounting software.

You probably will not get into too much hot water with the IRS if you take the total cost of your postage, packaging, and shipping materials as a current deduction on Schedule C of your federal tax return (that's the form on which you report your income and deductions from a "trade or business"), especially if the total amount of these expenses is relatively small.

What complicates the situation here is the "shipping and handling fee" you charge your eBay buyers. You will have to keep close track of the amount you actually spend on postage, packaging, and shipping materials, total them all at the end of the year, and then compare them to the total "shipping and handling fees" your charged your eBay buyers during the year. If your total shipping and handling expenses exceeded the total shipping and handling fees you received from eBay buyers, you can deduct the excess expenses on your tax return. If the total shipping and handling fees you charged your eBay buyers exceeded your actual shipping and handling costs, you must report the excess as income on your tax return.

Keep in mind that charging a flat shipping and handling fee regardless of your actual costs, while legal, may violate certain eBay policies (see pages.ebay.com/help/policies/listing-shipping.html). If your eBay buyers find out you are making money on your shipping and handling fees, they will feel cheated and will find a way to let the eBay community know about it, either by giving you negative feedback on eBay's Feedback Forum or by "flaming" you on the many chat rooms and bulletin boards on eBay's website.

If you value your reputation as an eBay seller, you will find a way to make sure your shipping and handling fees reflect your actual postage, shipping, and packaging costs. And while you're at it, start using the COGS method, which will help you keep track of what these actual costs are. You will make both your customers, and the IRS, very happy indeed.

Q. *What is "search interference," and how do I know when I'm getting in trouble?*

A. "Search interference" is a generic term referring to any attempt by an eBay member to divert traffic to his auctions and Buy It Now! sales by including terms in the auction header or item description that have nothing whatsoever to do with the item being sold.

Sellers of brand-name merchandise are particularly prone to search interference problems. Let's say you have a genuine Gucci handbag for sale on eBay. Assuming you have checked with the manufacturer to make sure it is a genuine Gucci handbag, you can include the word *Gucci* in your auction header and item description.

But let's say you're nervous that there won't be enough buyers looking for Gucci handbags when your auction is posted to give you a fair price. You may be tempted to put up the following header: "Gucci Handbag (Not Versace or Prada)."

Why would you do this? In the hopes that people searching on eBay for Versace or Prada products would see your listing on the first page of their search results. The problem is that your listing has nothing to do with Versace or Prada products.

This is a classic example of search interference, which is also known as "keyword spamming" (see Chapter 5).

Q. *I'm planning to sell a very rare antique on eBay. After searching through past auctions on eBay, I found the exact same item with a wonderful description prepared by an expert in this type of antique. Is there anything wrong with my copying this description, since it applies perfectly to my item and I really don't have the expertise to write a description on my own that's nearly as accurate?*

A. Yes, there is something wrong with this approach. Technically, you have infringed the copyright of whoever wrote the other seller's auction description (either the seller or the antique dealer who was helping the seller).

It isn't always clear on eBay exactly who "owns" an auction description, but in the absence of clear language saying that eBay or "the eBay community" owns it, then the copyright is owned by whoever wrote the words. You should get the other seller's permission before appropriating his auction description for your own use.

There's always the chance that your item is slightly different (perhaps not in exactly the same condition) as the item offered by the other seller, so copying the other description would put you in the position of offering for sale something slightly different from what you actually have. A lot of eBay community members (and more than a few lawyers) consider that fraud, so don't do it!

CHAPTER 4

Before the Auction Closes

When an auction is "pending," during the time between the auction "posting" and the auction "close," there isn't really much to do except watch the auction and respond to e-mail queries from buyers (and, of course, work on posting other auctions).

Yet, as the old saying goes, "there's many a slip 'twixt the cup and the lip." Here are some issues that frequently arise after an auction has been posted on eBay.

WHEN DOES A BID BECOME LEGALLY BINDING?

"Your bid is a legal contract . . ." You see that statement every time you bid for something on eBay. But is it true?

The short answer is yes and no.

To create a contract, there has to be both an "offer" and an "acceptance." In a live auction, when someone bids on something, the bid is construed as merely an "offer" to purchase the item, which is "accepted" when the auctioneer's hammer falls. So if I am bidding on a Chippendale table and am the high bidder, if I change my mind (say, I look at the table up on the auction stand and I see damage that I didn't see during the auction "preview"), I can retract my bid. This is done by shouting "Retract" or making a slashing motion across my throat with my hand—and when the hammer falls, the next highest bidder wins. Once the auctioneer's hammer falls, though, a legal and binding "contract" is created between me and the auction house (which, as discussed in Chapter 14, has the power to sell the goods by consignment).

This practice is not generally followed on eBay, though, because of the difficulties involved in communicating last-minute retractions online.

CAN A BUYER RETRACT A BID BEFORE THE AUCTION CLOSES?

eBay has a fairly detailed policy explaining when a buyer can and cannot retract a bid prior to an auction close. The policy is spelled out on the eBay site at pages.ebay.com/help/buy/questions/retract-bid.html.

Basically, a buyer on eBay can retract a bid:

➢ To correct a typographical error (say, typing in $100 instead of $10), as long as the buyer bids again quickly at the correct amount

➢ If the item description has "changed significantly" after the bid was placed (for example, as a result of additional information you posted in response to another buyer's inquiry about the item)

➢ If an incorrect telephone number or e-mail address was posted on your auction page, and the buyer cannot contact you to discuss the item because of that error

➢ At any time within one hour after placing a bid

➢ At any time more than twelve hours before the auction closes

➢ At any time prior to the auction close (with your consent)

In other words, a bidder can withdraw his bid for any reason as long as he does it more than twelve hours before your auction closes. After that, he can withdraw only with your consent or for one of the other specified reasons.

When bidders retract a bid, it becomes part of their "feedback" rating. Buyers with an abnormally high number of retractions may be engaging in "shill bidding" practices that are illegal. (We'll discuss this practice shortly.)

CAN A SELLER PULL AN AUCTION PAGE BEFORE THE AUCTION CLOSES?

Like an auction bid, which is merely an "offer to purchase" in the eyes of the law, putting an item up for sale on eBay is merely an "offer to sell." There is no binding contract until a buyer "accepts" the offer by submitting a winning bid at the auction close. So, if during a live auction the auctioneer decides to pull an item from the auction (say, because she discovered a flaw in the auction description at the last minute), she is free to do so for any reason before the hammer falls.

eBay's policies on "seller retractions" track the law that would apply in a live auction, and these policies are surprisingly seller-friendly.

Let's say you put a rare mechanical bank up for sale on eBay in a "reserve price" auction. A day after the auction starts, you receive a telephone call from a well-known, respected, and extremely wealthy collector of mechanical banks saying, "You know, I have been looking for that bank forever—sell it to me and I will pay you three times your reserve price, whatever it is." Can you end your auction early and sell the bank to the collector?

Now, eBay won't like this situation too much if they find out about it, because it deprives eBay of a "final value" fee. One of the surest ways to get booted off of eBay is to make a habit of steering eBay bidders to transactions outside of eBay (see Chapter 5). Yet, according to eBay's policy (see pages.ebay.com/help/sell/end_early.html), you can end your eBay auction early in the above example:

> ➤ At any time up to twelve hours before the auction closes, even if your reserve price has been met

➞ At any time less than twelve hours before the auction closes, but only
if your reserve price has not been met

In other words, it all depends on whether your reserve price has
already been met. If the answer is no, you can pull your auction at
any time. If the answer is yes, you can pull the auction up to twelve
hours before the auction closes. After that, you will have to have a
darned good reason to pull the auction.

When you end an auction early on eBay, eBay will e-mail the
bidders and tell them the auction has been terminated, but will not
explain why. Even though you are not required to do so, it is a good
idea to send your own e-mail to the buyers explaining the situation.
This way you'll "keep the peace" on eBay and avoid negative feedback. If you do not explain to buyers why you ended an auction
early, they are almost certain to smell a rat and assume you received a better offer from someone else, outside of eBay.

If you are not sure what to say, consider sending your bidders
an e-mail explaining that you have withdrawn the item "for further
study" because another bidder has pointed out to you that the item
may not be 100 percent as described. A buyer can hardly complain
about your ending an auction in order to make sure the item was
exactly "as described," since that's exactly what a responsible seller
should do. Just be careful—if you do pull an auction early for any
reason, do not put the item back on eBay a few days later with a
higher starting price or reserve price.

The eBay policy on ending auctions early is extremely seller-
friendly, and for a good reason. Because the vast majority of sellers
on eBay are inexperienced in their merchandise, situations will frequently arise where a seller realizes halfway through an auction
that the item is not as originally described. The policy is therefore
designed to give sellers the maximum amount of flexibility in
changing or ending their auctions to avoid problems with disgruntled buyers.

The policies also allow sellers to cancel individual bids in pending auctions if the bidder does not conform to the seller's require-

ments—for example, the bidder lives in a country to which the seller does not ship, or the bidder has an unusually high number of negative feedback postings. Before canceling anyone's bid on eBay, however, you should post Terms and Conditions on all of your auction pages (see Appendix B for an example) explaining the circumstances under which you will do so. Canceling someone's bid arbitrarily and without warning is one of the surest ways I know to generate negative feedback on eBay.

DISSEMINATING "INSIDE INFORMATION"

During an eBay auction, you will frequently receive e-mail messages from bidders (or potential bidders) asking questions about the item. When responding to these inquiries, be careful that you are not giving any of your bidders an unfair advantage in the auction.

Buying or selling securities based on inside information is a federal offense—and we can all think of celebrities who have gotten into legal trouble by doing so. While it is unlikely eBay will come after you if you demonstrate you prefer one bidder over another, it's not a good idea to discriminate among your buyers by giving some of them the "inside scoop" on an item.

Example: You have posted a mechanical bank for sale on eBay with digital photos of the front, back, and both sides of the bank. A bidder e-mails you and asks for a photo of the bank's underside because the base contains important information that mechanical bank collectors rely on in determining if a bank is authentic. You send the inquiring bidder the requested photo, but decide not to post the photo on your auction page because the auction has only a few hours to go and it's too much trouble.

Because of your decision, you have just given the inquiring bidder "inside information" that will give him an unfair advantage over other bidders in determining whether the bank is "as described."

While eBay technically doesn't require you to do so, it is good practice to include in your Terms and Conditions a policy that your e-mail responses to inquiries about any item will be posted to the auction page so that all buyers can see them. Failing that, you can copy all other bidders on your e-mails. See Appendix B for sample language.

ILLEGAL SELLING PRACTICES: DON'T EVEN THINK ABOUT THEM!

One of the surest ways to get kicked off of eBay is to be caught engaging in illegal bidding practices designed to "rig" an eBay auction. Not only do these practices violate eBay policies, they are criminal violations of the law in many states. If eBay catches you doing anything illegal, they will not only boot you off the site, but will send a nice letter to your state's attorney general's office telling them where they can find you. If you think any of your bidders are engaging in one of these practices, you should notify eBay immediately to head off any suggestion by a disgruntled buyer that you are in cahoots with these folks.

Shill Bidding

Sadly, this is a common practice in both online and live auctions. An auction seller appoints a friend or relative—a "shill"—to sit in the audience. If an item attracts only one or two bidders and looks likely to sell below the price the seller wants, the shill goes into action and starts bidding against the legitimate bidder, pulling out of the auction only when the seller's desired price has been reached. If the shill is too aggressive and wins the item, he pays the winning bid price and is quietly reimbursed by the seller after the auction closes. On eBay, of course, since the seller and the shill are in cahoots, no money will actually change hands if the shill wins. In fact, the seller and the shill will leave positive feedback for each other, boosting their positive ratings and making future shill bidding situations even easier. (You would never accuse someone with a 500 feedback rating of being a "shill" for an eBay seller, would you?)

A variation on traditional shill bidding involves the use of eBay's popular Second Chance Offer feature. Let's say a seller puts an item up for sale on eBay, and within a few hours before the auction closes, there is only one bidder. The seller notifies his shill, who puts in a "sniper" bid for the item at an extremely high price, in an effort to figure out what the legitimate buyer's maximum price is. The "sniper shill" wins the auction by $1 more than the legitimate buyer's maximum bid price, which the seller now knows thanks to the timely "snipe." (See the sidebar to learn more about sniping.)

The legitimate buyer has no reason to suspect foul play; after all, people get sniped on eBay every day. The next day, though, the legitimate buyer receives a "second chance offer" from the seller offering an "identical item" for the legitimate buyer's maximum bid price . . .

Shill bidding cannot happen without your consent and involvement. Someone who bids consistently in your auctions but is "always a bridesmaid, never a bride" is not your shill unless they are doing it at your request, although if the same user ID crops up over and over again in your auctions, be aware that other bidders may start to get suspicious that a shill bidding operation is going on. If eBay questions you about it, you will be in the difficult position of proving a negative—convincing eBay that there is no relationship between you and the perennially unsuccessful bidder.

Bid Rigging

Also known as a "ring," bid rigging isn't as common on eBay as it is in live auctions, but it can happen, especially in multiple auctions of identical items that don't attract a lot of bidders. In bid rigging, a group of buyers (usually antiques dealers) attend an auction and agree not to compete against each other for certain items. Ring member 1 bids on the first item, and nobody bids against him. Ring member 2 bids on the second item, and nobody bids against her. And so on.

If a bidder outside the ring starts to bid against a ring member, another member will try to discourage the outsider's bid by pointing out to him (in a friendly way) flaws in the item that the outsider presumably is not aware of. Have you ever bid for something on eBay and received a nice e-mail from a helpful person claiming to be an expert in the merchandise and pointing out "hidden flaws" in the item that were not disclosed in the seller's auction description? Have you ever been so grateful to this friendly stranger for his advice that you stopped bidding on the item? Were you then surprised to see the same item in the supposed expert's own eBay auction a couple of weeks later?

Bid Shielding

One form of bid rigging that does happen with some frequency on eBay is "bid shielding." In a shielding scheme, two buyers (or perhaps the same buyer with two different user IDs) drive up the bid price for an item so high above the item's market value that other, legitimate buyers drop out of the auction. Shortly before the auction closes, the two cooperating bidders both "retract" their bids, and one of them (or a third user ID) then places a lowball bid, $1 above the nearest legitimate bid, that wins the item.

eBay's policy limiting bid retractions within the last twelve hours of an auction has gone a long way to discourage bid shielding on eBay. If a bidder has multiple bids in an auction and retracts during the last twelve hours, only her most recent bid is retracted, not all of her bids. This forces "shielders" to retract each one of their bids individually—a practice that will almost certainly be picked up by the seller or eBay's Trust and Safety team.

Interfering with Other Sellers' Auctions

If you cause someone to breach a contract with a third party, you can actually be sued in just about every state. This practice is called "inducing breach of contract" or "tortuous interference with contract."

Let's say you put a rare antique up on eBay, in a fixed-price sale using eBay's Buy It Now! feature. It just so happens that another seller recently put up the same item, and there were several bidders in the other auction before it closed. While there is nothing wrong with e-mailing the underbidders in that other auction and telling them about your item, it would be illegal "interference with contract" to contact the winning bidder and offer to sell him your item at a lower price if he refuses to go through with his purchase from the other seller.

So far, so good. But what if the other auction is still pending? Can you send an e-mail to all bidders in the other auction? Suppose you contact them and say:

> "I see you are bidding on a genuine 1885 mechanical bank. You should be aware that this bank has the following problems: X, Y, and Z. If you are fussy about the condition of the banks you buy, you should be aware that I've got the same bank at my auction # _____ and it doesn't have any of these problems"?

Let's say you are an expert in mechanical banks, and all of the flaws you point out are, in fact, true. Sharing your comments with the bidders would not be a legal violation, technically, since there is no "contract" as yet between the bidders and the other seller. However, eBay's policy on transaction interference specifically prohibits members from e-mailing buyers in an open or completed auction to "warn them away from a seller or item," even though all of the members' allegations about the seller may well be true. For details of this policy, go to: pages.ebay.com/help/policies/transaction-interference.html.

Here's a tougher example, which I think falls into a gray area in eBay's policies: You send an e-mail to the other auction's bidders saying, "I see you are bidding on a genuine 1885 mechanical bank. If you are interested in this bank, I've got a similar one at my auction # _____ and you can Buy It Now! for $_____."

Unlike the previous example, you are not warning the other

• A Word About "Sniping" •

It happens to everyone on eBay sooner or later. Three seconds before an auction closes on eBay, you are the high bidder. Three seconds later, fifteen people outbid you by placing last-second bids for the item using one of several "sniper" software programs available on the Web, and you find yourself at the bottom of the pile.

Frustrating? Absolutely!

Illegal? No.

There is nothing illegal or immoral about sniping items on eBay. There are many legitimate reasons for even very nice people to become snipers:

- They wish to keep their user IDs confidential to discourage "parasite bidders" (also known as "auction stalkers"), or people who track your user ID to see what you are bidding on because "Cliff really knows about mechanical banks—anything he's bidding on is good enough for me!"
- They want to avoid shill bidding. When they snipe an item at the last second, the seller's "shill" doesn't have time to act.
- They want to keeping their identities secret from other eBay buyers who routinely bid against them because they are jealous, confrontational, or just plain don't like them.

Sadly, quite a few eBay bidders have told me in confidence that, in their opinion, "the only way you can get something you really want on eBay is to snipe it, because if you don't, someone is sure to snipe you!"

eBay doesn't care about snipers, and frankly, neither should you. As a seller, your goal on eBay is to get the highest price you possibly can for your stuff. And if snipers help you get better prices, so much the better. Just make sure that you are not sniping your own auctions in an effort to drive the bids up.

bidders about defects in the seller's merchandise. You are merely saying, "Hey, there's another one over here!" I don't think this action would be viewed as transaction interference, but there's always the chance the other seller might accuse you of diverting bidders' attention away from his auction. Whose side will eBay take? Heaven only knows . . .

I'm going to take a stand and say that as long as your e-mail message to other bidders contains only information they could get on their own (by finding your eBay auction without your help) and doesn't say anything negative about the other seller or his merchandise, I think you should be okay, at least under eBay's transaction interference policy.

But keep in mind that a "direct solicitation" of other bidders may not be necessary at all. You should do so only when that's the only practical way for another bidder to find out about your listings. If you have listed your item properly and in all of the right places, the people who regularly look for and buy this type of merchandise on eBay will find out about you without your having to chase them down. And no one can accuse you of "interfering" with their auctions just because you posted an identical item at the same time. Competition is a good thing, isn't it?

One last thing: If you should decide to send targeted messages to bidders in other eBay auctions, be careful not to send the same message to hundreds of eBay user IDs at the same time. An e-mail "blitz" targeting bidders of merchandise in certain categories could be viewed as spam, which violates another eBay policy. (See Chapter 5 for more about spam; see also the policy described at pages .ebay.com/help/policies/rfe-spam-ov.html.)

COMMON QUESTIONS

Q. *There's a seller on eBay who's notorious for putting up extremely phony stuff. Some friends of mine and I have made it a practice to bid on this guy's auctions and drive the price up to astronomical levels so that no legitimate bidders will fall victim to his shoddy merchandise. Then, when the auction ends, we simply don't respond to the seller's e-mails requesting payment. Can we get into legal trouble for that?*

A. Possibly. There's a name for people like you and your friends—vigilantes. In the Old West, vigilantes would take the law into their own hands and string up anyone they thought was guilty of a crime. The trouble is, they were wrong in a lot of cases, and ended up lynching the wrong guy.

If you think someone on eBay is selling bogus merchandise, eBay wants you to report it to them and let them deal with the seller. By taking the law into your own hands, you not only risk negative feedback from this seller, you may also be engaging in an illegal bidding "ring" (as discussed previously in this chapter) and may be thrown off of eBay for engaging in illegal auction practices.

Remember, what is "bogus" is often in the eyes of the beholder. The best advice here comes from the Bible: "Judge not, that ye be not judged."

CHAPTER 5

Marketing Your eBay Auctions

In business, nothing happens until something gets sold. And nothing gets sold unless buyers know that something can be bought.

When you first start selling on eBay, it's tempting to just kick back and let the buyers find you. But sooner or later, you realize

• Some Required Reading for eBay Marketers •

There are literally hundreds of books to help you sell stuff on the Internet. My personal favorites:

The 7 Essential Steps to Internet eBay Marketing, by Janelle Elms, et al. (New York: McGraw-Hill, $16.95), is a good general introduction to marketing on eBay and the Internet generally.

Search Engine Advertising, by *Entrepreneur* magazine columnist Catherine Seda (New Riders, Berkeley, CA, $29.99), is an all-time classic for anyone wanting to learn the basics of marketing on Internet search engines.

Blogging for Dummies, by Brad Hill (Hoboken, NJ: Wiley, $21.99), and *Blog Marketing,* by Jeremy Wright (New York: McGraw-Hill, $24.95), give advice on setting up your own blog on the Web.

Launching a Successful eBay Store, by Ron Mansfield (Indianapolis: Pearson Education, $24.99), gives you all the details about opening an eBay Store.

you have to reach out to buyers, both on and off of eBay, and direct them to your auctions or eBay Store.

When you run any sort of small business, whether on or off of eBay, marketing is "job one." Whatever else you may call yourself, you are always the "salesperson in chief."

Having said that, though, there are some rules you need to follow. This chapter highlights some of the legal issues you will face when marketing or promoting your eBay business.

IT'S THE SEARCH ENGINES, STUPID

There was a time, not too long ago, that I used to think the phrase *Internet marketing* was a contradiction in terms. Traditional marketing is all about pushing products to consumers, and on the Internet you cannot "push" or force viewers to see things they don't want to see. An entire industry of software products—from antispam filters to pop-up blockers—has sprung up overnight for the specific purpose of preventing marketers from getting their messages through to you when you're online.

You cannot "push" on the Internet, but you can "pull" people to your website. Online, consumers run free, like a wild stallion, going wherever their head takes them. You are the one who must corral the free-range consumers and lead them to your water. When people go looking for stuff on the Internet, what do they use? A search engine, of course. That's where your advertising focus should be—letting the consumers think they have found you, and have made the free choice to click on a link to your website and see what you've got to offer.

The first thing you have to do is "optimize" your website for search engines, so that when people go looking for the product or service you sell, the engine lists your website as one of the top-ten "hits" that show up on the search query results page. Optimization is as much an art as a science. It involves picking the most commonly used keywords that people use to search for your offerings, and making sure those keywords are embedded in your website so the search engine "crawlers" can find them.

If doing anything yourself on a computer gives you the willies, there is a growing industry of search engine optimization (SEO) consultants who, for fees ranging from a few hundred dollars to a few thousand dollars, can use advanced statistical methods to identify the keywords that will drive search engine traffic to your website. A search for "SEO Consultant" on any search engine will yield about 500,000 results, many from computer professionals in India and other parts of the world who may be willing to provide world-class service for a much lower rate than U.S. consultants. The Organization of Search Engine Optimization Professionals (www.seo pros.org) was formed in 2001 to develop best practices and standards for this industry. Go to their site and click on SEO Consultant Directory for a list of their members nearest you.

Once you have optimized your site for search engines, you don't just sit there waiting for the "hits" to happen. It is now time to engage in search engine marketing: creating ads for your website that will appear next to the search query results when someone is searching for the merchandise you sell.

Start with pay-per-click advertising on Yahoo! Search Marketing (searchmarketing.yahoo.com), because it's easier than Google Ad-Words (adwords.google.com) for new advertisers to figure out. When you buy a pay-per-click ad on Yahoo, Google, or one of the major search engines, you are "bidding" for placement on that engine's search results. You create a short ad (usually less than fifty words), tell the search engine how much you are willing to pay for each "click" from the ad to your website, and that's pretty much it. When a person is searching for something you sell, and he sees your ad, he clicks on the link to your site and the search engine automatically debits your credit or ATM card for the amount you indicated. Simple enough, right? Well . . .

Let's say I decide to place an ad for "small business attorney" on Yahoo. I create a wonderful ad and offer to pay that search engine five cents (the minimum amount for ads on Yahoo) each time someone clicks on my ad. My ad will appear on Yahoo, all right, but on page fifty of the search query results for "small business attorney." How many times have you searched for something and looked at the fiftieth page of the query results? To get anywhere with search engine marketing, your ad needs to appear on the first or second page of the query results. For that to happen with my "small business attorney" ad, I would have to pay the search engine about $50 per click. That can add up to a significant bill each month in a real hurry, and there's no assurance that anyone who clicks my ad and gets to my website (triggering a $50 fee for the search engine) will actually buy something once they get there.

So how do you get around that? Simple. Make your ad as narrow and targeted as possible. While a five-cent ad for "small business attorney" won't get me anywhere, a ten-cent ad for "NY small business attorney" will get me on page two of the query results. If I raise the ante to twenty-five cents, I'm on page one. Of course, that narrows the range of searchers, but the ones looking for a small business attorney in New York are the ones I really want, anyway. I will get fewer hits from the search engine ad, but (hopefully) a higher percentage of serious folks who will actually contact me once they get to my site and see how truly wonderful I am.

Once you've listed some pay-per-click ads on Yahoo, what next? If you're selling services, start blogging. Create your own blog (or weblog) to show that you're an industry leader. By sharing helpful information (or just some wild, crazy, and cool stuff), you will invite blog readers to hire you. On the Web, nothing beats "buzz marketing"—that is, having a friend, colleague, or someone other than your mom or PR person tell you, "Hey, Joe, you've got to check out this guy's crazy blog. He's a little off the wall, but he really gets what we're trying to do here!"

If you're selling products, look for sites with already heavy traffic, and try to become their affiliate. In an affiliate relationship, another party will let you have an ad on their home page in exchange for putting an ad on your home page (plus perhaps some cash). For example, if you're selling antique toys from the 1800s and early 1900s, an ad on the website of *Antique Toy World* magazine (www.antiquetoyworld.com) will be worth its weight in gold.

Here's a tip: Look for high-traffic sites that offer merchandise that complements, but is not the same as, your merchandise. One of the most successful Web merchants in the vintage art poster market doesn't sell posters at all, at least not online. Rather, he makes and sells the high-end, acetate-free folders you use to store vintage posters that you don't want to frame and hang on your wall. Just about every vintage poster website has a link to him, because all vintage poster collectors need these folders—and I don't think he paid more than a few dollars (maximum) for all that advertising. And if you ask him nicely, he has a few really good posters in the "back room" that he might be willing to part with . . .

Finally, if you are selling clothing, housewares, or any sort of collectibles, you should seriously consider opening an eBay Store (stores.ebay.com). For a monthly fee starting at $15.95, you can list dozens of items on eBay, and for a little more eBay will even help promote your eBay Store to the major search engines, so you don't have to figure out the finer points of pay-per-click advertising yourself. Have you ever searched for something on the Internet and had someone's eBay Store or auction listing pop up as one of the top listings? Enough said.

CLICK FRAUD

In search engine advertising's simplest form, known as "pay per click," you offer to pay a certain amount to a search engine each time someone searches you out and clicks on a link to your site. "Click fraud" happens when someone who wishes you ill (such as a competitor) clicks repeatedly on your ad listings without actually intending to buy anything, just to run up your bill. Before buying "clicks" on any search engine, find out about the search engine's "click protection system" and what they will and won't do to remove fraudulent clicks from your accounts. Also consider registering your site with a pay-per-click auditing service such as Who's

Clicking Who (www.whosclickingwho.com). For a fee, this service will track your search engine listings and identify potential fraudsters.

KEYWORD SPAMMING

If you have a registered trademark, you want to use it as a keyword so that people searching for that trademark see your website first. A "keyword spammer" is someone who uses your trademark (for example, by outbidding you for your trademark or including it in the invisible metatags search engines use to find your website) to siphon customers away from you. Most search engines will remove a keyword spammer's listings if you complain, but in many cases you will have to pursue legal action directly against spammers to get them to stop.

FALSE OR DECEPTIVE ADVERTISING

Any claim or statement you make about your products and services on your website is a legal warranty consumers can rely on, and such statements must be true, correct, and complete in all respects. If they aren't, you may be sued for false advertising. Avoid hyped-up claims unless you can back them up with hard data, and have an attorney review your product descriptions before posting them on your website, especially if you are disparaging or making fun of your competition.

DIRECTING BUYERS TO TRANSACTIONS OUTSIDE OF EBAY

While eBay encourages you to market your eBay auction listings and eBay Store on search engines and websites outside of eBay, they get a little testy—to say the least—if you try to send business the other way. One of the surest ways to get into hot water on eBay

• It's Okay to Tell People How Great You Are •

In Chapter 3, we pointed out that you cannot commit fraud by expressing an opinion. The same rule applies to your advertising and marketing efforts.

Putting phrases such as "the best [whatever] on eBay" is not fraud: It is what advertising people call "puffery," and it's perfectly acceptable—although not very helpful as a marketing tool. I mean, do you really expect me to say that I'm anything but the best small business lawyer on the face of the planet?

A better marketing tool—and just as acceptable—is to get somebody famous or highly respected within the eBay community to give your business an endorsement or testimonial that you can use in your advertising. The idea is that this person would not recommend your stuff unless she seriously believed it was good.

But you have to be careful with endorsements. If the person making the endorsement says "I use this product, and it's great!" that statement has to be absolutely, a hundred percent true—the celebrity must actually be using your product.

Also, every once in a while, today's celebrity is tomorrow's embarrassment. We can all think of famous actors, politicians, and business people whose careers crashed overnight because of a faux pas or momentary lapse in judgment. You don't want to be associated with a famous person (or worse, committed to paying a fee for his endorsement) who "melts down" and becomes the butt of jokes on all the late-night talk shows.

is to direct your eBay auction bidders to items you have for sale on your own website or anyplace other than eBay.

The policy on Offers to Buy or Sell Outside of eBay (see pages.ebay.com/help/policies/rfe-spam-non-ebay-sale.html) is such an important part of the eBay experience that it is worth citing in its entirety:

> E-mail offers to buy or sell listed items outside of the eBay site are prohibited. Offers of this nature circumvent eBay's fee structure and are a potential fraud risk for both buyers and sellers. . . .

Some examples of outside of eBay offers include:

➤ Using information obtained through eBay to offer to buy or sell a listed item outside of eBay.

➤ Canceling a listing to sell to a buyer who became aware of the item through eBay.

➤ Ending a listing early to sell the item at a higher price to the winning bidder.

➤ Offering to sell an item to a bidder in a Reserve Not Met listing.

➤ Offering to sell duplicate or additional merchandise to underbidders.

It is acceptable for sellers to end a listing early in order to sell an item at the current bid price to the high bidder. Bidders are permitted to contact sellers with requests to end a listing early; however, sellers are under no obligation to do so.

Although offers to buy or sell outside of eBay are not permitted, sellers may be able to sell items to underbidders by sending a Second Chance Offer.

The keyword in the eBay policy is *solicit*. If an eBay bidder happens to do an Internet search for you and finds out you have a website with merchandise for sale that isn't available on eBay, it's not against the rules for *the bidder to contact you*. What is against the rules is for you to contact bidders directly and "nudge" them in the direction of your website. You can, however, include a Web address in your About Me page on eBay, and as part of your signature when sending e-mails to people generally.

AVOIDING "SPAM" E-MAILS TO OTHER eBAY MEMBERS

Spam is e-mail that is both unsolicited and commercial in nature.

➤ "Unsolicited" means the e-mail has been sent without the permission of the person who received it.

➤ "Commercial" means the mail discusses the buying, selling, or trading of goods or services.

The CAN-SPAM Act of 2003 is a commonly used name for the United States law more formally known as the Controlling the Assault of Non-Solicited Pornography and Marketing Act of 2003. The law, which took effect on January 1, 2004, allows courts to set damages of up to $2 million when spammers break the law. Federal courts are allowed to send spammers to jail and/or triple the damages if the violation is found to be willful.

While not prohibiting the delivery of spam as such (doing so would probably violate the spammer's rights under the First Amendment to the U.S. Constitution guaranteeing freedom of speech, among other things), the CAN-SPAM Act requires that businesses:

- ➤ Clearly label commercial e-mail as "advertising."
- ➤ Use a truthful and relevant subject line.
- ➤ Use a legitimate return e-mail address.
- ➤ Provide a valid physical address.
- ➤ Provide a working opt-out option (allowing recipients to be removed from the spam list).
- ➤ Process opt-out requests within ten business days.

But never mind the CAN-SPAM Act. Spam is not permitted on eBay, period. While the eBay policy (see pages.ebay.com/help/policies/rfe-spam-ov.html) doesn't define precisely when communications with eBay community members rise to the level of "spam," it's pretty clear that you shouldn't automatically send e-mails to every eBay bidder who has bid on items similar to yours in, say, the last two years.

Having said that, though, building a mailing list of people who have bid on your eBay auctions and may want to hear about your new eBay auctions and other listings probably will not violate the eBay antispam policy, as long as 1) you ask their permission first to be placed on a mailing list, 2) you give them the chance to opt out of your list at any time, and 3) you do not promote your website or anything else you may be selling on sites other than eBay.

COMMON QUESTIONS

Q. *What are some types of search manipulation?*

A. The four primary types of search manipulation are:

1. *Keyword Spamming.* This is the practice of including brand names or other inappropriate keywords in a title or description for the purpose of gaining attention or diverting users to a listing. Keyword spamming is unfair to members who may be searching for a specific item and receive search results of listings that are not selling the item. Users often are confused and frustrated by such tactics.

2. *Brand-Name Misuse.* Do not include any brand names or company logos in your listings other than the specific brand name used by the company that manufactured or produced the item you are listing. Certain uses of brand names may also constitute trademark infringement and could expose sellers to legal liability.

3. *Comparisons.* Sellers are not permitted to compare items in their titles.

4. *Misleading Titles.* Make sure your title accurately describes only the actual item or items you are offering for sale.

Q. *What types of titles would not be permitted?*

A. Let me give two examples:

1. *Extra Brand Names in Title.* You are not permitted any use of a trademarked (brand) name in the title of a listing where products of that brand name are not being offered.

2. *Not This, Not That.* A title or description for a listing is prohibited if it reads, for example: "Gucci Purse (not Louis Vuitton, Armani, Prada)" or "I also sell Gap, Nike, Gucci, Rolex, etc." or "Please see my other listings for Beanie Babies, Pokemon, and Star Wars items."

Q. *How can I include a famous brand name in my auction listings without infringing their trademark?*

A. Generally speaking, reference to more than one brand name in a description is considered keyword spamming. Under some circumstances it may be permissible to refer to other brands for comparison purposes or if you are selling a group of items in a single listing. However, some uses of other brand names may be considered by the owners of the relevant trademarks to be infringements of their rights. For example, use of phrases such as "Chanel-like," "Movado-style," "Gucci" or "Prada" (in quotes), or "This X brand bag has leather just like a Coach bag" will likely lead to increased scrutiny of your listing by rights owners and the implication that the goods you are offering are not authentic. In such cases, the trademark owner may submit a sworn statement concerning the alleged infringement through eBay's Verified Rights Owner (VeRO) program and request that eBay end your listing early.

Of course, eBay realizes that many community members prefer to use a brand name for comparative purposes to best illustrate their item's particular style. However, eBay encourages everyone to first contact the trademark owner in question for guidance as to what is permissible, before making any questionable use of a brand name.

CHAPTER 6

After the Auction Closes

Since I first decided to write this book, I have dreaded writing this chapter, because I know that no matter what I say here, I will not be pleasing a hundred percent of my readers a hundred percent of the time. But here goes anyway.

WHEN BAD THINGS HAPPEN TO GOOD PEOPLE

From the beginning, eBay has been based on the premise that "people are basically good," and the statistics bear this out. According to eBay, 99.9 percent of all transactions on the online auction site go through without a hitch, and at any time more than 100 million items are available for sale on eBay.

Do the math in your head, and a fair number of transactions simply *don't* go as planned. If you are serious about building a business on eBay, you have to accept that sooner or later, you will find yourself in a sticky situation with a buyer and will have to make a tough—and fairly complicated—decision about how best to deal with it.

WHY DO BAD THINGS HAPPEN (SOMETIMES) ON eBAY AND PAYPAL?

One of the most beautiful things about eBay—and the core of founder Pierre Omidyar's vision for the company—is that anyone can sell anything to anybody there. And (as Shakespeare would say) "there's the rub."

When you buy something on eBay, you are (most of the time, anyway) not buying it from a professional merchant who is knowledgeable about the merchandise and about how to run a reputable retail business. Rather, you are buying it from someone who is . . . well, a lot like you! Someone who probably knows less about the merchandise than you do. Someone who knows even less about the proper way to run a retail business (until that someone buys this book, that is). Someone who doesn't see herself as a "professional," or even in business at all (see Chapter 1), and will take everything you say and do personally and emotionally as a direct threat to her honor, reputation, and self-esteem.

In other words, you are, in most cases, buying something from an amateur seller.

I don't have hard statistics, but I would be willing to bet serious money that the vast majority of "disputed transactions" on eBay arise from one of the following factors:

➢ Unrealistic expectations about what eBay or PayPal will or won't do to help their members resolve disputes (a subject discussed in the next section)

➢ Lack of selling experience on the part of one or both parties

➢ Lack of experience with the merchandise being sold on the part of one or both parties

➢ Poor communication (or no communication) between buyer and seller

➢ An inability on the part of one or both parties to separate "business" from "personal" considerations (or, if you prefer, "immaturity")

➢ Fear of confrontation (hey, it's a lot easier to give someone "negative feedback" or file an e-mail complaint with eBay than to call the other person directly and find out what's going on)

Please don't get me wrong. I am *not* naive, nor have I been co-opted by eBay or PayPal. There are some "bad apples" on eBay, just like there are some bad apples in any marketplace—people who "game the system" by taking unfair advantage of the open marketplace eBay tries to create for its community. Later in this chapter I'll describe some of the "games" these people play. However much eBay tries to get these people off of its network, they will always be with us, and sooner or later—despite your best efforts—you will bump into one. All I can say is, Welcome to the world of business.

Having said that, though, there aren't as many bad apples as one would like to think. The vast majority of disputes on eBay can be avoided or resolved by following some of the techniques described in this chapter. Most people *are* basically good, if you give them a chance to prove it to you.

SOME INCONVENIENT TRUTHS

Let's start by explaining how eBay and its partner PayPal operate.

About eBay

eBay is in the business of providing a marketplace—a "playing field" or "platform," if you will—on which businesses and individuals worldwide can buy and sell stuff *to and from each other.* That's the key to understanding how eBay works.

When you buy something on eBay, you are not buying it *from* eBay. You are buying it from another member of the eBay community, who may or may not be sophisticated, mature, or even basically intelligent. The good news is that anyone can be a "player" on eBay with a minimum investment of time, money, and experience. The bad news is that with such a low "barrier to entry," there's no way to ensure that you will be dealing with "class acts" every time you buy or sell on eBay.

If something bad happens to you on eBay, you cannot sue eBay, just like you cannot sue a "marketplace" in the brick-and-mortar world. If you buy something at a shopping mall and it falls apart before you even get it home, you can sue the store you bought it from, but you can't sue the owner of the shopping mall. If you buy something from a "classified ad" in your local newspaper and it turns out to be bogus, you can sue the person who placed the ad, but you can't sue the newspaper. Likewise, if you buy something from my mom at the local American Legion flea market, you can sue my mom (though I wouldn't advise it—she gives as good as she gets), but you can't sue the American Legion.

eBay works very hard to preserve its "neutral" status as a "marketplace." A number of powerful companies have sued eBay over the years claiming otherwise, but so far (as this book is written) those lawsuits have gotten nowhere.

About PayPal

Just as eBay is only a "marketplace" that facilitates transactions, PayPal is a "platform" to facilitate payments between individuals and businesses worldwide.

PayPal is not a bank, nor is it a credit card company. PayPal works very hard to ensure that it is not considered a bank, credit card company, or financial institution, because if that happens it will be subject to a vast and complex array of federal, state, and local regulations that would threaten (if not destroy) its business model.

The beauty of PayPal is that it enables sellers to accept credit cards without having to incur the expense of maintaining "merchant accounts" with each of the major credit card companies. The bad news is that when a seller or buyer has a dispute with a credit card company, PayPal cannot get involved—it has to undo or "rescind" the transaction to preserve its relationship with the credit card company and let the players duke it out, outside of PayPal.

About eBay and PayPal

If eBay or PayPal were to get too involved in the transactions that take place on their websites, they would be exposed to legal liability that would threaten (if not destroy) their business models, and no one would benefit from that. Even if that weren't the case, they would have to spend millions of dollars to hire the hundreds, if not thousands, of employees they would need to adjudicate buyer-seller disputes—employees that would not generate one penny of revenue for eBay or PayPal (unless eBay or PayPal were to charge fees for this service to cover their costs). They would have to figure out policies to ensure that decisions were being made consistently—that two dispute resolution "teams" in separate cubicles weren't reaching different conclusions on the same set of facts. They would have to figure out ways to publish decisions so that community members could follow them. They would have to figure out a mechanism for community members to "appeal" decisions, with the power to reverse prior decisions when circumstances change. Most important, they would have to work out a system of sanctions to enforce decisions in a way that would compel eBay/PayPal community members to abide by them.

In other words, eBay and PayPal would have to become governments, with their own regulators, bureaucracies, police force, and judicial system to enforce a complex and ever-growing set of rules. Not exactly what you want in a free and open marketplace.

About Getting Justice

The good news is that you can always sue a buyer who gives you a bad experience on eBay. The bad news is that you probably won't do that.

The vast majority of disputed transactions on eBay never end up in court, for two reasons:

> ➤ The parties are usually located in different states.
> ➤ The amounts involved don't justify the cost of suing someone.

If you are in California and get into a dispute with a buyer in Maine, you can sue the buyer in a California court, but here's what will happen: The buyer won't show up, and you will get a "default judgment" from the California court (which is what happens when the person you are suing doesn't show up to plead his case). You will then try to enforce the default judgment in a Maine court where the buyer lives, and the Maine court will not enforce the default judgment because the Maine citizen wasn't given the right to plead his case (many courts consider this a "denial of due process of law" under their state constitutions).

As for the cost of suing someone, the average attorney will want an up-front "retainer fee" of $5,000 to $10,000 to take on any sort of commercial lawsuit. If you are selling $10 bobblehead dolls on eBay, it will be hard to justify a $5,000 legal fee to collect a $10 judgment from a defaulting buyer (unless you are extremely wealthy and are willing to spend this much money for the satisfaction of seeing justice done).

If you do sue a buyer on eBay, you will probably do so in the small-claims court where the buyer lives, and despite the time and inconvenience involved, I encourage you to do so because it's frequently a very effective way for you to get justice. (Later in this chapter I'll give more advice on going to small-claims court as a way to get a long-distance buyer's attention.)

About Your eBay Business

While both eBay and PayPal offer certain services to help their community members resolve disputes—which will be described later in this chapter—they are not always going to take your side in the dispute or guarantee that you will always have a "perfect experience" when playing in their sandbox. Sometimes when you take advantage of eBay's or PayPal's online dispute resolution services, eBay or PayPal will rule against you, for very good reasons, and you and your ego have to be willing to take that risk. Before making any sort of ruling on your dispute with a buyer, eBay and PayPal will do everything possible to get you and the buyer talking so that you can settle it without having to involve eBay or PayPal at all.

Retailers in the brick-and-mortar world know that not every transaction goes smoothly. They know that a certain percentage of transactions each year will go sour and leave them holding the bag for something. Rather than weep and moan about the way of the world, they build that knowledge into their business plan and take precautions to protect themselves and keep the number of "bad deals" to an absolute minimum. Among these precautions are:

➢ Maintaining a reserve for "bad debts" on their books (which, by the way, are fully deductible for tax purposes, as covered in Chapter 9)

➢ Maintaining several bank and merchant card accounts, so that if one account is "frozen," they still have cash to operate

➢ Drafting and posting "policies" limiting their obligations and liabilities in the event of a dispute

➢ Avoiding troublesome buyers whenever they can be spotted in advance

➢ Being realistic and mature enough to know that not all disputes are worth pursuing, and that sometimes you have to cut your losses and move forward, even though you know you are a hundred percent in the right

When you are doing business on eBay, you are a "retailer" (see Chapter 1), and you have to do the same things brick-and-mortar retailers do to protect themselves and their businesses against bad deals. There is very little eBay, PayPal, or anyone else can do to change that.

What can I say? You-know-what happens on eBay as it does everywhere else, and the burden is on you to deal with it calmly, rationally, and in a businesslike manner.

GAMES BUYERS PLAY—DEALING WITH DEADBEATS

A sales transaction is really very simple. The seller delivers the goods to the buyer, and the buyer pays for them. Virtually all of the games that buyers play involve either 1) not paying for goods they've ordered or 2) paying for them and then trying to wiggle out of the deal once they know the goods have shipped.

Don't Ship Until You Get Paid

I am always amazed—*amazed*—that even some experienced eBay sellers, who should know better, routinely ship goods to the buyer before they have received payment. Yes, when you're selling hundreds of items each month on eBay, it's tough to keep track of who pays for what items, but—hey!—when you've reached that point, you can afford some wonderful software products (some of which are listed in Appendix A) that can help you do just that, so there's really no excuse.

The first rule in avoiding problems with "nonpaying buyers" is simple: Don't ship the goods until payment has been received! Period. End of story. World without end, amen.

Let's say it is several days after an auction closes. You have attempted to contact the buyer by e-mail on two occasions, and there has been no response. You have not received payment, but you've still got the goods in your hot little hands. The Terms and Conditions you post on every eBay auction page clearly states that if a buyer has not contacted you within X days, you can terminate the transaction and sell the goods to someone else. (You should always include this information in your auction "Terms and Conditions"—see Appendix B for suggested language.)

You have a number of options, such as:

> ➢ Relisting the item and "letting bygones be bygones"
> ➢ Using eBay's popular Second Chance Offer and offering the goods to the "underbidders" in your auction
> ➢ Posting negative feedback for the buyer on eBay's Feedback Forum (although this is not recommended because if the buyer is truly a "bad apple," he may turn around and post negative feedback on you)

If you've already shipped, however, you have none of these options. If (even worse) you have no proof of shipment, you're in even worse shape, because the buyer can now claim "I never received the goods, so why should I pay for them?" and it's your word against his.

No matter how frustrating it is to have a "nonpaying buyer," I wouldn't recommend leaving negative feedback. Why? Because if you do, Murphy's Law ("everything that can go wrong, will go wrong") comes into play. No sooner do you post negative feedback than the buyer e-mails you and says, "Sorry for the slow response, but I've been out of town on a business trip and just saw today that I won your auction—please confirm that you received my PayPal payment, which I sent this morning." Oopsie . . .

Bad Checks: When Do They Actually Clear?

It is a crime in just about every state—and a felony in most—to knowingly write a bad check. People who write bad checks should be in jail; it's that simple.

Yet every business gets a bad check every once in a while. The trick here, again, is not to ship the goods until you know with a hundred percent certainty that the check has cleared.

Most deposited checks clear within a day or two, but Federal Reserve Board Regulation CC gives banks the discretion to put much longer holds on certain types of higher-risk checks, including checks greater than $5,000, checks deposited into accounts of new customers, and checks that a bank suspects may not be paid. Most banks have a ten- to fifteen-day clearing policy for checks over $5,000.

So, to avoid problems with bad checks, simply adopt a rule (and put it in your Terms and Conditions) that you will not ship goods until twenty days after you deposit the buyer's check or "whenever the check shows up as clear on our monthly bank statement," whichever first occurs.

What happens if you get a bad check?

First, notify the buyer and give him X days to send you a good check. Accidental overdrafts do happen, even to good people. The person's identity might have been stolen. A creditor might have automatically debited his account without notifying him. Do not return the bad check to the buyer until you get a good one and it clears your bank.

Second, if the buyer fails or refuses to respond, notify eBay and post negative feedback on the Feedback Forum.

Third, call the police department in the buyer's hometown and let them know about the bad check. The desk sergeant will record this information in the local "police blotter," and it will very likely be picked up by the buyer's hometown newspaper, whose reporters scan the police blotter every day for juicy tidbits about local residents acting badly. (Trust me on this—I used to be a local police reporter for a daily newspaper.)

Lastly, send a letter by certified mail to the state attorney general's office in the state where the buyer lives, with a photocopy of the bounced check. (Go to your favorite search engine and type "[name of state] attorney general" to find the website.) If you have a choice of departments to send the letter to, send it to the consumer fraud department. Oh, and don't forget to "cc" the buyer, and include his home address on the "cc." Attorneys general love it when you make their work easier for them.

Credit Card Chargebacks

By far the most common, and most insidious, type of "nonpaying buyer" problem you will encounter on eBay is "credit card chargebacks." These are the bane of every online retailer, and it's almost guaranteed you'll have to deal with this problem if you sell long enough and hard enough on eBay.

Here's how a chargeback typically works. The winning bidder in one of your auctions pays for the goods using PayPal, but charges the purchase to a credit card rather than his bank account. PayPal charges the buyer's credit card and deposits the money into your PayPal account. You ship the goods when you confirm receipt of the PayPal payment (in most cases you don't even know that the buyer has paid by credit card).

The buyer waits a couple of days—just to make sure the goods have shipped and are out of your control—and then calls the credit card company claiming that the goods were "not in the condition described by" the seller. Because the credit card company views the buyer as their customer (and, let's face it, because credit card companies are reluctant to get involved in commercial disputes), they undo or "rescind" the transaction on the buyer's account and demand reimbursement from PayPal. PayPal, not wishing to use its own funds to pay the credit card company back, and desiring to maintain good relationships with the credit card companies on whom its livelihood depends, debits your PayPal account and reimburses the credit card company. If there isn't enough money in your account, PayPal might "freeze" your account until the matter is resolved.

Everybody wins in this arrangement . . . except you. You have parted with the goods, you don't have your payment, and often you don't even have a clue what the devil just happened. You sometimes don't know about a "chargeback" until you notice it in your PayPal account statement. You are happy to pursue the matter with the buyer's credit card company, but you don't know which one to contact. You send PayPal an e-mail asking for details, and you wait . . . and wait . . . and wait . . .

What's really tough about chargebacks is that they might be legitimate. If buyers have reason to believe you've delivered something different from what you promised on your auction page, they have every legal right to "stop payment" with their credit card company. Chargebacks are not crimes (like writing bad checks), so you can't do any of the nasty things listed in the previous section on bad checks. If you do, there's a good chance the buyer will sue you for "defamation of character" (think libel and slander).

When a buyer "charges back" a credit card payment, it still doesn't resolve the underlying dispute between you—did you or did you not deliver goods that conformed to your auction description? If a buyer claims that you didn't deliver the right stuff and offers to send it back to you if you "walk away," you are probably best advised to go along with that, get the goods back, and resell them on eBay (assuming the buyer hasn't trashed the goods in the meantime). If a buyer stonewalls you, then it's time to get nasty with the buyer's credit card company and PayPal.

It's difficult, but not impossible, to fight chargebacks. A useful resource is the Chargeback Bureau (www.chargebackbureau.com), a website where, for a subscription fee of $9.99 per month, you have access to all of the forms required by the major credit card companies to protest improper chargebacks. You also get guidance on how to fill out the forms, who to send them to, how to follow up on your protest, and other useful techniques to make the buyer's life as miserable as possible. You may not get the result you want, but you will definitely send the buyer a signal that you're not about to roll over and play dead.

One more thing . . . if a buyer ever pulls a chargeback on you, be sure to add him to your "restricted buyers" list, since you are well within your rights never to sell to him again. As we say in the legal business, "fool me once, shame on you; fool me twice, shame on me."

Dealing with Collection Agencies

Collection agencies really aren't much help to eBay sellers, because they are set up to collect only "undisputed" amounts. One of the surest ways to get a collection agency off of your back is to show there's a legitimate dispute over your obligation to pay for goods. All that most buyers will have to do is say, "The seller didn't deliver goods that conformed to her auction description," and the collection agency will have to back off. If a buyer admits that he owes you money and just can't pay, that's another story.

GAMES SELLERS PLAY . . . THAT GET BUYERS RILED UP

A sales transaction is really very simple. The seller delivers the goods to the buyer, and the buyer pays for them. Virtually all of the games that sellers play involve either 1) selling nonexistent goods, 2) delivering the wrong goods, or 3) delivering goods in damaged condition.

> ## • Things You Can't Say to a Nonpaying Buyer •
>
> Bill collectors are not known for being kind, gentle folks, but, believe it or not, there are rules about what you can and cannot say when you try to collect a debt from a nonpaying buyer.
>
> The federal Fair Debt Collection Practices Act prohibits you from doing certain things to collect debts that people, especially individual consumers (as opposed to businesses), owe you. For example, you cannot:
>
> - Imply that you are an attorney or government official (although you can threaten to sue)
> - Call before or after certain hours of the day or night
> - Imply that the debtor has committed a crime that will get him thrown in jail
> - Threaten to attach the debtor's wages or property unless you actually intend to do so
>
> Never leave a nasty collection message on a buyer's voice mail. If other members of the person's family are listening to messages, you may be liable for "defamation of character" (libel or slander) if your message is not a hundred percent accurate.
>
> The bottom line: Talk to a lawyer before you even think about making a collection call to a buyer.

The Goods Don't Exist

Whenever you are selling goods that you don't actually possess (think "consignment sales" and "drop shipping," as covered in Chapter 14), there's a risk that something may happen to the goods while your eBay auction is pending and that you won't be able to deliver them when the auction closes. The goods may be destroyed in transit to you, the "consignor" may have sold them to another buyer without informing you, the "drop shipper" may have run out of inventory of the item you want, and so forth.

If you are selling goods you don't actually possess, you should tell your buyers, either in the auction description or in your Terms and Conditions (see Appendix B). You should also reserve the right to terminate the auction and refund the buyer's payment if you are unable in good faith to deliver the goods within a reasonable time after the auction closes.

Of course, if you are selling stuff on eBay you know doesn't exist—and never has—you are engaged in fraud and deserve every bad thing that happens to you.

The Goods Get Damaged in Transit

This is probably the most common complaint you will get from difficult buyers on eBay. And a lot of times the complaint is made in good faith. I personally have bought items on eBay that have been trashed in transit to me, and I can tell you I wasn't a happy camper. Even though I knew it probably wasn't the seller's fault, I wasn't about to write off the purchase price.

The Terms and Conditions section of your auction page has to spell out who has the "risk of loss" between the time an auction closes and the time the goods are delivered to the buyer. There are normally two stages in this process: First, there's the "handling" phase, when the item is under your control and you are packaging it for delivery and dropping it off at the U.S. Postal Service, UPS, FedEx, or some other "common carrier." Then there's the "shipping" phase, when the item is in the control of the common carrier.

During the handling phase, the item is under your control, so the "risk of loss" is squarely on you. If you sell a Ming vase on eBay and it falls and shatters before you have a chance to package the item, there really is no other solution but to call the buyer (I would use the telephone, because e-mail is too impersonal, and you want the buyer to hear the regret and sorrow in your voice), explain the situation, and refund the person's money.

After you package the goods and deliver them to your common carrier, things get a bit tricky. What you want is for the buyer to assume the "risk of loss" as soon as you hand the package over to the common carrier, but—believe it or not—that's not always what the law says.

What the law says in many states is that unless you and the buyer agree otherwise, you remain liable for the risk of loss until the buyer actually receives the goods.

So what you have to do is put language in your Terms and Conditions stating clearly that the risk of loss passes to the buyer when you deliver the goods to a common carrier (in legalese this is called FOB, or "free on board"), and warning buyers that if they don't purchase insurance, you will not be responsible for any damage in transit.

The Goods Don't Conform to the Auction Photo or Item Description

In legalese, this is called a "nonconforming tender." You delivered (tendered) goods that are different from the ones you advertised or offered for sale. Most buyers trying to wiggle out of a "bad bargain" will claim that you "led them down the primrose path" by making claims about your merchandise you weren't prepared to deliver on, or that they discovered something wrong with the goods after you delivered them and, had they known about it in advance, they never would have placed a bid.

Who wins in this situation? The answer depends on a number of variables. For instance:

➤ What types of warranties did you make in your auction description, and did you disclaim them properly?

➤ Are you a "merchant" in the type of goods offered?

➤ Was the alleged defect "latent" or "patent"?

➤ Does the defect "substantially impair" the value of the goods for the buyer?

Let's tackle each of these circumstances one at a time.

Warranties. As we pointed out in Chapter 3, your auction descriptions about the merchandise you sell on eBay are "warranties" that a buyer can legally rely upon. If you do not properly disclaim your warranties, the buyer can reject your item and return it to you for a full refund if she can prove that the item doesn't live up to your warranties. See Appendix B for sample language to use to disclaim warranties.

Merchant Status. When a buyer receives defective merchandise, her first instinct is to accuse the seller of knowing about the defect and failing to disclose it. Commercial law draws a distinction between a "merchant"— someone who is in the regular business of selling merchandise of that kind— and someone who only occasionally sells that type of merchandise (the law doesn't give that person a name, so let's call him an "amateur seller").

If you are a merchant, the law requires you to disclose to buyers any defects in your merchandise if you "know" or "should know" (because of your experience in dealing with that merchandise) of the defect. The amateur seller is not required to make that disclosure, unless the disclosure is of such a nature that anyone of average intelligence would discover the defect.

> Example 1: You are a dealer in laptops and are selling "new" laptops you acquired from a freight liquidator. The laptop manufacturer has just come out with a new model that supports newly released versions of Microsoft Office that the older version you are selling won't support. Because you are a dealer in laptops, you may be required to disclose this "defect" to potential buyers.

> Example 2: A consignor gives you an 1890 mechanical bank to sell on eBay. You are not an expert in mechanical banks generally and don't know of anyone who is, so you properly disclaim all warranties when writing your auction description for the bank. However, the bank has a broken internal spring such that when you pull the lever, the bank fails to "do its thing." You fail to disclose this defect in your auction description. The buyer will be entitled to reject the bank and get his money back. Even though you are not a "merchant" in mechanical banks, you would have discovered the defect had you tested the bank before putting it up for auction, and even "amateur" sellers should test the merchandise to make sure it works.

"Latent" vs. "Patent" Defects. If a defect is so obvious that it shows up on your auction photo (rust spots, say, on a mechanical bank) or during a cursory examination of the item, it is called a "patent defect." When it comes to "patent" defects, you don't have to rub the buyer's nose in them and say, "Be sure to notice those rust spots over there." On the other hand, unless you are

• The Color You See Isn't the Color I See •

Colors are a particularly sticky subject on eBay, because they are literally "all over the spectrum." Often a buyer trying to wiggle out of a bad bargain will claim that the color of the item received didn't match the color on your auction photo.

Sometimes it's your fault—for example, if you didn't set the resolution properly on your digital camera when you took the photo, or didn't light the object properly, so the color showed up darker than it actually was.

But a lot of times it's the buyer's fault. Colors often show up slightly different due to the way you set your monitor. If a buyer is using an older monitor and has set it to a different pixel resolution than someone using a newer monitor, the color of the object may show up differently on each screen.

There really is nothing you can do about this situation except disclose to potential buyers that you are not responsible for differences in color due to differing monitor resolutions, and you can be flexible with your return policy if a buyer really makes a stink about it. (Appendix B has sample language you can use in your Terms and Conditions about your auction photos.)

a "merchant" in goods of the kind you are selling on eBay, you are not obligated to tear the mechanical bank apart and look for every conceivable flaw that only an expert in banks would discover—these are called "latent defects." Be sure to state clearly in your Terms and Conditions that you are not responsible for "latent" defects that would only be discovered upon a professional inspection of the item you are selling on eBay.

<u>*Defects That "Substantially Impair" the Value of the Goods.*</u> If a defect is relatively minor and wouldn't prevent a "reasonable person" from enjoying the goods in the manner normally intended, the buyer probably won't be allowed to reject it and get his money back. So, for example, if you are selling a briefcase on eBay and clearly disclose that it is "used," a buyer who discovers a couple of minor scratches on the briefcase that didn't show up on the auction photo has no right to complain that you sold him "nonconforming" goods.

If, however, a bidder for the briefcase e-mails you and states clearly that he intends the briefcase as a gift for his son, who is about to graduate from law school and start his first job with a Wall Street law firm, then the buyer will be able to reject it and get his money back if he discovers undisclosed scratches on the briefcase. (Although what father would buy a used briefcase for his son and pass it off as new . . .)

RESOLVING SELLER-BUYER DISPUTES: THE FIVE PATHS TO TRANQUILLITY

Here's a brief unpaid political announcement.

If I had to pick the biggest unmet need in the online commerce world right now, it would be the lack of a reliable, efficient, and inexpensive way of resolving disputes between buyers and sellers. Although eBay and PayPal have made heroic efforts to set up dispute-resolution services for their members, the holy grail of an "ultimate authority" that will deliver a final resolution of all conflicts and enforce them strictly does not yet exist in the online world.

Having gotten that off my chest, we still need to ask the musical question: How exactly *do* you resolve disputes on eBay or PayPal? There are a number of alternatives, all of which involve time and a good deal of patience on your part, to say nothing of the cooperation of the "other guy."

Basically, resolving a dispute with a buyer on eBay or PayPal is a five-step process, as follows:

Step 1: "Before You Accuse Me, Take a Look at Yourself . . ."

Many eBay sellers are too quick to blame the buyer when their own conduct contributed to the problem. Before you accuse a buyer of fraud, bad faith, or worse, take a moment out, sit down calmly, and ask yourself some soul-searching questions:

> ➤ Did I know something about this item that I kept out of my auction description for fear it would turn off buyers?

> ➤ Were my auction photos clear and well-lit?

> ➤ Did I take the time to write a clear, sufficiently detailed description of the item, or did I "rush" the item onto eBay with just a few words of explanation?

➤ Did I say anything in my e-mails to the buyer that might have been misconstrued?

➤ Were my selling policies clear? (You would be amazed how many eBay sellers "cut and paste" their selling Terms and Conditions from another eBay seller's pages and don't even bother to read them before using them. You may be guaranteeing your buyers "automatic refunds" within five days and not even know it!)

If it's clear that you and the buyer were both somewhat at fault, always give the buyer the benefit of the doubt. A local grocery chain in the Northeast has a large slab of granite outside the front door of each of its stores. Chiseled on each stone is the following:

RULE 1: THE CUSTOMER IS ALWAYS RIGHT.

RULE 2: IF THE CUSTOMER IS EVER WRONG, REREAD RULE 1.

Few buyers on eBay have ever left negative feedback for an eBay seller who treated them with respect and "bent over backwards" to look at the problem from both sides in an effort to achieve a fair result. On eBay, arrogance plus attitude equals negative feedback and frustration.

Step 2: Research Your Buyer and Look for Behavior Patterns

Now that you've eliminated yourself as a source of the problem, it's time to do a little homework on the buyer.

➤ Check the buyer's feedback rating. If she has an 800 rating with 100 percent positive feedback, it's highly unlikely you are dealing with a crook, and you should not be afraid to deal with her.

➤ Check eBay's community pages and search under the buyer's user ID to see if she is a chronic complainer or has a "chip on her shoulder."

➤ Check the buyer's other purchases and see if there's a pattern that would explain her objection. For example, if the buyer is buying lots of different motorcycle parts for the same make and model of bike, then clearly she is building or restoring a motorcycle and may have ordered the wrong part from you in the mistaken belief it would fit her bike. It is plausible that she didn't discover the mistake until after the part arrived.

➤ Do a little searching on the Web. If the buyer is running for public office, or is a high-ranking clergyperson in your community (or— gulp!—a faculty member of eBay University), you have lots of leverage over her because she cannot afford the negative publicity of a commercial dispute that would almost certainly (with your help) find its way into the local newspapers.

Step 3: Deal Directly with the Buyer

Far, far too many eBay sellers go "running to Mommy," filing a fraud complaint on eBay or PayPal or leaving negative or neutral feedback on the Feedback Forum without making any effort whatsoever to contact the buyer directly and working with him to resolve the dispute.

When it's clear you've got a difficult buyer on your hands, send him an e-mail asking for his telephone number. Then pick up the telephone and call the person.

Do not engage in lengthy conversations via e-mail! At best you will waste your time; at worst you will "escalate" the dispute into a holy war. When you hit a snag with a buyer, nothing beats picking up the telephone and making human contact with that person. In my experience negotiating deals for my law clients, I find people are a lot less likely to "posture" or play "mind games" when they can hear a person's voice and know that they're dealing with a fellow human being. Also, it is far too easy to miscommunicate in an e-mail message. While e-mail is a terrific time-saving tool in general, it was not meant to handle sensitive communications.

In your phone conversations with the buyer, avoid a confrontational posture unless it is absolutely apparent that you are dealing with a jerk. Remember what Grandma told you: "You can catch more flies with sugar than you can with vinegar."

Step 4: Consider Mediation Through eBay and PayPal

If your conversations with the buyer go nowhere, or you are unable to make contact with the buyer despite repeated efforts, it's time to consider the dispute-resolution services offered by eBay or PayPal.

In using these services, it's important to manage your expectations. That is, while these services are better than nothing, do not expect that eBay or PayPal will spend enormous amounts of time and money helping you "get justice" from a difficult buyer.

Mediation vs. Arbitration. When using eBay's and PayPal's dispute-resolution services, remember that they are primarily "mediation" services, not "arbitration" services (although some of these services give you the option of "escalating" the dispute and having an eBay or PayPal customer service representative make a decision for or against you).

When you mediate a dispute, a third party (called a "mediator") sits down with both you and your adversary and attempts to broker a negotiated solution. The mediator may point out the faults in each of your positions, and point out possible solutions, but ultimately the mediator's goal is to get the two of you to shake hands and work out your own settlement. The mediator does not decide the case and rule in someone's favor.

"Arbitration" is much more like an actual court case. You and your adversary each present your side of the case; the arbitrator asks questions of both sides and (like a mediator) tries to get the two of you to see things the same way. But in an arbitration, the arbitrator has the power to decide the case and rule in favor of one of you. If you have agreed to "binding" arbitration, you are required to either follow the arbitrator's decision or appeal it to a court oflaw.

Both eBay and PayPal will go to great lengths to get the two of you to "see the light of reason" and come to your own negotiated settlement. They will not cram a decision down either of your throats unless you or the buyer specifically request them to do so.

But even if they do "rule" on your dispute and insist that one of you take a certain course of action, remember that there is no assurance you will get a ruling in your favor. Like any party in a real lawsuit, you "rolls the dice" and you "takes your chances."

eBay's Dispute-Resolution Processes. The most common disputes that can be settled using eBay's and PayPal's dispute-resolution mechanisms are:

1. *Unpaid Items.* The buyer hasn't paid for something he successfully bid for on eBay. These disputes are almost always started by the seller who hasn't received payment.

2. *Items Not Received.* The buyer has paid for the goods but hasn't received them within a reasonable time. These disputes are almost always started by the buyer.

3. *Items Significantly Not as Described.* The buyer paid for the goods but received something that (the buyer thinks) is different from the item you described in your auction listing. These disputes are almost always started by the buyer.

4. *Feedback Disputes.* A buyer, unhappy with the outcome of your transaction, has posted negative or neutral feedback on you, and you wish to have the negative or neutral feedback removed from eBay's Feedback Forum. These disputes can be started by either the seller or the buyer.

If any of these disputes involve a transaction in which the buyer paid using PayPal, the dispute will be referred to PayPal's Resolution Center (described below), because unlike eBay, PayPal has control over the parties' funds and can move the parties' money back and forth to reflect their settlement agreement. If the transaction involved payment by check, money order, credit card, or any other means, you will be dealing with one of eBay's dispute-resolution processes.

eBay has developed a number of systems to resolve these four types of dispute (for a full description, click on the Community tab on eBay's home page, then click on "Security and Resolution

Center"). They are all pretty similar, and rely to a large extent on cooperation between you and your buyer.

For "Unpaid Items," "Items Not Received," and "Items Significantly Not as Described" disputes, eBay's dispute-resolution process will take you through three steps, and you can choose a fourth if you're really courageous.

First, the party starting the dispute will be subjected to a "Problem Diagnosis"—a series of computer-generated e-mail messages that are designed to eliminate claims based on common misconceptions. For example, a buyer who starts an "Item Not Received" dispute less than twenty-four hours after an auction closes will be told that no human seller can possibly pack, process, and ship items in that short a time frame.

Second, if the dispute has not been resolved in the "Problem Diagnosis" phase, the parties will participate in a "Tech Assisted Negotiation." Both you and your buyer will receive programmed e-mails from eBay's customer support staff designed to push you ever closer to an actual settlement.

Third, if the "Tech Assisted Negotiation" does not result in an actual settlement, the parties will be encouraged to mediate their dispute using one of the independent dispute-resolution firms with whom eBay has business relationships, such as SquareTrade, based in San Francisco (discussed below).

If you feel very strongly that you are in the right, you can elect a fourth step—to "escalate" the dispute and have it resolved by one of eBay's customer service representatives, who are based in Salt Lake City, Utah. The assigned representative will evaluate the e-mail correspondence between the parties and make a determination (like "Judge Judy") about which party is in the right.

Keep in mind that while eBay's customer service representatives are trained to handle disputes to a certain extent, they are not lawyers or judges. As with any judge or arbitrator in the non-eBay world, some representatives have more experience with certain types of claims than others, and in any event there can be no assurance that the representative will rule in your favor. If an eBay customer service representative rules against you, and if you do not do what the representative tells you to do within a prescribed time period, you may well be suspended or expelled from the eBay site for "contempt of court," just like in a real courtroom proceeding.

Disputes concerning feedback are handled in a different way on eBay. If a buyer has unfairly posted negative feedback in the Feedback Forum and you are able to persuade him to withdraw the negative feedback, the two of you can go to eBay's "mutual feedback withdrawal" tool in the Feedback Forum and get the negative feedback removed. In certain extreme situations (such as those in which the negative posting contains obscene or racist language), eBay will remove the negative posting (or at least delete the offending language) if you bring it to their attention. In all other cases, eBay will refer you to one of the independent companies that provide online dispute-resolution services to eBay—such as SquareTrade or NetNeutrals.

Mediation Through SquareTrade. SquareTrade, based in San Francisco (www.squaretrade.com), is an independent company that provides online dispute-resolution services to the eBay community. It is primarily a mediation service, although it offers an arbitration service (discussed below) for certain transactions on eBay Motors. While SquareTrade helps resolve a variety of eBay-related disputes, it is best known for resolving feedback disputes between eBay sellers and buyers.

If a buyer has posted negative feedback in the Feedback Forum and refuses to withdraw it, SquareTrade can recommend that the negative feedback be withdrawn (sometimes with conditions). Here's how it works:

1. If you request SquareTrade to mediate the dispute, the buyer agrees to the mediation, and the mediation results in a settlement signed by both parties requesting that the negative feedback be withdrawn, SquareTrade will recommend to eBay that the feedback be withdrawn.

2. If you request SquareTrade to mediate the dispute, and the buyer agrees to mediation but then stops communicating with you and SquareTrade,

SquareTrade will send notices to the buyer for ten consecutive days asking her to rejoin the mediation. If the buyer fails to respond and there is nothing in SquareTrade's file to indicate that the buyer won't withdraw the negative feedback under any circumstances, then SquareTrade usually will recommend to eBay that the negative feedback be withdrawn.

3. If you request SquareTrade to mediate the dispute, and the buyer does not respond at all to SquareTrade's notices for fourteen consecutive days, then SquareTrade will review your case. If there's nothing in the file to indicate the buyer intended to participate in the mediation (for example, the buyer sent an e-mail to SquareTrade saying, "Sure, I'll participate, but first I have to recover from open-heart surgery next week"), then SquareTrade usually will recommend to eBay that the negative feedback be withdrawn.

SquareTrade does charge a fee, currently $29.95 per dispute.

Unlike eBay and PayPal, which allow their members to "escalate" disputes and have them resolved by trained customer service personnel, SquareTrade does not arbitrate or resolve disputes (with one exception, discussed below). If you and your buyer cannot reach agreement within a reasonable time, the SquareTrade mediation ends and the negative feedback against you will stand.

The one exception is SquareTrade's "independent feedback review" process, which is offered only to sellers that sell on eBay Motors. For a higher price (currently $100), a seller who is not happy with the progress of the mediation can elect to have SquareTrade make a determination about whether or not negative feedback should stand based on the information available to SquareTrade at that time. SquareTrade offers this service because on eBay Motors the average transaction price is so high that a single negative feedback posting could crush a seller's business on eBay entirely.

One last thing about feedback disputes on SquareTrade: Even though SquareTrade recommends to eBay that a negative posting against you be removed, eBay has the ability to reject SquareTrade's recommendation. And eBay may do so if it believes either 1) that your buyer has not been given an adequate opportunity to respond to SquareTrade's notices (for example, because the buyer recently changed an e-mail or mailing address), or 2) that your "track record" with other buyers justifies leaving the negative feedback intact (for example, if there are numerous "seller infractions" recorded against you that SquareTrade didn't have access to when you filed your claim there).

eBay has access to much more information about its members and their transaction histories than SquareTrade does, and for reasons of privacy eBay will not disclose that information to Square-Trade without the member's consent. If a buyer hasn't responded to your SquareTrade claim because of a recent address change, you (not SquareTrade) will be notified of this, and you will have to begin your claim all over again.

PayPal's Dispute-Resolution Center. Like eBay, PayPal offers a number of mediation services to address issues such as:

> ➤ Claims for undelivered or "nonconforming" items
> ➤ Credit card chargebacks (as discussed previously)
> ➤ Claims alleging unauthorized activity in the buyer's account involving a payment to you.

If your dispute with a buyer concerns "Unpaid Items," "Items Not Received," or "Items Significantly Not as Described," and the buyer paid using PayPal, your dispute will be referred to PayPal for resolution, since PayPal has the ability to enforce your settlement by moving the parties' money back and forth between accounts. PayPal does not, however, get involved in feedback disputes.

For further information, log onto PayPal and click on the Resolutions Center tab.

The Bottom Line on eBay and PayPal Dispute Resolution. The dispute-resolution processes offered by eBay and PayPal are fine, as long as you and the buyer agree to cooperate, negotiate fairly and in good faith to resolve the dispute, and communicate well with each other. Frankly, if that were the case, the two of you probably could resolve the dispute directly without having to involve eBay or Pay-

Pal at all. When the buyer won't respond to your repeated e-mails, or "goes negative" without attempting to negotiate with you in good faith, the eBay and PayPal services are useful but limited. There is no all-powerful "Judge Judy" at either eBay or PayPal whose sole mission in life is to give you the justice you deserve. Your success at resolving a dispute with a buyer will depend to a large extent on the amount of time, energy, and patience you are willing to put into it. Don't expect eBay, PayPal, or SquareTrade to do the work for you.

Step 5: Go to Small-Claims Court

So you have a deadbeat customer or client who owes you money. You have made repeated demands for payment, you have threatened to charge interest on the overdue debt, and you have made a personal appeal to your debtor's sense of honor and fair play. Nothing has worked. The buyer hasn't paid a cent. Like they say on television, it's time to . . . take them to court!

In most cases, it isn't worthwhile to bring a lawsuit in state or federal court to collect a small amount of money (less than $5,000 in many states). Your lawyer alone will charge an up-front retainer of $5,000 to $10,000 to take on a new case (so-called "contingency fees," based on a percentage of the judgment you win, are usually not charged in commercial or breach-of-contract cases), and then there are the court costs, the time you lose attending depositions and hearings, and so forth. However, every state has a system of small-claims courts that you can use to collect judgments for small amounts of money . . . if you have the nerve.

But, Cliff—I can already hear you saying—*the buyer lives halfway across the country!* That's precisely why you should consider filing a case in the buyer's local small-claims court. Being served with legal papers—even in small-claims court—does wonders to get the attention of long-distance buyers, precisely because they're not expecting it! Once a buyer sees you are taking the dispute seriously, you will "get his attention," and he will be more likely to respond to avoid having to go to court. Especially if you draw up a quick-and-dirty press release and mail it, along with copies of the legal summons, to all local newspapers in the buyer's community. ("Local Merchant Sued in eBay Tussle" isn't the kind of headline your buyer would like to read, right?)

Travel expenses to a buyer's community to appear in small-claims court are a deductible business expense (see Chapter 9). That could be a plus, if the buyer lives in a nice place like Las Vegas . . .

Make no mistake, however. When you bring a suit in small-claims court, you do most of the work yourself, and pleading your own case before a real-life judge can be one of the scariest events of your life, even if you know you are 100 percent right. Yet sooner or later, if you run your own business, you will get into a situation where you have to bring an action in small-claims court to collect an overdue debt (or, God forbid, defend yourself against someone who thinks you owe *them* money). Here is a quick "survival guide" for surviving a small-claims court proceeding.

➤ *Get the pamphlet.* The bar association in just about every state publishes a short guidebook, in pamphlet form, that takes you step by step through the small-claims court process in that state. This pamphlet (which may be called something like "Guide to the Use of Our Small-Claims Courts") is usually available free of charge or for a small fee (less than $5) to cover postage. To find the address and telephone number of the state bar association where your buyer lives, go to your favorite Internet search engine and type "state bar associations" or go to www.findlaw.com/06associations/state .html, where you'll find links to the home pages of virtually all state bar associations nationwide. Once you reach your state bar association, ask for their publications department.

➤ *Prepare, prepare, prepare.* I cannot say this enough—almost always, the victory in small-claims court goes to the party that is better prepared. If you claim that someone owes you money, but 1) you never delivered a proper invoice stating when payment is due, 2) you failed to make a formal written demand for payment, and 3) the debtor has some serious objections to making payment (such as your products and services didn't work as you promised), your path to success in small-claims court will be rocky indeed.

When you appear in court, be sure to bring copies of all relevant corre-

• Want to Become a Small-Claims Court Wizard? •
Watch Lots of Television!

Please don't laugh—I am absolutely serious!

Here's a little secret. You know all of those courtroom television shows like *Judge Judy, Judge Joe Brown,* and *Judge Mills Lane?* They are all modeled on small-claims court proceedings! If you've never watched any of these shows before (I warn you that you are likely to get hooked on them), check out the website at www.tvjudgeshows.com, where the strengths and weaknesses of each show are thoroughly discussed. The judges in these TV shows are (or were), after all, real-life judges, and the judge in your small-claims court case is highly likely to behave the way the ones on TV do. By doing some research on your favorite show's website, you might even be able to find an episode that featured a case similar to your own and order a videotape of it.

And how do these judges behave? In a nutshell, here's what happens: The judge listens patiently to the arguments for both sides, asks a couple of questions to understand something better, and then asks some fundamental questions: Who is in the right here? Who is telling the truth, and who is playing games? In most cases, the answer will be patently obvious after only a few minutes; don't be surprised if your debtors bring a check to court and pay you off in the courtroom lobby because they don't want the embarrassment of having to justify their position before a judge. The judge rules in favor of the person who is in the right (or telling the truth) and explains why he ruled the way he did.

So what does that tell you? It means that if you bring an action in small-claims court against someone, you had better make darn sure there aren't any serious holes in your case that would lead the judge to think, even for a moment, that you are the "wise guy" in the proceeding.

spondence (e.g., contracts, invoices, purchase orders, warranty forms) that back up your case, in case the judge asks to look at them. Where your case is less than "airtight," ask yourself where the weaknesses are, and be prepared to explain why those weaknesses occurred. Being organized, and having ready answers to the judge's questions, sends a strong signal to the judge that you really care about the outcome of the case, and that you are the one who deserves to win.

➤ _Stay away from lawyers._ You can sometimes be _too_ prepared for a small-claims court action, however. While many attorneys will be happy to spend an hour or two with you to help you prepare for your case and anticipate the judge's questions, be careful not to overdo it. Lawyers are barred from many small-claims courts, and judges always frown upon parties who appear to have been overly prepared, or "horse-shedded," by their attorneys. If you do not normally use phrases like "May it please the court," "I object, your honor," and "Please let the record show" in your everyday speech, _do not,_ under any circumstances, use them in a small-claims court.

➤ _Be on time._ You absolutely must show up on time for your court date. In case of an emergency, if you cannot possibly attend your hearing, contact the court clerk's office and try to get a postponement, or "continuance," of the court date. Be sure to call your debtor as well. In most states, each party is entitled to one continuance if both parties agree. Otherwise, your request for a continuance will have to be approved by the court—and remember, you are not there to explain why you need the continuance. If you fail to get a postponement and do not show up for your trial, the judge or magistrate may dismiss your suit and you may be prevented from suing again for that money owed you.

➤ _Keep it simple._ Now comes the stressful part. When you begin your presentation to the court, you should explain why the defendant owes you money. Answer any questions the judge or magistrate asks you as clearly and directly and possible, and _do not ramble._ Show the judge any bills, receipts, or letters that you have brought along as proof of your story (be sure to know in advance if you must bring originals or whether photocopies will suffice). If you have a witness, your witness will be allowed to tell what he or she knows after you speak. Next, the person you are suing will explain what her position is. Each party has a right to question a witness. If the other party fails to show up, ask the judge for a "default judgment," because in some states the judge is not obligated to grant default judgments unless you request one.

➤ _Get your money._ If the case is decided in your favor, the party you sued will be ordered to pay. In most states, the judge has the power to order the defendant to pay in installments if it's clear the defendant cannot afford to pay the full amount in a lump sum. If the person who owed you money refuses to pay by the date ordered by the court, or if the payments are stopped later on, you should apply to the court clerk's office for an "execution" to be issued against the party's wages, property, or bank account. Once the execution is issued, you will be required to give the execution to a sheriff, bailiff, or court officer who will serve the execution on the appropriate employer, banking institution, or other person who will have to pay the amount directly to the court officer. The court officer will then pay you.

USING COMMON SENSE, OR "REVENGE IS A DISH BEST SERVED COLD"

When you go to law school, one of the first cases you are required to read is the case of *Pierson* v. *Post*.

Pierson and Post were country squires who lived on neighboring properties in upstate New York in the late 1700s. One fine day, Pierson and Post were out fox-hunting with their drinking buddies. The two hunting parties flushed out a fox, and both parties gave chase. The fox was ultimately killed by Post's party . . . but on Pierson's land.

The two squires immediately begin squabbling over who was entitled to claim the fox pelt—the squire who had killed the fox or the squire on whose land the fox was killed. Country squires being a rather testy lot, they sent the matter to court.

The case dragged on in the New York courts for nearly fifty years. It bankrupted the estates of both Pierson and Post, and was finally settled by their great-grandchildren (the original Pierson and Post having moved on to that great fox warren in the sky) because they could no longer afford to pay the attorneys' fees (which over the years totaled more than $1 million in today's money).

Please don't get me wrong. I'm all for "truth, justice, and the American way." When you sell on eBay, nothing—and I mean "nothing"—eats at your insides like a buyer who's playing games with you or acting dishonestly. At eBay University seminars, I'm often regaled with stories of "buyers gone bad" by people who I honestly think would commit murder if the offending buyer were to show up at just that moment.

But remember the lesson of *Pierson* v. *Post*. Sometimes it isn't

• How to Be a Class Act on eBay •

You can tell a truly great eBay seller by the way she handles problems. While 99.99 percent of all eBay sales go through very smoothly, every once in a while you hit a snag. For example, what do you do when the buyer pays for the item, you ship it, and the item is damaged or destroyed while in transit to the buyer? Now, the buyer has a right to be dissatisfied (it wasn't his fault, after all), and you want to be flexible in your dealings with dissatisfied buyers, otherwise they will post negative feedback about you on the eBay site and ruin your reputation. Still, you don't want to have to "eat" the cost of the item because, after all, it wasn't your fault, either.

Here's an actual e-mail exchange between a seller and a buyer where this problem occurred. The item in question was a movie poster from the 1960s valued at $200.

Buyer: Hi, Joe. Sorry to be the bearer of some bad news, but the poster I purchased from you on eBay last week [auction #_____] was totally destroyed in transit to me here. The mailing tube looked as if it had been stomped on by King Kong. As a result, water got into the tube, which thoroughly soaked the poster. The damage clearly occurred somewhere between your post office and mine, because the tube is stamped by my local post office in several places "received in damaged condition." I will return the poster along with the original tube so you can see what happened. Please credit my PayPal account when you have had the chance to examine the damage.

Seller: I really don't know what to say. You did not purchase insurance, which was offered in the eBay invoice that I sent you. We offer shipping insurance through the eBay invoices we send to the buyers. Some folks buy it, some don't. We let the buyer decide. If they buy it and the poster is damaged, we file a claim and get the purchase cost back. If they don't, then we cannot file a claim. That's not an oversimplification, that's how it works. It really isn't fair to ignore the insurance and then expect us to reimburse you for the damaged poster, or at least I don't think it is. Do you think that is fair?

Buyer: What you say makes a lot of sense, and I realize I may have to eat the cost, because I'm not about to risk negative feedback over a $200 purchase. For future reference, though, you should be aware that legally—in most states I'm aware of—the seller bears the risk of lost or damaged goods in transit unless this risk is expressly assumed in writing by the buyer, insurance or no insurance. If your policy is "no refunds without insurance," your auction pages should contain a clear statement that the buyer assumes all risk of lost or damaged goods. You should explain that, to be assured of a refund in the event your item is lost or damaged in transit, the buyer must buy insurance at the rate offered, as there will be no refunds or exchanges if you do not purchase insurance.

Seller: When I buy items on eBay, I know that if I do not buy insurance, then I am taking the risk of it arriving safely. We generally have three to five mailing tubes that are totally damaged in the course of a year, and invariably they are uninsured, and everyone's reaction is the same—it's our fault and we need to reimburse for the purchase. It is never the buyer's fault that they opted not to insure, and I do mean never. Knowing that this does happen from time to time, we do have a policy for our good customers like you. We extend a credit for half of the purchase price—in your case $100—and strongly recommend that they go for the insurance the next time they buy. You are welcome to use the credit for a website purchase or eBay should you participate.

Buyer: I think that's a very fair way to resolve the situation, and be assured I will buy insurance in your auctions from now on. I am sometimes a seller on eBay, and I "feel your pain" in this situation more than you realize. Thank you for being a mensch—I will post positive feedback on eBay later today.

This is a textbook example of how to resolve a dispute on eBay, but take note of a few lessons here:

- The seller and buyer in this case were well known to each other, had engaged in a number of successful transactions, and had a strong motivation to preserve their relationship.
- Both the seller and buyer treated each other with respect in their exchange—both sides firmly but politely stood their ground, and neither side let it get "personal."
- The seller clearly made an exception for this buyer by offering to "split the difference," and made it very clear he wouldn't do this in every situation.
- The amount of the buyer's loss wasn't very large. If this had been a $2,000 item, much more would have been at stake and things might have gotten a bit nastier.

By the way, this buyer is correct about the law: If your policy is "no refunds unless buyer buys insurance," that's fine, but you must state it clearly in the auction Terms and Conditions you include on your eBay auction pages. Otherwise, you will be the one buying insurance, especially for big-ticket, one-of-a-kind items.

worth spending millions of dollars and fifty years of courtroom time over a fox pelt.

There's an old Spanish saying that "revenge is a dish best served cold." When you're selling on eBay, time is your biggest asset—it's even more valuable than money, because once you spend it, you can never earn it back again. Even if you're a hundred percent in the right, it isn't worth spending hundreds of hours of your time to recover $50 someone's ripped off of you. In that time, you could post hundreds of auctions and make a hundred times the amount of money you're fighting for. Write off the expense, put the bad buyer on your "restricted" list, and get on with your life.

If, however, it is worth your time and trouble to pursue the matter and preserve your reputation as a "no-nonsense seller" on eBay, then go for it. Do everything you can to get justice; just don't stop selling while you're at it.

• Getting a Tax Break on Your "Bad Debts" •

When you are selling on eBay, you are engaged in a "retail" business, and like any retailer, you will find out sooner or later that some transactions simply don't go as you would like them to. If you doubt that, go to any local department store on December 26 and watch what happens at the "returns" counter. Are ALL of those items being returned defective in some way, as the buyers are claiming? Of course not . . . they are being returned because the recipient changed his or her mind, didn't want the item, or wore the item several times for his holiday parties before deciding it didn't "fit" exactly as it should . . . (please don't get me wrong; I hate people who do that as much as you do, but they're a fact of life for retailers).

As Internet retail (including eBay) becomes more and more a part of our lives, buyers will expect you to provide them with the same rights and privileges they have at their local department stores or "brick-and-mortar" retailers. Like all retailers, you will have to:

- Weigh the benefit of strictly enforcing your "no refunds or exchanges" policy against the cost of doing so (lost business and "negative feedback" on eBay from disappointed buyers).

- Assume that a certain percentage of your transactions on eBay (hopefully a very small percentage) will result in a "no sale," even though you accurately described the merchandise and there is nothing wrong with it.

The way retailers have done this since time immemorial is to write off debts once they have become uncollectible. The IRS requires you to make a "reasonable effort" to collect your debts, but once all of the following events have occurred . . .

- The buyer has indicated in no uncertain terms that he will not pay for the item.
- The buyer has refused to return the item, or has not responded to your repeated attempts to contact him and demand either payment or return of the item.
- The item is of such small value that it is not worth your time and effort to pursue the dispute on eBay's or PayPal's dispute resolution centers.
- You are nervous about leaving "negative feedback" for the buyer because you are afraid he will retaliate with negative feedback for you, and your feedback score is low enough that you can't afford even one "negative."

. . . you probably have a shot at deducting the winning bid amount as a "worthless or uncollectible" debt.

If you do not treat your eBay selling as a "business" but rather as a "hobby," it is more difficult to deduct bad debts. Unlike business bad debts, which can be deducted even if only "partially" worthless, "nonbusiness bad debts" can be deducted only when you can prove the debt is "totally" worthless. That means you will have to "go to the wall" to seek collection before you deduct. What is more, while business bad debts are fully deductible against your business income, "nonbusiness bad debts" can be deducted only as short-term capital losses, which can be deducted against short-term capital gains but not against ordinary income (such as the salary from your day job).

For more information, see IRS Publication 535, "Business Expenses."

COMMON QUESTIONS

Q. *Why doesn't eBay do more to chase down the bad guys on eBay? We frequently report bad people and bad situations to eBay, but nothing ever seems to happen.*

A. Some variation of this question is raised virtually every day on eBay's community bulletin boards, chat rooms, and online workshops. I'm not an eBay employee, and I'm not qualified in any way to speak on behalf of eBay, but I think the best answer to this question is to ask a couple of related questions.

"Why doesn't the IRS track down every tax cheat and audit every individual and business they suspect of cheating on their taxes?"

"Why doesn't the FBI chase down every bank robber?"

"Why doesn't the Securities and Exchange Commission pursue every person who engages in a questionable stock trade?"

These are basically all the same question. And they all have the same answer: lack of manpower.

At any given time there are millions of "active" listings on eBay. To monitor every one of them, or even every "problematic" listing a member complains about, would take tens of thousands (or perhaps hundreds of thousands) of employees working full-time at it. And mistakes would sometimes be made. Tell me, what would generate more unhappiness within the eBay community—a complaint that isn't responded to, or an innocent auction seller's listing being "pulled" because of a hasty or ill-considered review by an eBay employee?

If you think someone is engaged in questionable practices on eBay, it is up to you to contact that person, figure out what's going on, and if it becomes apparent to you that the person is engaged in shady practices, provide negative feedback for that person on eBay, being fully cognizant of the fact that person will probably "flame" you as well.

eBay does look at member complaints, but like almost all law enforcement agencies (including the IRS), it focuses on those that pose the greatest harm to the eBay community as a whole, those that threaten eBay's basic business model, and those that may require a change in eBay's policies. To ask them to do more than that is to ask them to exercise greater surveillance and enforcement power than the IRS, the FBI, or the SEC.

To which I ask: Do you really want that?

CHAPTER 7

Leaving Feedback on eBay's Feedback Forum

In the vast majority of transactions on eBay, if things go wrong it doesn't make sense to sue someone because:

➤ The buyer lives in a faraway state.

➤ The amount of money involved is relatively small (and even if you can find an attorney willing to take a case, he will want an up-front retainer of $5,000 to $10,000).

➤ State courts are reluctant to enforce "default judgments" entered in another state (that's where you sue somebody and they just don't show up), so you will have to bring the lawsuit in the buyer's home state and duke it out there, where the buyer will have the "home court advantage."

Recognizing these difficulties early on, eBay created the Feedback Forum as the main way for sellers to alert each other about difficult buyers, and vice versa. The idea is that if you have a bad experience with someone on eBay, you can leave negative or neutral feedback for that person, which is recorded in his feedback count. If there are enough negative and neutral ratings for certain buyers or sellers, the eBay community will steer clear of them. The forum actually gives people an incentive not to do anything on eBay that would generate negative or neutral feedback.

This is a noble idea in principle, although after you've been selling on eBay for a while, you will realize there are "holes" in eBay's feedback system. If you leave negative feedback for me, am I just going to sit there and take it, accepting that I'm a miserable human being who doesn't deserve to live, let alone sell on eBay? Of course not! What I will do is . . . leave negative feedback for *you*! Now you've got a problem. You've got a negative feedback rating that you didn't deserve (because you did nothing wrong) and that eBay won't remove unless you jump through a lot of hoops (basically you have to work it out with your buyer through the SquareTrade mediation program, as discussed in Chapter 6).

A lot of eBay sellers who have bad experience with buyers simply don't leave negative feedback because they are afraid of retaliation. When such people get into sticky situations with buyers, they avoid conflict at all cost, "take one for the team," and get on with their lives. Feedback squabbles can take up a lot of your precious time and energy, and if it happens more than once, you will sooner or later become discouraged about selling on eBay at all. Still, leaving negative feedback for someone can be a very effective way to punish bad behavior, as long as you are really careful about doing it.

IF YOU CAN'T SAY ANYTHING NICE ABOUT SOMEONE . . .

My dad always used to tell me that "before you get mad at somebody, count to ten, and if you're still mad, make sure you have 100 percent of the facts before you do anything that could come back and haunt you later on."

I couldn't give you any better advice about using the Feedback Forum. Often there are two sides to every argument, and the buyer has some right to be upset in most disputed transactions on eBay (either because of something you did or didn't do, or because of the way eBay or PayPal handled something, or because of something that happened in transit between you and the buyer).

Before yielding to the temptation to leave "negative" or "neutral" feedback on someone, make sure you have all of the facts, and that you have given the buyer at least a chance to tell her side of the story. If the blame for a bad transaction is "a little bit me, a little bit you" (in the words of another old Monkees' song), the best course is simply not to leave feedback at all and hope the other person does the same.

The good news is that the Feedback Forum only gives you eighty characters (including spaces and punctuation) to get into trouble there. But be careful: These same rules apply to things you say about other eBay community members in eBay's community bulletin boards, chat rooms, and other spaces in the Community section of its website. And you have a lot more room there to get into real legal trouble.

DEFAMATION OF CHARACTER

If you are saying anything bad about someone in the Feedback Forum (or, for that matter, on any of eBay's community bulletin boards) that isn't 100 percent true, that you either know isn't true or post in the heat of anger (without at least making some effort to determine if it's true or not), or that you said with the intent to hurt the other person's reputation (and when, pray tell, is negative feedback *not* intended to hurt someone's reputation?)—then, in all these instances, you have "defamed that person's character," and the individual can sue you for it.

Example: Your buyer wants to return merchandise because it arrived in damaged condition. You used extreme care in packaging the merchandise before you shipped it out. You post negative feedback as follows: "Buyer trashed the merchandise and falsely claimed it arrived broken." Had you investigated the matter, you would have discovered that the merchandise fell off the U.S. Postal Service truck and was run over by several cars before it was retrieved—damage that couldn't have been prevented by the best packaging in the world. You have defamed your buyer and will suffer the consequences.

In the old days, defamation of character was broken down into two categories: "libel," if the defamation was in written form, and "slander," if the defamation was verbal. This distinction doesn't really apply to eBay, since e-mail messages are considered written and therefore anything bad you say about someone on eBay is potentially libel.

IT'S A MATTER OF OPINION

Note that defamation of character applies only to statements of *fact*. If you are merely expressing an opinion about something or someone, and make it clear that it is only your opinion and not a statement of fact, you cannot be sued for that.

Example 1: "Cliff is a terrible lawyer; I wasn't at all happy with the way he handled my case." I won't like that comment very much, but there's nothing I can do about it because it is merely your opinion, which you are entitled to. The correct response is, "Sticks and stones may break my bones, but names will never hurt me." (Or, as they say in Brooklyn, "Yuh mudda.")

Example 2: "Don't use Cliff as your lawyer; he has been sued for legal malpractice ten times in the last month." This is a statement of fact that is either true or false. If it is false (and I assure you that it is), I will come after you in court like the hammers of hell.

If you're not sure whether something is an opinion, try saying it out loud with the words "I think . . ." or "It is my opinion that . . ."

at the beginning. If it makes sense, it's probably an opinion. If you're still not sure, don't make the statement until you are.

TRUTH IS AN "ABSOLUTE DEFENSE"

Of course, if what you are saying is 100 percent true, and you can prove it, then go for it! You cannot defame someone by uttering an absolutely true statement, although there are other ways to hurt people with the truth (see the sidebar).

• Invading Someone's Privacy •

The subject of privacy doesn't really apply to the Feedback Forum, but it comes up occasionally on eBay's community bulletin boards and chat rooms. If you are a regular contributor to these forums, you will probably get to know some of the other regulars rather well after a while. While that's a wonderful thing, and something eBay generally encourages, you have to be careful about inadvertently posting information about other people on eBay that they wouldn't want to be disclosed publicly.

If you make a public disclosure about someone else that is absolutely true but is not the sort of thing any reasonable person would want to be made public, you may be exposed to legal liability for invading that person's privacy.

For example, you carry on a regular e-mail correspondence with Joe, an "eBay buddy" with whom you hang out in eBay's community chat rooms. In the course of that correspondence, you learn that Joe's daughter has been killed in an auto accident. Without asking for Joe's permission, you post a message on your eBay bulletin board telling everyone about Joe's daughter's death and asking them to contribute funds to "help Joe through this difficult time." While your intentions are admirable, and the statement is 100 percent true (and therefore not "defamation of character"), Joe may be able to sue you for invading his privacy and announcing his grief to the entire world.

WHAT TO DO WHEN YOU ARE "FLAMED"

As you become more and more of a serious player on eBay, it becomes harder and harder to maintain an absolutely positive feedback rating. Look at any eBay seller with more than 1,000 feedback ratings and you will probably see at least one negative or neutral statement. This happens either because:

➤ There are just some buyers you cannot make happy, no matter what you do for them.

➤ When you have dozens or possibly hundreds of eBay auctions going on at the same time, it is physically impossible for you to give each and every buyer the tender loving care they deserve.

Don't get me wrong—I'm not saying you should just roll over and accept negative feedback as a "fact of life." If someone wrongly posts negative feedback on you, you should definitely:

➤ Contact the person and try to work it out. Then, if you are able to work it out, go to SquareTrade and get the "negative feedback" removed.

➤ Respond to the negative feedback, but be careful to include "just the facts, ma'am." Anyone viewing the negative posting will see your response at the same time and get "both sides of the story."

➤ Even better, respond to the negative feedback as follows: "Sorry this went wrong—call me at [your toll-free telephone number] and I will give you a full refund and a 10 percent discount off of future purchases." This way, people viewing the negative feedback will see the sort of seller you are.

I do think, though, you should use common sense when it comes to negative feedback. If I look at a seller's feedback and I see a 7,000 rating with only two negative postings (unless they are the most recent two postings), I'm not going to worry about them too much, and neither should you.

COMMON QUESTIONS

Q. *What can be done if you leave feedback for a person, but she doesn't leave feedback for you?*

A. Nothing can be done. Feedback is not compulsory. You can send a nice note asking for feedback, but most people seem to resent this approach. Feedback is entirely voluntary. Leave it if you like, but don't necessarily expect anything in return.

Q. *What is feedback manipulation, and how do eBay users manipulate feedback?*

A. The eBay policy regarding feedback manipulation is spelled out online at pages.ebay.com/help/policies/feedback-manipulation.html. Basically, the policy states that "feedback left or received where the feedback's primary value is to artificially enhance a member's reputation rather than provide commentary on genuine transactional experience is not permitted."

As such, offering to sell, buy, or barter feedback is not permitted. In addition, registering multiple accounts (or working with others) in order to exchange feedback to artificially increase your feedback score is not permitted.

Q. *I want to create a new user ID, but a lot of eBay sellers won't sell to my new user ID until I have at least a 20 positive feedback rating, and that will take a while. Can I place bids on my own auctions using the new user ID so that I can build up the required minimum feedback rating?*

A. This is a classic example of feedback manipulation—friends bidding on each other's auctions without the intent of actually going through with the transaction, but doing it just to build up each other's feedback ratings. Don't do it!

Dealing with Taxes

CHAPTER 8

"Aw, Do I Hafta Pay Taxes?"

The short answer is yes. Sorry about that.

When people ask, "Do I really have a business on eBay?" what they are really asking is, "Do I have to pay taxes on the money I earn from selling on eBay?"

Sadly, it makes no difference whether your eBay selling is a "business" or a "hobby"—taxes are a fact of life in the United States, and you will have to pay them no matter how you classify your eBay selling in your own mind.

A lot of people in the eBay community don't think of themselves as being in business. To these folks, selling on eBay is more of a hobby. But here's the sad truth: If you made any amount of money (i.e., profit) selling merchandise on eBay last year, the IRS doesn't care if you think of yourself as a business person or a hobbyist. They want you to report your eBay selling profits as income on your tax return, and they want you to pay income taxes (and sometimes other taxes) on that income. If you are making money doing *anything* in life, you have to pay income taxes on it. There is no "minimum threshold" below which you are free from income taxes, as many folks believe.

LIVING IN A FEDERAL SYSTEM, OR THREE LAYERS OF TAXATION

We live in a "federal" system. There are three levels of government in the United States—the federal, the state, and the local—and each one of them is given the power under the Constitution to levy taxes. This means that when you run a business, you are subject to three (and sometimes more) levels of taxation.

Most people know that when they start a business, they have to sign up for a federal tax ID number or Employer Identification Number (EIN), even though they don't have employees. They often forget, though, to sign up for state and local taxes—the other two "layers"—and that's where they get into trouble.

When you start a business, make sure your accountant (or whoever does your taxes) signs you up for all federal, state, *and* local taxes. And if he doesn't know what you're talking about . . . get another accountant!

INCOME TAXES

If you have even $1 of income (profit) in an eBay selling business, you have to pay income taxes on it. Period. End of story. World without end, amen.

It doesn't matter whether your eBay selling is a hobby or a business (see Chapter 1). If you make money (profit), the government wants a piece of it.

If you do not want to claim your eBay selling as a business, you report your income (profit) as "hobby income" on Schedule C, Profit or Loss from a Trade or Business, of your Form 1040 for the year. You *cannot* take deductions against "hobby income" unless you have losses from other hobbies.

Example 1: You made $1,000 in profit from selling on eBay last year. You also sold some mechanical banks in a live auction and took a $500 loss on those. You can "net" the $500 loss against the $1,000 profit and pay tax only on the $500 balance as "hobby income."

Example 2: You made $1,000 in profit from selling on eBay last year. You also lost $500 playing the stock market. Because the $500 loss is considered an "investment loss" and not a "hobby loss," you will not be able to deduct the $500 loss against the $1,000 profit, and you will have to pay taxes on the whole $1,000 profit as "hobby income" (although you may be able to deduct the $500 loss in other ways).

Income taxes are not imposed on your gross income (i.e., revenue). Instead, they are imposed on your *taxable* income—basically your gross income (profit) from selling on eBay, less deductible business expenses (described in Chapter 9) and certain credits.

Unless you have organized your eBay selling business as a corporation or subchapter "S" corporation (in which case your tax return will be due on March 15), all tax returns for your eBay selling business will be due on April 15 of each year.

But, as already noted, income taxes are imposed by all three levels of government: federal, state, and local. So, an eBay selling business based in Yonkers, New York, pays taxes to the IRS (federal government), the State of New York, the County of Westchester, and the City of Yonkers. Very few eBay selling businesses are based in Yonkers, New York.

SELF-EMPLOYMENT TAXES

But that's not all. If you make more than $400 in income (profit) from your eBay selling business this year, you will have to pay self-employment taxes in addition to your income taxes.

Remember when you worked for someone else, in those days long ago? Remember that when you received each paycheck, certain "payroll" or "employment" taxes (with acronyms such as FICA and FUTA, which you never bothered to figure out) were taken out of your paycheck?

Well, congratulations! Now that you're self-employed (i.e., you run your own business), you get to deduct these taxes from every penny you make in your eBay business! "Payroll" taxes are described in Chapter 12, but they basically amount to about 15.3 percent of your self-employment income (basically, your profit from selling on eBay) and are tacked *on top* of your income taxes.

So, to summarize: When you run a business on eBay, you have to pay 1) income taxes on every penny in profit you make and 2) another 15.3 percent in payroll taxes on top of that.

QUARTERLY ESTIMATED TAXES

It gets even better, folks. If you make more than $1,000 in income (profit) from selling on eBay, you can't just wait until April 15 of next year and pay all of this in a lump sum.

Noooooooooo. . . .

You see, the government knows you a lot better than you think. The government knows that if they let you keep all that money you earned on eBay, you will "blow it" at the racetrack, on some useless article of clothing, or on hobby purchases on eBay. The government worries that you may not be disciplined enough to keep enough cash in reserve to pay your taxes when they're due, so they require you to estimate your tax liability and pay in installments four times a year.

Make a note of these dates: April 15 (yep, the same day you pay last year's taxes), June 15, September 15, and January 15. When you're self-employed, these become the four worst days of the year. They are the dates on which your estimated taxes are due.

There are two ways you can "estimate" your taxes:

1. *The "Safe Harbor" Method of Estimating Taxes.* If you're in a business (like selling on eBay) where your income fluctuates from month to month, the IRS allows you to use this method. Basically, you look at your tax liability

• Cliff's Survival Secret for Estimated Taxes •

Estimated taxes are the bane of every self-employed person's existence (including mine, so join the club), but they really aren't all that bad as long as you remember one thing:

YOU HAVE TO HAVE ENOUGH CASH IN YOUR CHECKING ACCOUNT TO PAY THE TAXES WHEN THEY COME DUE!

If the payment date for your estimated taxes approaches, and you see you owe the IRS $10,000, but there's only $2,000 in your checking account, you got a big problem there, hot shot!

Here's a tip. When you open your business checking account for your eBay business at your local bank, spend a couple of extra bucks and open an interest-bearing savings account as well (most banks will offer one for a small extra fee).

Then, at the end of each month, look at your checkbook register and your PayPal account statement, total up your "gross income" (don't worry about expenses and deductions at this point), take 35 percent of the total, and write a check to your savings account. Remember, you're earning interest on this amount.

Then . . . *forget the money is there!* Conduct your business with whatever is left over in your checking account (the remaining 65 percent).

When an estimated tax date approaches, calculate how much you owe and write the check first from your savings account until there's nothing left. If you still owe money to the IRS, write the balance from your checking account.

What you are doing here is "escrowing" for taxes, and it may well save your life as an eBay seller. When people start seeing money flow into their checking accounts, their immediate response is, "Oh, boy, this is great! I can live on all of this!"

Not true, because 35 percent of that money (actually, a little more when you take state and local income taxes into account) actually belongs to the government. It is not yours, and never was. All you can live on is the remaining 65 percent. The sooner you learn to live on just that 65 percent, the easier your life as a self-employed business person will be.

Note that the 35 percent is a rule of thumb, not the law. If your eBay selling involves lots of deductible expenses, you may be able to get away with escrowing only 30 percent. If your business has very few deductions, you should consider escrowing 40 percent, just to be safe. I have found, through trial and error, that the correct escrow amount usually falls between 30 percent and 40 percent. But, as they say on TV commercials, "your experience may vary."

for last year, increase it by 10 percent, divide by four, and that's what you pay on each of the quarterly "estimated tax" payment dates.

Example: Last year you paid $40,000 in taxes to Uncle Sam. You really don't know what your income will be this year. So you take 110 percent of $40,000 (or $44,000), divide by four, and pay $11,000 to Uncle Sam on each of the four "estimated tax" payment dates. (Don't forget to add a small sum for your state tax authority as well.)

Simple, huh? There's only one problem. At the end of the year, you "crunch your numbers" and find out your actual tax liability for the year was $50,000. The good news: The IRS won't charge interest and penalties on the $6,000 balance (the $50,000 you owe minus the $44,000 you paid). The bad news: The whole $6,000 will be due in a single lump sum on April 15. And next year's estimated taxes will be based on your $50,000 total tax liability, not the $44,000 you paid. (In other words, you will take 110 percent of $50,000—or $55,000—divide by four, and so on.)

I would bet serious money that most eBay sellers don't see a 10 percent increase in business every year, so that leaves the second way of calculating your estimated taxes for the year, otherwise known as . . .

2. *The "SWAG" Method of Estimating Taxes.* Don't know what SWAG means? There are two popular definitions:

    ➢ Silly Wild-Assed Guess

    ➢ Scientific Wild-Assed Guess

Whichever definition you use, it all boils down to the same thing. As you get close to each of the four estimated tax payment dates, you sit down, crunch your numbers, and make your best SWAG as to what you owe the IRS for the three-month period ending on that date. The number you come up with is what you pay the IRS on the due date, and you cross your fingers and pray really hard that you were right. If, at the end of the year, it turns out you were wrong, you owe the balance in a lump sum on April 15, together with interest and penalties on the overdue amount.

The vast majority of eBay sellers (and, to be frank, just about all self-employed professionals) use the SWAG method to determine their estimated tax liability.

SALES TAXES (ON WHAT YOU SELL)

Now that you've paid your federal, state, and local income taxes, it's time to talk about "sales" and "use" taxes—the primary taxes you will have to pay for selling stuff on eBay.

There is no federal sales or use tax, although occasionally you hear talk about Congress imposing one someday. Sales and use taxes are imposed by state, and sometimes local, governments. Talk to your accountant or tax adviser to find out what sales and local taxes you have to pay when you sell on eBay.

Taxes on In-State Sales

When it comes to sales taxes, the general rule is this: Whenever you sell something on eBay and the buyer is a resident of your state, you have to pay sales tax to your state tax authority.

It's really that simple. When you first set up your eBay selling business, you should register with your state tax authority for a "sales tax permit." It consists of two parts:

➤ You will get a state tax ID number (called a "resale number") that you use when paying sales and use taxes.

➤ You will be given a form of "resale certificate," which you give to your vendors whenever you buy something for resale on eBay. That way the vendor will not charge you sales tax for what is essentially a wholesale transaction.

If your state tax authority doesn't send you the resale certificate form, it's usually available as a free download from your state tax authority's website. Just type "[name of state] department of revenue" into your favorite search engine. Then click on "forms and publications," then "sales tax forms" to find the resale certificate form.

Remember, *there is no sales tax on wholesale transactions, only retail transactions*. I hear occasionally about eBay sellers who pay sales tax when they buy merchandise from vendors, and then turn

• If You Don't Warn Your Buyers Up-Front, •
You Can't Charge Them Sales Tax

Whenever you buy something at retail, the vendor usually tacks the sales tax on to the total amount. You don't even think about it.

So it comes as a surprise to many early-stage eBay sellers that under the laws of most states, you *cannot* add sales tax to the buyer's winning bid amount, *unless* you tell them first you're going to do so!

The Terms and Conditions you prepare for your eBay auction pages (see Appendix B for sample language) should *always* contain a sentence that says: "Residents of [name your state]: State and local sales taxes will be added to your winning bid."

If you don't tell your bidders up-front that you will add sales tax to their winning bids, you are still required under state law to pay the tax when it comes due. That means you'll have to "eat" the tax by deducting it from your profits.

• Sales to Nonprofit Organizations •

You are required to collect and pay sales tax when you sell on eBay to residents of your state. What if the resident happens to be a charitable or nonprofit organization?

The short answer is that you don't have to charge sales tax, but only if the purchaser is a genuine or bona fide charity.

For an organization to qualify as a bona fide charity, it must obtain an exemption from taxes under Section 501(c)(3) of the U.S. Internal Revenue Code. When the IRS grants an exemption, it issues a "501(c)(3) letter" to the charity.

If you sell something on eBay and the purchaser claims exemption from sales tax as a charity, ask for a photocopy of the purchaser's 501(c)(3) exemption letter from the IRS. If the letter appears genuine, it's okay to forgo charging the purchaser sales tax.

If the purchaser cannot produce an exemption letter, *charge them sales tax*. A lot of nonprofit organizations haven't gone through the trouble of getting a tax exemption from the IRS, and this is the price they pay for not getting that piece of paper.

around and charge that sales tax to their winning bidders. That's just wrong!

The way it's supposed to work is as follows:

> ➤ When you buy merchandise from vendors that you intend to resell on eBay (otherwise known as "inventory"), you give your vendors a copy of your resale certificate, and you *do not* pay sales tax on that purchase.
> ➤ When you resell an item on eBay to someone in your state, you add the sales tax to the winning bid amount, collect it from the winning bidder, and then remit it to your state tax authority (usually once a quarter, but in some states once a month).

Some vendors cannot legally sell you product at wholesale—everything with them is a retail transaction. For example, franchise operations can only sell at retail. If you buy from them, you must pay sales tax, and hope you can make a profit when you resell the item on eBay. See Chapter 9 for information on deducting unreimbursed sales taxes on your federal and state income tax returns.

Taxes on Interstate Sales

At the time this book was written, the laws are such that you have to charge sales tax only when the winning bidder in your eBay auction or Buy It Now! sale lives in the same state you do. If the winning bidder lives in another state, you *do not* have to charge sales tax—unless the buyer's state and your state have entered into a mutual "sales tax" agreement.

For example, New York and Connecticut have entered into such an agreement, and about a dozen Midwestern states have entered into an "interstate tax compact." If you live in a state that has signed such an agreement, and you sell stuff on eBay to a buyer who lives in one of the other states that are a party to that agreement, you are required to collect the other state's sales tax and pay it to the other state's tax authority.

I know, I know . . . nobody you know has ever done this, but it is the law.

Here's the way it works: Let's say you live in Connecticut and you sell something on eBay to a buyer who lives in New York. You are supposed to collect New York state and local sales taxes and pay them to the Connecticut tax authority (there's a form for that, which you can obtain as a free download from the Connecticut state tax authority's website). Then, when they receive your payment, Connecticut will "remit" the sales tax to New York.

I can hear you sniggering right now. . . . Yeah, I don't know if Connecticut will actually remit the tax to New York, either. But, if you follow this procedure, neither New York nor Connecticut can come after you for unpaid sales taxes down the road, and that's all you should care about!

"Drop Shipping" and Consignment Sales

Are you selling merchandise on eBay for people who live in another state? Here's where sales taxes get a bit tricky.

The best way to explain this situation is to illustrate it. Let's say you have an eBay business in Connecticut and you are contacted by people in Nebraska who ask if you'll sell their grand piano on eBay. You put the piano up for sale on eBay, and the piano sells. Here are the sales tax rules, regardless of whether you took possession of the piano:

➤ If the winning buyer lives in Connecticut, you have to charge Connecticut sales tax.

➤ If the winning buyer lives in Nebraska, you have to charge Nebraska sales tax and remit the tax to Nebraska (there's a special form for that, which your accountant can find for you if you can't find it yourself on the Nebraska tax authority website).

➤ If the winning buyer lives anywhere else, you won't have to charge sales tax.

In other words, you charge sales tax if the buyer lives in the same state as either you or the person or business for whom you are selling on eBay.

• The Streamlined Sales Tax Project (SSTP) •

Currently, you *do not* have to charge sales tax on eBay when the winning bidder lives in another state . . . unless the buyer's state and your state have an "interstate compact" that says otherwise.

You should be aware, though, that there's a movement afoot in Congress to change all that.

Since the vast majority of e-commerce transactions are "interstate" in nature, state governments have lost a ton of tax revenue from the millions of Americans who are buying and selling products on the Web. And they are hopping mad about that.

About twenty-five states have adopted something called the Streamlined Sales Tax Project (SSTP). It is a law that, if approved by Congress, would allow states to charge sales tax on interstate transactions over the Web. Shocking? And how!

The only reason it hasn't happened yet is because of some U.S. Supreme Court decisions from the 1990s ruling that states cannot tax interstate commerce. As long as those rulings remain in place, the SSTP cannot be enforced by any of the states that have so far adopted it. If Congress overrules those court rulings, though, the SSTP will go into effect and state tax authorities will have a field day auditing the eBay community for unpaid sales taxes.

Worried about the SSTP? You should be! The Government Relations team at eBay has made it a top priority to fight any bill in Congress that would lead to approval of the SSTP. To join in their efforts, go to www.ebaymainstreet.com and sign up to receive periodic e-mails with "form letters" you can send to your representatives in Congress, telling them not to do anything that would tax e-commerce, and eBay in particular.

You should also make sure to warn potential bidders that they may have to pay sales taxes on their winning bids. In the example just given, your notice on the eBay auction page would say something like this: "Note to residents of Nebraska and Connecticut: State and local sales taxes will be added to your winning bid."

In many states, if you fail to give buyers that notice, you will be prohibited from adding sales taxes to their winning bids and will have to deduct the tax from your winning bid when the buyer pays you.

USE TAXES (ON WHAT YOU BUY FOR YOUR OWN "USE")

Prepare for a shock. In addition to collecting and paying sales taxes to your state tax authority, you may also be required to pay "use" taxes on the things you buy on eBay. Every state that has a sales tax also has a use tax. In most of these states the use tax applies only to businesses, but in many states the use tax applies to both businesses *and* individual consumers. Look closely at your state income tax form—if there's a line item for "use tax," it means your state has a personal or individual use tax.

A use tax is the opposite of a sales tax—I like to call it the sale tax's "evil twin." You pay use tax on:

➤ Items you buy for your own consumption (*not* the inventory you are reselling on eBay)

➤ Items for which you *did not* pay a state sales tax

Example 1: You go to your local office supply outlet and buy paper clips you intend to use in your business. You pay your state sales tax at the register. You *do not* have to pay use tax on the paper clips, because you paid sales tax on them. There is no "double dipping" when it comes to use taxes.

Example 2: You live in Connecticut, and you buy a laptop computer on eBay from a seller in California. You intend to use the laptop computer yourself to help you run your eBay selling business. You will have to pay use tax on the winning bid amount you paid for the laptop.

Example 3: You live in Connecticut and buy a laptop on eBay from a seller in California, except this time you are buying the laptop for resale to someone else. You do not have to pay use tax on the laptop, because it is "inventory" and not "for your personal consumption."

Got all that?

If I had to pick the biggest tax problem most small retail businesses have right now, it's the failure to understand and comply with their state's use tax laws. (If you want to know what can happen if you ignore these taxes, see "A 'Use Tax' Horror Story" in Chapter 13.) Even though your state may not be auditing use tax aggressively right now, it's only a matter of time before *some* state tax authority contacts eBay and requests records of purchases their residents have made on eBay for which use tax may be due.

OTHER TAXES

Most states have income, sales, and/or use taxes. But there are other taxes you have to watch out for in some states. When starting an eBay selling business, you should talk to your accountant and get a list of every state and local tax you will have to deal with. Let's go over the most common ones.

Personal Property Taxes

Many states impose a personal property tax for individuals on luxury goods such as automobiles and yachts. Some states go further, though, and impose their personal property tax on business equipment and supplies.

If your business is subject to a personal property tax, it usually works the same way as the real estate taxes you pay on your home. Your local government sets a "mill rate" showing how much tax you have to pay. You figure out the value of your business equipment and supplies each year and pay the tax accordingly.

Example: You own business and equipment and supplies worth $5,000 (whatever you paid for them). Your town's mill rate is $25 for each $1,000 of your property's assessed value. You will have to pay $125 ($25 × 5) in personal property taxes this year. Next year your property will be worth only $4,000 due to depreciation, so you will have to pay $100 ($25 × 4) in personal property taxes next year—unless your town changes the mill rate, of course.

Inventory or "Floor" Taxes

An inventory or "floor" tax is a percentage of the market value of your year-end inventory (the merchandise you didn't sell on eBay during the year), and it is calculated in much the same way as a personal property tax. There are numerous exemptions from the tax, though. Most states have an exemption for goods sold in "interstate commerce," which should apply to most inventory sold by eBay sellers. Other states have exemptions for specific types of goods whose manufacturers have extremely powerful lobbyists in the state legislature.

> Example: Your state imposes a 5 percent floor tax. On December 31, you have $5,000 worth of bobblehead dolls in your basement that you weren't able to sell on eBay. Unless an exemption applies to these items (maybe you can write some of them off as "worthless goods"), you will have to pay a $250 tax to your state tax authority.

Most states that have floor taxes are gradually phasing them out, except for certain items such as cigarettes and other tobacco products. Not only are these taxes politically unpopular, but they are difficult as the dickens to calculate and impose a real hardship on small businesses that don't have the resources to track the "market value" of each line of goods they sell.

Business Entity Taxes

For years, many states have had "minimum income taxes" for corporations that must be paid each year, whether or not the corporation is making money. When the limited liability company (LLC) was first adopted in the mid-1990s, owners of corporations howled about the fact that unincorporated businesses such as LLCs weren't subject to these minimum taxes.

In response, many states adopted a "business entity tax" for LLCs, subchapter S corporations, and other "pass-through" or unincorporated business entities (see Chapter 2). A business entity tax is usually a flat tax (in Connecticut, for example, it's currently $250) and is payable on April 15 of each year.

Excise Taxes

Finally, certain types of goods may be subject to excise taxes in your state. These are flat taxes, and they are usually imposed on goods that require a state license to sell (think alcohol, cigarettes, and gasoline).

If you need a license to sell something on eBay (see Chapter 2), there may well also be a state excite tax on those items, so check with your accountant to learn the details.

COMMON QUESTIONS

Q. *How does the IRS collect information on what is sold on eBay, or do they rely on the sellers to provide it?*

A. To date, the IRS does not collect information on what is sold on eBay; the IRS relies on sellers to be honest and thorough in filling out their tax returns.

Having said that, though, it's only a matter of time before someone (probably a state tax authority) demands information from eBay about selling activity in their state so they can pursue sellers for unpaid sales and use taxes. To anyone's knowledge it hasn't happened yet, but you don't want to wait until it does to get into compliance.

Q. *If I pay my taxes quarterly, what will the effect be on my filing process at the end of each year? What federal forms do I use to file my taxes quarterly?*

A. If you are paying quarterly estimated taxes, you have "prepaid" your 2005 taxes and would report these payments on your 1040. If at the end of the year you owed more in taxes than you paid in estimated taxes, you will have to pay the balance due, together with interest (and be sure to increase your quarterly estimated payments for 2006). If you overpaid, of course, you will be entitled to a refund.

Q. *A few months ago I started selling a few things from my family's estate. They were collectible and did very well. I would like to sell on a regular basis now, but I doubt that I will make the same amount of money per sale. How will I deal with quarterly taxes if they are going to assume I will be making more than I actually will? Or am I misunderstanding how quarterly taxes work?*

A. There are two ways you can pay estimated taxes this year. You can pay 110 percent of the taxes you paid last year (divided by four, of course, because estimated payments are made quarterly), but this will probably result in your paying more than you should.

   If you think you will make less than $1,000 in profits this year, then you can forgo paying estimated taxes altogether. Otherwise, you should total your sales each quarter, do a rough calculation of the taxes you think you will pay on that quarter's sales, add another $20 or $30 for good luck (don't laugh—a lot of people do that), and make the quarterly payment accordingly. It's not perfect, and you'll probably be a little over or a little under at the end of the year, but it's the best you can do in an imperfect world.

Q. *I didn't realize I'd have to file eBay on my taxes! I thought it would be like a garage sale!*

A. Hate to burst your bubble, big guy, but you have to pay taxes if you make money selling stuff at a garage sale. Where I live, they even send sales tax auditors to flea markets pretending to be buyers . . .

Q. *What if I fail to pay estimated taxes?*

A. If you fail to estimate properly, you will be subject to penalties and interest on the amounts you failed to pay. If you underpay one quarter and then overpay the next quarter, you still have to pay penalties for the three months you were underwithheld.

Q. *If I sell something on eBay that was worth $10 about fifty years ago, and I get $200 for it, do I have to pay tax on $190?*

A. Yes. The IRS rules for calculating the capital gains tax on the sale of an asset do not take inflation into account. So, if you bought the item for $10 fifty years ago and sold it this year for $200, you must report a capital gain of $190 and pay tax on it.

The one exception is for items you were willed from a deceased relative or other person. Let's say your Aunt Matilda bought the item for $10 fifty years ago and left it to you in her will when she died in the year 2000. The item had a fair market value of $150 on the day your Aunt Matilda died.

Under those circumstances, if you sell the item on eBay for $200 this year, you will report a capital gain of only $50 (the difference between the $200 winning bid and the $150 value on the date of Aunt Matilda's death) and will pay taxes on only the $50.

Tax Deductions for eBay Sellers

Probably the biggest selling point for anyone thinking about starting their own business is "when you're self-employed, life is deductible!"

Well, sometimes . . .

If you are selling on eBay and filing Schedule C on your tax return, there are quite a few things you can deduct. This chapter summarizes the most common deductions eBay sellers can take and points out a few misconceptions about things that can and cannot be deducted.

THE "HOME OFFICE" DEDUCTION

Since the vast majority of eBay sellers work out of their homes, the "home office" deduction will probably be the single biggest deduction they take on their tax returns each year. It's so important to the eBay community that it deserves an entire chapter all its own, so see Chapter 10.

DEDUCTING EXPENSES VS. "INVENTORYING" THEM

One of the biggest misconceptions eBay sellers have about taxes is that they can deduct things such as postage, shipping supplies, packaging materials, and sales taxes they pay to vendors for goods that they later sell on eBay.

Bad news . . . you're really not supposed to deduct these costs, although a lot of eBay sellers do. You're supposed to "inventory" them by adding them to your "cost of goods sold."

Cost of Goods Sold (COGS)

Generally, when a retailer (that's you) incurs out-of-pocket costs buying or selling inventory, the costs are not deducted outright as business expenses. Rather, you add them to whatever you paid for the item and deduct them from the final sales price when you actually sell the item on eBay.

For example, you buy $100 worth of inventory for sale on eBay, plus $10 for a cardboard box that the item fits in. You then sell the inventory on eBay for $200. You would include the $10 cardboard box in the "cost of goods sold" and report $90 ($200 minus the $100 item cost minus the $10 box) as income on your Schedule C, paying taxes on that amount.

Examples of items that eBay sellers should inventory (i.e., add to COGS) are:

➢ Postage
➢ Shipping fees
➢ Handling fees
➢ Shipping and packaging materials (such as plastic peanuts and bubble or blister pack)
➢ Sales taxes you pay to vendors

What If the Buyer Reimburses These Costs?

Most eBay sellers charge their buyers a "shipping and handling fee" precisely to cover the costs of postage, packaging materials, and other selling expenses. If you charge your eBay buyers a shipping and handling fee, then you cannot deduct the cost of these items, nor is the shipping and handling fee treated as "income" to you. It's a total "wash," as if you took the buyer's shipping and handling fee out of one hand and paid it to your supplier with the other hand at the same moment.

For example, you buy $100 worth of inventory for sale on eBay, plus $10 for a cardboard box that the item fits in. You then sell the inventory on eBay for $200, plus a $10 "shipping and handling fee" to cover the cost of the box. You would include the $10 cardboard box in the cost of goods sold and report $100 ($210 minus the $100 item cost minus the $10 box) as income on your Schedule C, paying taxes on that amount. The $10 shipping and handling fee would offset the $10 you added to your cost of goods sold for the box.

Any sales tax you charge your eBay buyers (as opposed to sales tax you pay your vendors) is treated in the same manner. It's a "wash" and is neither income to you nor a deductible expense.

Now, let's look at another example: You buy $100 worth of inventory for sale on eBay. You then sell the inventory on eBay for $200. Because your buyer lives in the same state you do, you add your state's 5 percent sales tax ($10) to the winning bid amount. Because the $10 sales tax has to be paid over to your state tax authority, whether or not the buyer reimburses you for it, it would not be part of the item's cost of goods sold. So, you would report $100 ($210 minus the $100 item cost, minus the $10 sales tax obligation) as income on your Schedule C, paying taxes on that amount.

If the buyer didn't pay you the $10 sales tax (perhaps because you didn't tell him you would add sales tax to the winning bid—see Chapter 8), the sales tax would reduce your income on the sale. So you would report $90 ($200 minus the $100 item cost, minus the $10 sales tax obligation) as income on your Schedule C, paying taxes on that amount.

What If You Go Ahead and Deduct These Costs, Anyway?

Having said all that about the cost of goods sold, you will probably not get into too much hot water with the IRS if you deduct unreimbursed shipping and packaging materials, postage, and sales taxes

• Charging Your Buyers More for Shipping • Than Your Actual Costs

This is not a recommended practice for any eBay seller. Not only might it violate eBay policies and get you kicked off of eBay, but it may also violate consumer protection laws in your home state. If winning bidders find out you are inflating their winning bid by overcharging for postage or shipping materials, you are almost certain to generate negative feedback on eBay's Feedback Forum—not a good thing, especially for new sellers.

If you do engage in this practice, you still have to pay taxes on the "excess" shipping fees, which are income to you. The proper approach when filling out your tax return—and what the IRS would prefer you to do—is to total all the shipping fees you receive from winning bidders on eBay and report the total as "Other Income" on Schedule C. Then, total up your actual postage and shipping costs and report the total as deductible "Materials and Supplies" on Schedule C. If you do it right, the "net income" subject to tax is the total amount of your excess shipping and handling fees, which is where you should end up.

Be forewarned: If you are ever sued by an eBay buyer (or eBay itself) for "fee gouging," the first thing a lawyer will ask to see are copies of your Schedule C.

as an office expense on your Schedule C, especially if the total amount you paid was relatively small and it's too much of a hassle to track it as part of the COGS of a much larger inventory for which you didn't pay for shipping and packaging materials.

Just keep accurate records (such as sales register receipts) of the amount you paid for these items, because you may have to justify your deduction if you are ever audited by the IRS or your state tax agency. And when you get a little bigger, start recording these costs the right way.

SOME COSTS eBAY SELLERS CAN DEDUCT

Once you start making money on eBay, almost everything you spend money on—from advertising to insurance to travel—is deductible as a "business expense." Let's go through these expenses, one by one. If you want more information, go to Intuit Corp.'s eBay Tax Center and access the "What's Deductible" page (www.tax center.turbotax.com/ebaytaxtips/deductiblechecklist).

Also check out some of the books, IRS publications, and other resources listed in Appendix A.

Advertising and Marketing

For eBay sellers, advertising and marketing costs cover such things as:

- ➢ Billboard advertising
- ➢ Business cards
- ➢ Consulting fees paid for search engine optimization of your website
- ➢ Design costs (e.g., logo, website, letterhead design)
- ➢ Flyers and brochures
- ➢ Mailing list rentals and purchases
- ➢ Market research expenses
- ➢ Pay-per-click advertising
- ➢ Radio ads
- ➢ Signs
- ➢ Sponsorships of junior sports (e.g., Little League baseball teams)
- ➢ Stationery used for business
- ➢ Phone book ads and listings

Automobile Expenses

The IRS gives you two choices when it comes to deducting motor vehicle expenses. You can either *deduct your mileage* (the current rate is 44.5 cents per mile, but it changes every year, and sometimes even during the year) or you can *deduct the actual cost* of maintaining the car (e.g., gas, oil changes, garage repairs, car washes, and so forth).

Either way, the IRS will not allow you to deduct 100 percent of your mileage or expenses if you use your car or truck for both business and personal uses. You must keep track of how much time you use your car for business as opposed to personal use.

We recommend that you buy a mileage log (available on eBay, or from any store or website that sells office supplies), keep it in a convenient place (such as under the driver's side visor) along with a pen or pencil, and record your actual business mileage on a daily basis. This mileage log will come in handy when you prepare your annual taxes and if you are ever audited.

What counts as mileage? Basically, any miles you travel while actually conducting business on eBay. As examples:

➤ Driving between your home office and your post office or UPS Store to check your private mailbox and pick up ordered items that you are planning to sell on eBay

➤ Driving to and from your home office to your post office or UPS Store to drop off items you have sold on eBay for shipment to the buyer

➤ Driving to a seller's home or office to pick up items you plan to sell on eBay

➤ Driving to and from garage sales, flea markets, and the like to purchase goods for sale on eBay

➤ Making personal deliveries of items you have sold on eBay to local buyers

➤ Driving to and from a local meeting of an organization of local business people or eBay sellers, such as a networking group

Example: You leave your home office in your SUV with your three children and several packages of goods you have sold on eBay that have to be shipped. You drive three miles to your children's school and drop them off. Then, you drive another two miles to your post office and mail the packages before returning the five miles to your home office. You can deduct the two miles you drove to your post office and the five miles you drove back to your home office, but you cannot deduct the three miles from your home office to your kids' school.

If you conduct your eBay selling from an office or retail location outside your home, however, you cannot deduct the miles spent driving to and from that office or retail location—that's considered a "commuting expense" and therefore a personal, not a business, expense.

If you use the "actual cost" method instead of the mileage method, you will still need to keep tack of your mileage, because that is the most accurate way to figure out what percentage of your automobile use is business-related versus personal. In addition, you should keep copies of all receipts for gasoline and oil changes and collect them in a special file folder so that you can document all automotive expenses during the year.

Consignment and Drop-Shipping Fees

Consignment and drop-shipping arrangements are discussed in Chapter 14.

The better approach, and what the IRS would prefer you to do, is to total up all your sales of consigned goods and drop-shipped items and report them as income, then total up all the amounts you paid your consignors and drop shippers (after deducting your consignment fee or commission) and report that total as a deductible business expense. If you do it right, the "net income" subject to tax is the total amount of your consignment and drop-shipping fees and commissions, which is where you should end up.

Make sure you send a Form 1099 to every consignor and drop shipper you paid more than $600 (total) during the year, and mail it by January 31 of the following year. Duplicate copies of the Form 1099 must also be mailed to the IRS and your state tax agency by February 28 or 29 of the following year.

Copyrights and Trademarks

If you are just starting up an eBay business, and your total start-up expenses, including trademark and copyright registrations, do not exceed $5,000 total, then you can deduct them in the year in which you paid them. Otherwise, copyrights and trademarks should be amortized over a fifteen-year period, which means you deduct one-fifteenth of the total cost each year.

Debts and Losses

The only good news about "nonpaying buyers" is that you can deduct them on your tax return. You can, for example, deduct the costs of:

- ➤ Bad or bounced checks from your buyers
- ➤ Bad debts
- ➤ Bankruptcy filings
- ➤ Casualty losses (if not covered by insurance)
- ➤ Credit card chargebacks
- ➤ Damages for breach of contract (including punitive damages), unless imposed by a government agency
- ➤ Net operating losses (if you paid more for goods than you received from selling them online)
- ➤ Refunds on returned goods that are added back to inventory
- ➤ Shoplifting losses
- ➤ Stolen equipment (to the extent that it's not depreciated)
- ➤ Stolen inventory (as part of the cost of goods sold)
- ➤ Uncashed checks (checks that you may have written in December that were not cashed until the following year because the recipient uses the cash method of accounting and does not want to report the income this year)

Donations and Gifts

If you are a sole proprietor, partnership, or limited liability company (LLC), you cannot deduct charitable contributions on your Schedule C, not even amounts from your winning bids that you give to charity under the eBay Giving Works program. Since these unincorporated businesses are "pass-throughs" for tax purposes (see Chapter 2), you can, however, deduct them as personal charitable contributions on your Form 1040, under "charitable contributions." To take the deduction, though, these costs must total more than 2 percent of your personal adjusted gross income, and that might be a tough target to hit in a given year.

Other donations and gifts you can deduct include:

➢ Business gifts up to $25 in any one year

➢ Charitable contributions you made as an individual

➢ Flowers given as gifts to employees or clients for birthdays or illness

➢ Greeting cards to business clients or employees

➢ Prizes to customers and suppliers

➢ Rebates you pay to others (as long as they are not illegal "kickbacks")

Online Selling Fees

All of the following expenses are deductible:

➢ Insertion, option/enhancement, and final value fees charged by eBay

➢ PayPal fees

➢ Other marketplace fees (such as Yahoo, Shopping.com, and Amazon .com)

➢ Third-party fees for use of software and services that facilitate business on eBay (such as Andale, MarketWorks, or Vendio)

➢ Merchant account transaction fees (from an online merchant credit card account).

Under certain circumstances, if you use your PayPal ATM/debit card to pay your eBay and PayPal fees, you are entitled to a "cash back bonus" of between 1 percent and 1.5 percent. The better approach—and what the IRS would prefer you to do—is to total *all* your cash back bonuses during the current tax year and report them as "Other Income" when filling out your Schedule C. Then report your total eBay and PayPal fees you paid with your ATM/ debit card for the year (without taking the bonus into account) as "Commissions and Fees" on Schedule C.

Education

When you don't get what you want, what you get is an education. And it's all deductible. That includes:

• Can You Deduct Your Dog? •

At eBay University seminars, I am often asked about the tax rules governing guard dogs. It seems that a lot of eBay sellers are chaining their Chihuahuas to their inventory at night and claiming a deduction. I've got two words for those folks: "animal abuse."

If your dog qualifies as a guard dog, you can deduct expenses (such as her food, kennel stays, grooming, etc.), but you can't deduct the dog itself. You can only depreciate the dog over its "useful life"—usually the average life expectancy of the particular breed and sex as determined by a local breeder.

Here are Cliff's Rules for determining if you have a real "guard dog" on your hands:

- If the dog is smaller than a breadbox, it's not a guard dog.
- If the dog responds to strangers by licking them and exposing its belly, it's not a guard dog.
- If the dog has a name like Peaches or Fluffy, it's not a guard dog.
- If there's no evidence your dog is actually guarding your inventory (e.g., the dog's house is in the backyard, but you store your inventory in the basement), it's not a guard dog.
- If the newspaper deliverer and postal carrier are afraid to leave packages by your front door, you're a little nervous around the dog yourself, or the dog is a "rescue" formerly owned by an abusive drug dealer, you've got a shot at deducting it.

No guarantees, though—your dog may be tough, but some IRS agents are a lot tougher.

> Books (if business related)
> Magazines and newsletter subscriptions (if business related)
> Newspapers
> Consulting fees you pay to others
> Seminars (for the purpose of maintaining or improving a skill required in your business), such as programs offered by eBay University or sponsored by the Professional eBay Sellers Alliance (PESA)
> Conferences and conventions (such as eBay Live! or PESA Summit)

Employees

You are not considered an "employee" of your own business for tax purposes (see Chapter 2). But if you have real, actual employees, you can deduct the following:

- Bonuses to employees (not yourself)
- Compensation to employees (including family members, but not yourself)
- Day care for employees' children (not your own)
- Disability insurance for your employees (not yourself)
- Expenses incurred by employees that you reimburse
- Employee wages and benefits
- Employment agency fees
- Employment/payroll taxes (see Chapter 12)
- Family members on payroll (see Chapter 12)
- FICA (Social Security) taxes paid for employees (see Chapter 12)
- Fringe benefits to employees (such as educational assistance, athletic facilities, or achievement awards)
- Federal unemployment tax (see Chapter 12)
- Health insurance for your employees (not yourself)
- Life insurance for employees (not yourself)
- Long-term care insurance for employees (not yourself)
- Medicare tax paid for employees (not yourself)
- Payroll expenses (other than for yourself)
- Payroll taxes
- Pension plans
- Retirement plan contributions for employees (such as SEP-IRA, 401K)
- Salaries to employees (not yourself)
- Unemployment taxes (including state disability funds)
- Wages paid to employees

Equipment (IRS Section 179)

If you bought equipment to use in your eBay selling business this year, you can deduct up to $105,000 worth on your tax return this year. That includes purchases such as personal computers and laptops, photo studio equipment, mannequins to display jewelry and clothing, and computer software.

Fees, Dues, and Licenses

Take every deduction you can, including:

➤ Accountants' fees
➤ Advances to professionals (prepaid fees)
➤ Association dues (if business related)
➤ Attorneys' fees
➤ Audits
➤ Bank charges for business (not personal) accounts
➤ Bookkeeping fees (including QuickBooks Pro and eBay Accounting Assistant)
➤ Business association dues
➤ Business licenses and registrations
➤ Club dues (if business related)
➤ Commissions to finders or brokers for referring sales
➤ Consulting fees you pay to others
➤ Contract preparation fees
➤ Credit card fees and interest (if business related)
➤ Customs fees, duties, and tariffs
➤ Dues to business groups
➤ Employment agency fees
➤ Fax machine
➤ Finance charges for purchases made with a credit card
➤ Homeowner's association fees
➤ Import fees

> Independent contractor fees (i.e., payments to accountants and book-keepers)
> Internet access fees
> ISP fees for maintaining your website
> Legal fees
> Merchant account fees (i.e., accounts that relate to a seller's ability to take credit card payments)
> Membership fees (if business related), such as a Rotary Club or other business networking organizations
> PESA (Professional eBay Sellers Alliance) membership dues
> Referral fees you pay to others (if legal)
> SquareTrade fees
> Trade show admissions

Insurance

You can take deductions related to:

> All insurance for employees, other than yourself or your spouse
> Health insurance for yourself, spouse, and dependents (unless you are eligible for insurance through your "day job")
> Insurance premiums for business insurance (e.g., liability, business interruption, property/casualty)
> Long-term care insurance for yourself, spouse, and dependents (with some limits)
> Payments to a state unemployment compensation or disability fund

Inventory (What You Sell on eBay)

Generally, the stuff you sell on eBay cannot be deducted until it is sold. You figure out the cost of goods sold (discussed previously) and deduct it from the final sales price (the winning bid in your eBay auction) to figure out the amount of the deduction. Items remaining in inventory at the end of the year (December 31) are an "asset" and cannot be deducted.

Postage

Postage cannot be deducted right away, but must be added to your cost of goods sold and deducted from the final sales price (the winning bid in your eBay auction) when the item is sold.

Shipping Materials

Shipping materials, such as boxes and peanuts and bubble pack used for wrapping merchandise, cannot be deducted right away, but must be added to your cost of goods sold and deducted from the final sales price (the winning bid in your eBay auction) when the item is sold.

Software

Software that you purchase can be depreciated over three years or less, if the software has a shorter useful life. For example, tax preparation software such as TurboTax Personal and Business for eBay Sellers (see Appendix A for a description of this program and other eBay-related software products) is only good for one year, so it probably could be deducted outright in the year you buy it.

Start-up Costs

You can deduct legal fees, accounting fees, and filing fees for setting up a corporation or limited liability company (LLC) up to $5,000. Beyond that, you must amortize (or write off) your start-up expenses over fifteen years.

State and Local Taxes

Taxes you have to pay to sell and buy on eBay (especially sales and use taxes) are covered in detail in Chapter 8. Taxes that are deductible include:

> ➢ Inventory or "floor" taxes (if imposed by your state) on the year-end value of your eBay inventory
> ➢ One-half of self-employment taxes you pay (note, however, that you take that deduction on your Form 1040, not on your Schedule C)

➢ Personal property taxes on equipment and supplies (if imposed by your state)

➢ Sales taxes you pay when you buy goods for resale on eBay

➢ Sales taxes you pay when you sell goods on eBay (unless you are reimbursed for these sales taxes by the buyer, in which case it is a "wash")

➢ Telephone service taxes (for a dedicated business telephone line)

➢ Use taxes (paid to your state when you buy items from out-of-state vendors for use in your business—not for resale—and when you don't pay sales taxes)

Travel and Entertainment

These expenses, when associated with your eBay selling business and separated from your personal expenses, are deductible:

➢ Business trips: Round-trip airfare, meals, and lodging, and perhaps entertainment

---

• What If Some of the Stuff You're Selling • on eBay Is Personal Stuff?

The Internal Revenue Service wants you to keep separate records of your business expenses (which are deductible) from your personal expenses (which are not). It's very important when you're a sole proprietor (see Chapter 2) to differentiate your business from yourself. The best way to do that is to have a separate business checking account, a separate tax ID number for your business (don't use your Social Security number, even though the IRS allows you to), a separate "trade name" or "DBA" (for "doing business as . . .") for your business, and so forth.

You might even consider using a second eBay ID for the personal items, which will make tracking your sales correctly much easier.

If you mix your personal and business sales (what the IRS calls "commingling"), it's much easier for the IRS to claim that your personal income is actually business income and/or that your expenses are for personal, not business, use (especially when the expense could be either one).

- ➤ Entertainment expenses (50 percent only)
- ➤ Grooming expenses (if traveling on business)
- ➤ Lodging (when traveling on business)
- ➤ Meals while traveling on business (50 percent only)
- ➤ Meals with customers and suppliers (50 percent only)
- ➤ Parking costs (out of town)
- ➤ Per-diem rates for employee expenses while traveling (see IRS Publication 1542 for details)
- ➤ Prepaid expenses, such as Yellow Pages advertising you paid for this year that will appear in next year's telephone directory

Website

The Web is where you make all eBay sales, of course. Therefore, you can claim deductions for:

- ➤ Web-related design costs
- ➤ Internet access fees
- ➤ Website hosting

SOME THINGS eBAY SELLERS CAN'T DEDUCT

Topping the list of things that aren't deductible are the two biggest expenses you incur—your own compensation and your time.

➤ *Owner's Compensation*. Generally, when you are self-employed, you cannot deduct your own compensation, although you can deduct compensation paid to your employees.

There's one exception: If you form a corporation for your business (see Chapter 2) and hire yourself as an employee of the corporation, you can pay yourself a regular salary just like any other employee, as long as you withhold income and employment taxes from each paycheck, just as for any other employee. This saves you from having to pay quarterly estimated taxes, and it may cause you to pay less in employment taxes than if you are self-employed. Unless you are making more than $100,000 a year selling on eBay, however, the tax savings are probably not worth the trouble of forming a corporation and dealing with all the employment tax forms you will have to fill out each month and quarter.

➢ *Time.* Sadly, while time is often the single biggest expenditure you make in a business selling on eBay, it is not deductible.

Other expenses that are not deductible are:

➢ Antiques and artwork (unless they are inventory)
➢ Bribes and kickbacks
➢ Campaign contributions
➢ Clothing (except for uniforms all employees are required to wear while on duty)
➢ Club dues
➢ Commuting expenses (i.e., travel to and from work)
➢ Consigned goods (see Chapter 14 for the proper tax treatment)
➢ Disability insurance for yourself
➢ Estimated tax payments
➢ Expenses to have your spouse attend a business-related convention or conference (unless your spouse is an employee)
➢ Fines and penalties for breaking the law
➢ Gardening and lawn care expenses for a home office (see Chapter 10)
➢ Grooming expenses (except when traveling on business)
➢ Group health insurance for yourself
➢ Income taxes
➢ Life insurance on yourself
➢ Meals at work
➢ Reserves for bad debts (as opposed to the debts themselves)
➢ Self-insurance (which, after all, isn't really "insurance" but just cash you pay out if something bad happens to your business)

For a more detailed list, access the "What's Not Deductible" page at Intuit's eBay Tax Center (www.taxcenter.turbotax.com/

ebaytaxtips/nondeductiblechecklist). Also check out some of the books, IRS publications, and other resources listed in Appendix A.

COMMON QUESTIONS

Q. *I am a retired police officer. I knew I wanted to sell toys on the Internet as my retirement job and started doing so last year. How do I handle those toys I have been collecting and storing for many years and want to put up for sale now? How do I handle starting inventory for tax purposes? Many of the things I bought several years ago are highly collectible now.*

A. I think you are asking how you report the "cost of goods sold" of these items when you don't have accurate records of how much you paid for them.

You may have to rely on your memory about how much you paid for the item. In that case, record the cost, but keep some type of written "memo to the file," such as "purchased at Danbury antiques fair, March 1966, for $10." You can also look at old auction catalogs and ads in antique toy collector's magazines to see what specific toys were selling for at roughly the time you bought them. The IRS usually will accept that type of information.

Another (less reliable) approach is to show your toys to a local antiques dealer who's been around a while and get a rough written estimate of how much these items were selling for "way back when." Many dealers collect old catalogs and magazines and will do this research for you, for a fee of course. Just don't sell your toys if the dealer offers to buy them— you'll often do better on eBay.

Q. *I want to improve my understanding of import and export laws and rules. The university in my town has a great class. There is also a very good class in Tampa, Florida, about forty miles from my favorite vacation islands (Sanibel and Captiva). Can I take the Florida class and still deduct the air tickets, the class cost, and hotel and grub?*

A. If you are already an eBay seller and have at least some international sales, you should be able to deduct all travel expenses, including hotel, meals, and entertainment—within reason.

If you are a newbie and are just thinking about selling on eBay someday, be careful: The IRS does not allow you to deduct educational expenses for getting into a "new" business, and the rules are highly technical here. You might want to hold off until you actually have sales before you sign up for this seminar.

Q. *Please address the issue of net operating loss (NOL) for business. Can bad years be safely woven in with better ones? Is this a red flag? Should losses be carried forward?*

A. Generally, if you have an NOL for a tax year ending in 2005, you must carry back the entire amount of the NOL to the two tax years before the NOL year (the carry-back period), and then carry forward any portion of the NOL you cannot use for up to twenty years after the NOL year (the carry-forward period). You can, however, choose not to carry back the NOL and only carry it forward. See IRS Publication 536 for more specific information.

While taking net operating losses is certainly not an "audit trigger," you want to make sure you're doing it right. If you find out next year that you should have taken a net operating loss in 2005, you will have to amend your 2005 tax return to claim the deduction retroactively, and that just might wake some "sleeping dogs" at the local IRS office.

Q. *If I sew my company name on sweaters or other apparel, can I deduct the dry cleaning?*

A. I've always believed that creative people have a reward in heaven . . .

The IRS, however, will allow you deduct clothing only if it's a "uniform" you require your employees to wear while performing their jobs. Personalized sweaters for a one-person business is stretching that interpretation a wee bit too much, I think.

Q. *I am currently accounting for the COGS of each item as it sells. Over the course of a year, we purchase quite a few items that we do not end up selling (because we don't think they will sell for a minimum amount that we try to maintain). Some of these items are donated, others are simply thrown away. Can I account for these as part of my COGS, and if so, how?*

A. You can write off the stuff you throw away as "worthless inventory"—you can take either the cost of those goods or their fair market value, whichever is less. As for merchandise you donate to charity, the same rule applies (lesser of cost or fair market value).

However, if you are anything but a sole proprietorship (e.g., an LLC or corporation), you cannot take them as a charitable deduction. You should take them as a charitable deduction on your personal Form 1040.

Make sure you have a written appraisal of stuff you donate or throw away. That way if you claim "fair market value" as the basis for a deduction, you will have some support if the IRS audits you.

Q. *I sell on eBay, and I also have a second part-time business that involves traveling to clients' homes. My question is, which business should I take my traveling/mileage deductions on? On a typical workday, I drive to the post office to ship and receive eBay-related mail, then onward to a client's home, then back to my home office.*

A. You are exactly the reason why they invented "mileage logs" for small businesses.

Seriously, if it's not too much of a hassle, buy yourself two "mileage logs"—one for your eBay selling business, the other for your other business—and record your mileage in "real time."

Here's a time-saving tip: If you know the distance to and from your post office, you probably don't have to record it each time. Just count up the number of trips you make each day and record that in your mileage log. You can do the math next year come tax time.

Q. *If I choose to take my vehicle deduction as the 44.5 cents per mile, does this mean that nothing else is eligible for deduction (such as a percentage of my car insurance)? I realize that general maintenance, repairs, and gasoline would be included in the per-mile deduction, but I need to know how insurance fits in there.*

A. You can deduct either your mileage or your actual auto-related expenses, whichever is greater. So, if you take the mileage deduction, you can't deduct your car insurance, and vice versa.

Q. *In my eBay selling business, I sometimes take money out of the business checking account to pay my personal bills. How do I deduct these with-drawals for tax purposes?*

A. You don't. As the sole owner of an unincorporated business, you cannot pay yourself a deductible salary. Instead, you must report 100 percent of all profits from the business as your personal income each year, regardless of whether you withdraw the money from the business checking account. There is no need to report periodic withdrawals from your business check-ing account (called "draws" in tax language) on Schedule C.

If you have employees in your business who are not also owners, then you can pay them a fixed salary each week or quarter and deduct it from your business income. Amounts you pay to employees who are also own-ers, however, are not deductible (see Chapter 12).

Q. *What expenses qualify as business start-up costs?*

A. Start-up costs are business expenses you have before you start your busi-ness selling on eBay. General preliminary costs, such as researching whether you want to sell on eBay, are not deductible, but conventional expenses of setting up your eBay selling business are deductible. For ex-ample:

- ➢ Legal and accounting costs of getting a tax ID number and/or forming a limited liability company (LLC)
- ➢ Office stationery and business cards
- ➢ Pre-opening advertising (such as in the Yellow Pages)
- ➢ Rent, telephone, and other expenses you incur before you make your first sale on eBay

If you haven't made your first sale on eBay, wait until you do. Everything you spend money on after that point is deductible as a "business expense," and you won't have to worry about IRS start-up cost rules.

Running a Business Out of Your Home

THE "HOME OFFICE" DEDUCTION

The vast majority of eBay sellers are small, family-owned businesses that operate out of a private home, apartment, or garage. If you are among these folks, the "home office" deduction is probably the largest single deduction you can take on your tax return each year, and with a few exceptions (which will be discussed in this chapter), I think you're crazy not to take it.

No Longer an Audit Trigger

Don't believe what other people may tell you, or what you might read in some older, pre-2000 tax guides. Taking the "home office" deduction is *not* going to trigger an audit that will automatically expose you and your tax return to review by the IRS. Back in the 1980s and 1990s, the IRS did audit aggressively in this area, but Congress and the courts have done a lot since then to clarify the rules under which you can legitimately take the home office deduction, and so many people are taking the home office deduction now that the IRS doesn't have time to chase them all down.

• Cliff's Rules on Using Tax-Advice Books and Software •

You have to be careful what you pick up at used-book sales. In just about every eBay presentation I give around the country, someone steps up to the microphone during Q&A and says, "Cliff, you said a few minutes ago that we should consider doing X when we report something-or-other on our taxes. But this book I've been using says we should do just the opposite. Who's right here?" When I press the person for information about the book, it almost always turns out to be a 1988 tax guide the person picked up at a tag sale, used-book sale, or library sale, and the information she is relying on is woefully out of date.

Here are two rules about tax advice:

1. If you are using a tax guide that has a "year" printed on the cover and the year is anything other than the current year (or next year), throw it away! Do not recycle it, do not give it to your local library, do not sell it on eBay. Shred the bloody thing and get a new one. It has absolutely no worth to anyone else.
2. If you are using tax preparation software and are not updating it each month or calendar quarter (that's every three months) as recommended by the software publisher, delete it from your computer!

Using out-of-date tax information is not only a waste of time; it can actually harm your business. A lot of things that weren't deductible in 2000 are deductible now, and vice versa.

There is absolutely *no reason why you shouldn't take the home office deduction* if you are indeed conducting your eBay activities out of a bona fide home office.

But, because the home office deduction is easy for people to abuse if they are not careful, you have to make sure you are disciplined in how you use your home office, keep good records, and follow the rules closely. That way, if you are ever audited (not because you took the home office deduction, but for other reasons), your home office will stand up to IRS scrutiny.

The Six Steps to Taking the Home Office Deduction

Step 1: Pick your space. If you have an empty spare bedroom in your home, a second floor over your garage, an "in-law apartment" or other clearly defined space in your home, this is where your home office should be, because it will be easy to measure. You can use a portion of a room as a home office, but be sure the boundaries between your office and personal spaces are clearly defined.

Your home office has to be the *only area* where your eBay selling activities take place. If you work sometimes out of your home and sometimes out of an office, you may not qualify for the home office deduction.

If you use areas in your basement, garage, or attic as storage space for your inventory, you can add it to your home office space in order to take the deduction. You cannot deduct your entire basement, though, if you use only a portion of that space to store inventory.

<u>*Step 2: Get rid of stuff that doesn't belong in a home office.*</u> When the IRS audits a home office, the first thing they look for is furnishings, artwork, or accessories that do not belong in an office of any kind.

Cliff's Rule: When furnishing your home office, you should have only those decorative items and furnishings that would be appropriate in a real office or cubicle. If you wouldn't have something in a real office, it shouldn't be in your home office.

For example, your desk, computer, photo studio, and shipping area should all be part of your home office space. You can have a stereo system in your home office (which you can deduct), as well as appropriate artwork (which you cannot deduct). However, you *cannot* have cribs, kitchen or bathroom items, or inappropriate artwork in your home office. If you

• How Duct Tape Can Save Your Life •

Believe it or not, a roll of duct tape can help you out a lot if you are ever audited by the IRS for taking the home office deduction.

Most eBay sellers store their inventory in a basement, attic, garage, or barn, but they don't use the entire basement, attic, garage, or barn for their eBay business. While the IRS will let you deduct the portion of your room or space that you actually use to store inventory, they will not let you deduct all of it.

Duct tape to the rescue! Use it to mark the boundaries of the "business" portion of your basement, attic, garage, or barn, so that if you are ever audited, the IRS agent can see clearly where your home office space ends and your personal space begins.

sell rock concert posters on eBay, you can have rock concert posters on the wall of your home office. If you sell Oriental antiques on eBay, you shouldn't have rock concert posters on the wall of your home office, but you can have Oriental silk screens on the wall. Deductions are discussed in greater detail in Chapter 9.

Step 3: Measure your home office. To take the home office deduction, you have to know the square footage of both your entire home (wall to wall) and your home office space.

Don't do the measuring yourself, as it's easy to make mistakes (usually not in your favor). Instead, have a contractor measure your home office space professionally and give you something in writing with the exact measurements, in case you are ever audited.

Step 4: Determine your "home office percentage." This is a fraction, in which the numerator (top number) is the square footage of your home office space, wall to wall, and the denominator (bottom number) is the square footage of your entire home, wall to wall.

So, for example, if your home office space is 1,000 square feet, and your entire home, wall to wall, is 4,000 square feet, your "home office percentage" is:

$$1,000/4,000 = 0.25 \text{ or } 25\%$$

Step 5: Apply the home office percentage to your household expenses. If you have a home office, you can deduct your home office percentage of just about all of your household expenses, such as taxes, utilities, and housecleaning fees. However, you *cannot* deduct expenses for activities that take place outside of the home, such as lawn care and gardening, since by definition a home office must be "within" a home.

If you own your own home, you can also depreciate it for tax purposes, but watch out. If you later sell your home at a profit, you will have to pay a 25 percent capital gains tax on the total depreciation deductions you took while you were living there. (This tax does not apply to expense deductions you took for your home office.)

Step 6: Keep good records. While the home office deduction is typically not an audit trigger, you do have to keep good records in case you are ever audited. Be sure to keep the following records:

➢ Copies of IRS Form 1098 showing the interest you paid on your mortgage each year

➤ Property tax bills (and canceled checks)

➤ Utility and insurance bills

➤ Canceled checks for housecleaning, pet sitting, and other services

➤ A copy of your lease (if you rent the house or apartment in which your home office is located)

In addition to the six steps to taking home office deductions, there are some *special rules* worth noting as well:

➤ You cannot deduct more than the net profit your business makes each year (but like other operating losses, you can carry these forward into future tax years).

➤ You must fill out IRS Form 8829 and submit it with your 1040 each year if you are taking the home office deduction.

What Happens When You Sell Your Home?

Until 2003, if you took the home office deduction for more than three of the five years before you sold your house, you had to pay capital gains taxes on the "business" portion (i.e., home office fraction) of your home. In 2003, however, Congress changed the rules and no longer requires payment of this tax. As long as you live in your home for at least two out of the five years before you sell it, the first $250,000 (for single taxpayers) or $500,000 (for married taxpayers filing jointly) of profit is not taxable.

You will, however, have to pay a capital gains tax (called a "depreciation recapture") in the year you sell your home, equal to 25 percent of the total depreciation deductions you took on your home office since May 6, 1997—but *only* the depreciation deductions, not every other deduction you took for your home office. And if you didn't depreciate your home for tax purposes (which is a complex decision requiring the assistance of your accountant or tax adviser, since there are a lot of variables that could influence the decision one way or the other), you won't have to pay even that.

What Happens If You Have More Than One Home Office?

It may sound funny at first, but you actually can have more than one home office, although not at the same time. This can happen in two very common situations:

> ➤ You live in State A but have a summer or winter residence in State B, where you spend a portion of each year. (A fair number of people called "snowbirds" live in the Northeast during the summer months and winter in Florida.)
> ➤ You begin the year living in House 1 but sell the house during the year and move into House 2, where you continue your home-based eBay selling business.

You can still take the home office deduction in both of these cases, but you cannot take more than one home office deduction for the same period of time. You will have to "prorate" the deduction. So, for example, let's say you move from State A to State B on June 30. All income (profits) that you made from selling on eBay during the period January 1 to June 30 will be reported to the IRS (federal government) and the State A tax authority. All income (profits) you made from selling on eBay during the period July 1 to December 31 will be reported to the IRS (federal government) and the State B tax authority.

What Happens If You Rent Rather Than Own Your Home?

If you rent a home or apartment, you can take the home office deduction for the home office percentage of your rent and other household expenses.

Since you do not own your home or apartment, however, you cannot depreciate it for tax purposes.

You are also required to give your landlord a Form 1099-MISC each year showing how much of your rental payments (not other expenses) you deducted. Your landlord will absolutely love you for doing this (*not*), so be sure to give your landlord a "heads up" before giving the nasty surprise come tax season next year.

• Can You Take a Home Office Deduction • for Someone Else's Home?

Let's say you are running your eBay selling business out of your home, but you are using someone else's home (such as a friend's or relative's) to store your inventory. You can take the home office deduction for your own home office, but you will not be able to deduct your inventory space under the home office deduction.

To take a deduction for off-site storage space (i.e., space that is located on land you do not own), consider having an attorney draw up a lease for the space, have the owner of the other home sign it as "landlord" (you would sign as "tenant"), and pay the other homeowner a reasonable rent for the space. That way, you could deduct the rent you pay the other homeowner for the use of her garage, attic, basement, or barn. Make sure you are paying a fair market rent.

Do not conduct any other business at the other homeowner's address, or else you open yourself up to an IRS charge that you are not conducting your eBay selling business "solely and exclusively" from your home office. Also, don't let your relationship with the other homeowner get too "cozy," because if you do there's a risk the other person may be considered your partner in the eBay business (see "Avoiding an 'Accidental Partnership'" in Chapter 12), which will have significant legal and tax ramifications for you.

Remember that when doing business with friends, family members, or neighbors, you should treat them as if they were total strangers. Have them sign the same paperwork you would require if it were me or another third party on the other side of the table.

DEALING WITH LOCAL ZONING LAWS

I was once approached at an eBay University program by an individual with the following question: "A number of gated communities in my area are making new rules that prohibit people from buying and selling merchandise on eBay out of their homes. Their argument is that there are too many UPS trucks going in and out of the development each day picking up the eBay parcels. Is it legal for them to do that?"

While it sounds like these communities are going about it in a very heavy-handed way, the short answer is yes. It's perfectly legal for a gated community, condominium association, or residential subdivision to ban residents from engaging in commercial activities within its boundaries.

And it's not just gated communities that can enforce such rules. Prepare for a shock: Every business that operates out of someone's home is, technically, an illegal business.

Now you're probably saying to yourself, "Wait a minute! There are at least five people on my block working from their homes. The IRS allows you to take a deduction if you operate a home-based business. How can you say they're illegal?"

They're illegal because just about every city and town in the United States has adopted a zoning ordinance, dividing the community into residential, commercial, and other zones. Unless you live in a progressive community that allows "mixed use" zones, virtually every zoning ordinance prohibits the operation of a commercial business—with a few time-honored exceptions such as family dentists and visiting nurses—in a zone designated as "residential."

So why are so many people working out of their homes without getting into legal trouble? The answer has to do not with the law but with its enforcement.

Every community with a zoning ordinance has established a planning board or zoning board that oversees the zoning law and grants exceptions (called "variances") from the ordinance. But I'm not aware of a single community that has adopted a special police force to make 100 percent certain people aren't running businesses out of their homes. You've never had any government official knocking on your front door asking you if you're operating an illegal business, have you?

As a practical matter, if you're operating a business out of your home, you usually won't get into hot water with your local zoning authorities unless your neighbors turn you in. And when will your neighbors turn you in? When you're conducting business in such a way that you're "changing the residential character of our neighborhood." Maybe the local kids can't play stickball in the street because they're too busy dodging the UPS trucks going to and from your home office. Or the neighbors are being kept awake at night because of the loud noises or foul odors emanating from your basement. You get the idea.

What the gated communities are objecting to isn't the operation of a home-based business per se, but rather the increased vehicle and truck traffic that business is generating. And the courts will probably back them up.

So how can you operate an eBay business out of your home without getting into legal trouble?

Simple. First, find out if there's a UPS Store, Mail Boxes Etc., Navis Pack & Ship Center, or other franchise in your area. There almost certainly will be one. These franchises will provide you with a private mailbox—essentially a post office box that has an actual street address (such as "123 Main Street, # 456").

Next, if you expect to have lots of inventory delivered—and by lots, I mean more than a few items at a time—find the nearest self-storage facility (you can find the ones nearest you at www.self storage.org) and rent some storage space for your inventory. Because the mailbox outlet and the storage facility are both located within your community's commercial zone, they don't violate your local zoning ordinance. Therefore, your business won't, either.

Then sign up for a private mailbox—the average rental is around $300 per year, fully deductible—and use your mailbox address as your only mailing address for all shipments and correspondence to your suppliers and customers. Keep your inventory at the storage facility, and make sure all incoming shipments are dropped off there, or pick them up at the mailbox outlet and bring them to the storage facility. Use your home only as the "executive office" where you post your eBay auctions, work on your e-commerce site, keep your business records, and pack your boxes, though most mailbox franchises will do packing for you as well, for a fee.

Then once or twice a day—no more than that, please, especially if you live in a gated or other closed community—visit your storage facility, fill your car with your outgoing shipments, drive them down to your private mailbox address, and have the postal service, UPS, or FedEx pick them up there.

One last thing: Don't tell the neighbors what you're up to. Every neighborhood has a Gladys Kravitz (for you *Bewitched* fans) or a Martha Huber (*Desperate Housewives*) who just can't keep her nose out of your affairs. If your business isn't too visible and isn't interfering with their lives, most neighbors will adopt a "don't ask, don't tell" policy. After all, they probably don't want you finding out about *their* home-based business . . . at least until you bump into them at your local private mailbox outlet!

COMMON QUESTIONS

Q. *Can you talk about the requirements for the decor of a home office? I've had a home office set up for the past twenty years. It is decorated to suit my taste in decor and collectibles and also has custom bookcases with books I enjoy. Are you saying I must completely remove everything not associated with eBay sales in order to claim it?*

A. Not at all. You can have appropriate decor in your home office if it's something you would have in a "real" office. So, for example, a bookcase with general business books (not eBay specific) is perfectly okay. A bookcase full of romance novels (unless, of course, you sell romance novels on eBay) probably wouldn't be.

If you sell Oriental antiques, by all means put Japanese prints on the wall. Rock posters, on the other hand (unless they are anime-themed or in Japanese for a Budokan concert), probably should go elsewhere.

Always keep in mind that when the IRS audits a home office, the first thing they look for is inappropriate furnishings and decorations. If you have any doubts about a specific item, it's probably safer to remove it than to take the risk of blowing your home office deduction.

Q. *Where can I find a list of deductions associated with a home office? I am curious if expenses such as my trash service or my water bill are included. Also, if my Internet service is used 100 percent of the time for conducting* *business (my husband and I run two separate businesses that require In-ternet service), can I deduct the entire cost instead of the home office per-centage?*

A.   IRS Publication 587, "Business Use of a Home," is your first stop. The "home office fraction" of both your trash service and your water bill is deductible. If you can prove your Internet service is used exclusively for your eBay business, you should be able to deduct the entire cost on Sched-ule C, but be really careful here, lest the IRS auditor find even one video game on your PC.

Recordkeeping for eBay Sellers

I hear this plea all the time: "I've been selling on eBay for a while. I realize now I have a business, but I can't find information about my sales to date. Help!"

When you register as an eBay seller, you are given a Seller's Account, which appears as part of your free My eBay page. The Seller's Account records all of your selling transactions on eBay, including the fees you pay, but is kept active for only a limited time. Completed auctions listed under "Items I've Sold," for example, are kept active for up to sixty days, and the "Account Status" page (found under My Seller Account Summary) records transactions for up to four months. Your e-mail invoices to buyers (if you send them through eBay, which too few sellers do) are kept on the system for up to eighteen months.

The bottom line: If you use your My eBay page as the only way to keep track of your sales records, you must—I mean *must*—print this information out every month, so you have a hard copy of your eBay sales data.

If you use PayPal, you're in a little better shape. The Transaction History section will preserve data going back three years, but only (of course) for your PayPal transactions. If you have also accepted checks, money orders, or credit card payments as an eBay seller, you will not find those reflected anywhere in your PayPal Transaction History.

When you create a Seller's Account on eBay, you can elect to receive free monthly Sales Reports from eBay showing your total sales, your successful listings, your average sale price, and your total eBay and PayPal fees. If that isn't enough information, you can sign up for Sales Reports Plus, which helps you keep track of your selling performance by category and auction format. A detailed comparison of the two products, both of which are currently offered free to eBay sellers, is available at: http://pages.ebay.com/salesreports/compare.html. To subscribe:

➢ Go to your "My eBay" page and find the "My Accounts" section.
➢ Click on the "Subscriptions" link in that section.
➢ Scroll down to "Sales Reports" and follow the prompts. Be sure to select the "e-mail notification" option so that eBay sends you an e-mail each time your current Sales Report is updated.

There are two drawbacks to eBay Sales Reports, though. First, you have to view your reports at least once every sixty days (for Sales Reports) or ninety days (for Sales Reports Plus), or else eBay cancels your subscription automatically. You can always resubscribe, but you won't get sales data for the intervening period you were "offline."

Second, you still have to print your eBay Sales Report pages (one at a time) to have a permanent record of your sales, since eBay will keep your Sales Reports online for only six months (two years for Sales Reports Plus).

To save your transaction data for longer periods of time (such as the six years the IRS suggests you keep records relating to your income and expenses), it's best to use one of the eBay auction management software products available on the market, such as eBay Accounting Assistant, AuctionHelper.com, or Zoovy.com. Once your eBay sales data resides on your personal computer rather than one of eBay's computer servers, you can sleep a little more easily at night knowing your data will be ready whenever you are (just be sure to back up your files periodically).

Now, let's create a brief checklist of the information you will need to prepare your tax return if you sell on eBay.

KEEPING TRACK OF YOUR eBAY INCOME

If you are filling out Schedule C, you will need to keep on hand all paperwork necessary to document the income you received from your eBay selling activities. This paperwork includes:

1. The check register for your business checking account, showing deposits made from sales for which the buyers paid by check or money order.
2. Your online sales reports, or monthly printouts of "all selling" activities as recorded on your My eBay page. (It's essential to print out these reports at least once a month so you have a hard copy record of all transactions on eBay.)
3. Credit card merchant account statements, showing amounts paid to you by buyers using their American Express, Visa, MasterCard, or Discover cards.
4. PayPal account statements (available online), showing amounts eBay buyers paid to you using their PayPal accounts.
5. "Sales history" files on Selling Manager, Selling Manager Pro, or eBay Accounting Assistant (if you use any of these programs to track your eBay sales).
6. Form 1099-MISC for amounts you received as an "independent contractor" working for others, including people for whom you sold goods on eBay.

KEEPING TRACK OF YOUR eBAY SELLING EXPENSES

If you fill out Schedule C, you will need to keep handy all paperwork necessary to document your eBay and PayPal fees, including:

1. Records of the eBay fees you paid from your My eBay page, from your eBay Sales Reports, or from online fee calculators such as HammerTap's FeeFinder software (www.hammertap.com).

2. Records of the PayPal fees you paid.

3. Records of fees you paid for your eBay Store (if you have one).

4. Amounts you spent on inventory, if you have any—including the cost of raw materials if you make the products you sell online, customized packaging expenses, sales taxes you paid to vendors for items you later sold on eBay, and postage and packing material expenses that *were not* passed on to your buyer as part of your "shipping and handling fee."

5. Detail of any estimated taxes, both federal and state, paid during the year—including copies of the Form 1040-ES you file each quarter, copies of the comparable form you include with your state estimated tax payments, or copies of the canceled checks, and the amounts applied from your prior year tax return.

6. Your mileage log for travel expenses incurred while engaging in your eBay selling business.

7. Receipts for expenses incurred while attending the eBay Live! conference and trade show, any other conference of eBay sellers (such as regional or national meetings of the Professional eBay Sellers Association), or any other trade show, conference, or convention for buyers and/or sellers of the type of merchandise you sell on eBay

8. Receipts for amounts you paid to:

   ➢ Your bookkeeper and accountant

   ➢ Your attorney

   ➢ Your property/casualty and liability insurer

   ➢ Staples, OfficeMax, Office Depot, and other places where you bought equipment and supplies for your business

   ➢ Your state tax agency for sales, use, personal property, inventory, and other business taxes

   ➢ Your landlord (if you rent commercial or retail space for your eBay business)

   ➢ The publishers of newspapers, magazines, and other publications that help you sell on eBay or run your business more efficiently

   ➢ Booksellers for books that help you sell on eBay or run your business more efficiently

➢ Advertisers (including pay-per-click advertising on Yahoo! or Google)

➢ Your telephone company (for a telephone or fax line dedicated to your eBay business)

9. Invoices from the people you bought inventory from for sale online.

10. Records showing how much you originally paid for goods you sold online during the year (including monthly printouts of the "all buying" section of your My eBay page, if you purchased items on eBay for resale on eBay).

11. Form 1099s you sent to your consignors and drop shippers for sales of their goods on eBay during the year.

IF YOU HAVE EMPLOYEES . . .

You should have on file:

➢ Form W-4 filled out by each employee

➢ Form I-9 filled out by each employee

➢ Form 940, Employer's Annual Federal Unemployment Report

➢ Form W-3, Transmittal of Wage and Tax Statement

➢ A copy of each W-2 you mailed to each employee by January 31 of each year for wages paid during the preceding calendar year (you did do this, didn't you?)

➢ Copies of claims statements for medical insurance expenses you paid for your employees (other than you and your spouse)

➢ Copies of canceled checks or other documentation for out-of-pocket expenses incurred by your employees (such as travel and lodging for required business trips) that you reimbursed

IF YOU TAKE THE "HOME OFFICE" DEDUCTION . . .

You should keep handy the following records if you use part of your home for business:

➢ Documents specifying the number of square feet of the home office you use for selling on eBay, as well as the total square footage of your

• "Getting It All Together" •

Even in the age of the Internet, most of the documents you will need to do your taxes each year are in paper form. You should always have paper copies of any Internet record, such as your My eBay selling pages, and you have to have a place to put them so you can access them quickly.

If you are filing Schedule C, go to your nearest office supply store and get yourself a box or two of three-tab file folders (I prefer legal size) and at least five expandable manila folders (also legal size, since the file folders need to fit into them).

Take the first few file folders and label one for each bank account, credit card account, PayPal account, and eBay user ID that you use to sell on eBay. Put these files in the first manila folder and label it "Basic Documents." All of your bank and credit card statements, printed-out My eBay pages, eBay Sales Reports, and PayPal account statements should go in this folder, because they are the most important pieces of paper you will need to do your taxes.

Now get the "chart of accounts" you use to sell on eBay—that's the spreadsheet that lists every item of income and expense in your eBay business—and label each remaining file folder with a "line item" from your list. Don't have a chart of accounts? You can buy a "starter" one for $14.98 from Allegro Accounting in Portland, Oregon (www.allegroaccounting.com); however, keep in mind no two eBay businesses are exactly alike, so you will have to "customize" your chart of accounts to reflect what actually happens once you start selling on eBay.

Once you have a file folder for every "line item" in your chart of accounts, organize them in your four remaining manila folders as follows:

*   All file folders for "income" items go in the second folder, which you will label "Income."
*   All file folders that relate to your eBay business expenses go in the third folder, which you will label "Schedule C Expenses."
*   All file folders that relate to household expenses you are deducting as part of the "home office" deduction go in the fourth folder, which you will label "Home Office Expenses."
*   All file folders that relate to personal expenses (such as charitable and medical deductions) go in the fifth manila folder, which you will label "Personal Deductions."

> As receipts, documents, bank statements, and sales reports arrive that relate to any "file folder" item, put the original in the appropriate folder (I do this on Friday afternoons each week, just before leaving the office). That way, when it comes time to do your taxes, all your paperwork is where it should be and you won't be scrounging through shoeboxes looking for evidence of that PayPal rebate you had last February.

home (preferably, measurements taken and put in writing by a professional contractor)

➤ Receipts for expenses related to the home-office deduction, such as:

1. Utility bills (oil, gas, electric)

2. Canceled checks for housecleaning services

3. Cable and Internet access bills

4. Telephone bills (other than for a line dedicated to your business on eBay)

5. Water, sewer, and trash-hauling bills

6. Pest control bills

➤ If you rent your home or an apartment, the total amount of rent you paid your landlord during the year

COMMON QUESTIONS

Q. *One of my friends from the Philippines has a problem with his PayPal account. I am helping him by receiving money from his buyers and sending money to his sellers. Am I liable for taxes for this activity? How do I prove to the IRS that I simply act as a conduit for the transactions? Does the IRS have access to my PayPal records?*

A. First of all, the IRS does not yet have access to your PayPal records; although they are certainly free to do so, they have not, to date, subpoenaed records from either eBay or PayPal as to anyone's sales activity. If you are simply doing a favor for a friend and are not collecting a fee for your services, then you are neither incurring income nor paying expenses for tax purposes. It is a "wash" from your perspective, and "silence is golden" is probably the best advice here.

If you think there's a serious risk your friend won't report the profits from his eBay sales as "income," you can protect yourself by filing a Schedule C showing all of the eBay sales you have made for your friend, and all of the amounts you remitted to him. So you'll be showing the IRS that "there's nothing to see here; just move along." But I think that's overkill if your friend is a serious eBay seller and knows he has to pay taxes. Also, you shouldn't be doing this kind of favor for someone who's likely to get you into legal trouble.

Q. *I made around $2,200 last year, after taking into account all eBay, PayPal, and shipping fees. I sold mostly personal items last year, mostly at a loss. How do I prove to the IRS that I didn't make any profit? I don't have receipts for any of the items I sold, and I don't even remember the price when I bought them.*

A. Clearly it would be a mistake for you to report this activity as a "business."

Seriously, if you are sure you lost money and do not want to deduct your loss against other income, then "silence is golden" might be the best advice here. Just keep on hand whatever records you have (even informal or anecdotal ones, like "my mom told me she spent $10 for that vase"), just in case the IRS picks up on your eBay sales. If that's too scary, then make the most conservative estimate of your losses and report it as a "capital loss" on your personal Form 1040. If the amount is relatively small, you will probably be below the radar screen of the IRS (but please don't quote me on that).

Going forward, start keeping records of your eBay selling activities, because if you are making money selling on eBay, you can treat it as a "business" and qualify for the deductions we're talking about in this book.

P A R T

4

Growing Your Business

Staffing Your eBay Selling Business

Selling on eBay is a labor-intensive enterprise. It takes a lot of time and effort to find merchandise to sell on eBay, research each item, write interesting and accurate item descriptions, take digital photos, assemble the information in an auction page, respond to buyer e-mails, pack and ship the goods, and so forth.

At some point all eBay sellers realize that in order to "run" their business, they have to delegate some or all of the routine, day-to-day operations to someone else. It is time to hire your first employee.

EMPLOYEES ARE EXPENSIVE, AND THEY HAVE RIGHTS

When you hire your first employee, though, your legal and tax obligations increase by a factor of ten. In this country, labor is viewed as more than just a commodity. In the United States, employees have rights. I'm frankly proud to live in a country where workers cannot be abused or beaten, made to work excessive hours without pay, or forced to work under sweatshop conditions. But all of the rights our nation grants to employees makes life a bit more expensive and difficult for employers.

That's why, before you hire anyone, you should sit down with a strong pot of coffee and figure out if adding an employee or two will be worth all the extra effort you will need to spend making sure their rights are respected and their expectations fulfilled.

SHOULD YOU EVEN HIRE EMPLOYEES?

Too many small business owners rush into hiring their first employee on the theory that "there's lots of work here I don't want to do," so they think that by shoveling that work onto someone else's shoulders, they'll have more time to do the things they want to do.

Fair enough. But while hiring employees will certainly save you time, you need to do a little cost-benefit analysis to figure out whether adding an employee will also add to the bottom line of your business. As a friend of mine, a professor of statistics at a local university, once put it: "In business, if you can't quantify something, it's only a rumor."

You have to ask yourself two burning questions:

1. _How much will this new employee cost?_ When figuring out employee costs, most employers look just at the employee's "base salary"—that is, the amount of wages the employee is being paid each week or month before taxes are taken out. That's a big mistake. The true cost of an employee is often much greater than that because of benefit costs (including sick days, vacation days, and the like) and "allocated overhead," meaning you have to provide the employee with a desk, a computer, and other equipment and supplies, and all of that stuff costs money.

    A good general rule of thumb is that the total costs of an employee are three times (300 percent) his base salary. So an employee who is making $20,000 a year (pretax) in base salary is actually costing your business somewhere in the neighborhood of $50,000 to $60,000 when benefits, overhead, and other costs are factored in.

2. _How much revenue will the new employee generate?_ Now that you've figured out the employee's total cost to your business, it's time to figure out if you

can actually make more money by hiring the new employee than by "slogging on" by yourself alone.

Let's say you are thinking of hiring someone to help you post your eBay auction pages. Assuming you will be paying this person $X an hour (pretax), your typical eBay auction generates $Y in revenue, and your typical "success rate" (the ratio of total auctions posted to items sold on eBay) is Z, how many auction pages will the new employee need to post on average each hour, day, or week to cover your expenses? I realize that's somewhat simplistic, but that's the sort of pencil-breaking analysis you have to do.

Once you know the employee's "breakeven point" (i.e., the number of auction pages the employee has to post each hour, day, or week to cover your expenses), you then have to ask: Is it physically possible for the employee to meet that goal? If your analysis shows that a new employee would have to post 100 auctions a day to cover her base salary, benefits, and overhead, then it doesn't make sense to hire the employee, because nobody can post auctions that fast.

A lot of employees in small businesses should never have been hired in the first place—not because they're not good workers, but because it just didn't make economic sense to hire them. You can save yourself (and your employee) a lot of heartbreak and frustration by doing a little simple math before you post your classified ad in your local newspaper's "help wanted" section.

THE THREE TYPES OF WORKERS, AND HOW TO TELL THEM APART

Everyone who works with you in your business—I mean *everyone*—falls into one of three broad categories. They are either partners, employees, or independent contractors.

Partners

If someone is your business "partner," that person can:

> ➤ Get a percentage of profits and losses after all expenses of the business have been deducted from your revenue.

• How Do Partners Get Paid? •

Technically, partners don't get a salary. Instead, they get a percentage of the partnership's income. But partners have to pay their bills each month like everyone else. How do they take money out of the partnership checking account?

Here's how partnerships are supposed to work, taxwise. Let's say A and B are 50/50 partners. At the end of each month, A and B sit down, pay all of the partnership's bills for the month, and keep some money in the checking account to pay future bills. Whatever's left over (the profits) is split 50/50 between A and B, and they each take out their one-half of the profits. That's called a "distribution" in tax language.

Now take a different example. Let's say A, B, and C are equal partners (one-third each), but C is the person doing all of the day-to-day work, while A and B are passive investors. The partners agree that C can take out the first $5,000 of partnership income each month to pay her living expenses. At the end of the month, the partners sit down, pay all of the partnership's bills, deduct C's $5,000 payment, keep some money in the checking account to pay future bills, and whatever's left is split three ways (including C).

In this example, C's $5,000 withdrawal each month is called a "draw," while the three-way split at the end of the month is a "distribution," as in the first example.

All three partners have to pay income and self-employment tax on both their draws and their distributions. If C doesn't feel comfortable paying estimated taxes on her draws, the partners can agree to have taxes voluntarily withheld from each $5,000 payment to C each month. It will be difficult to withhold taxes from any partner's distribution since, by definition, you don't know what that is until the end of each month, when you know how much money the partnership has made.

➤ Make contributions to capital, and be required to make additional contributions to cover cash shortfalls if the partnership agreement so provides.

➤ Bind your company to legal agreements, even if you disagree. Each partner can bind all the others, even if the others don't know what the renegade partner is doing. Lawyers call this "joint and several" liability.

> Get an IRS Form K-1 at the end of each tax year that reports how much income he received from the partnership, both as "draws" and as "distributions" (see the sidebar).

A partnership interest is an "asset," so if a partner dies, it goes to the deceased partner's heirs under his will. This means that once someone becomes your business partner, the only way to get rid of him (legally) is to buy him out for a price he is willing to accept. If he's decided he doesn't like you anymore, it's going to be a long drawn-out negotiation.

Employees

When people are your "employees":

> You "direct and control" their activities. You can tell them what to do, when to do it, where to do it, how to do it, and so forth.
> They are paid a regular salary, not a share of profits (although they can receive commissions, bonuses, and other "incentive compensation").
> You withhold income and employment taxes (described a little later in this chapter) from their paychecks.
> They receive a W-2 at the end of each tax year telling them how much income they received from you and how much tax was withheld from their wages.

Independent Contractors

When people are working with you as "independent contractors":

> You do not "direct and control" their activities, because they are out-side of your organization.
> They can work for other companies (though, hopefully, not for any of your competitors).
> You don't withhold income or employment taxes from their pay-checks—that is, the contractor's responsibility.
> They receive a Form 1099 at the end of each tax year telling them how much income they received from you (if paid more than $600). Independent contractors are often known informally as "1099s."

• Avoiding an "Accidental Partnership" • with an Independent Contractor

Remember back in Chapter 2 we said that partnerships were so easy to form, you could actually form one by accident? Here's how that can happen with an independent contractor.

You hire Joe to help you with your eBay business for a few hours each week. Because Joe is a student, he's free to schedule his work hours, so you make him an "independent contractor." Over time, Joe becomes a trusted and valued helper. You know you can leave the business for days or weeks at a time and Joe will take care of everything just fine while you're away.

You begin to trust Joe. You allow Joe to sign contracts with regular customers, answer phone calls, and tag along on sales meetings. Whenever customers, suppliers, or anyone else sees you in your store, there's Joe right at your side. You start giving Joe a share of your business profits on top of his hourly payments because of his value to your company.

One day, you do something wrong—something really stupid. Your company gets sued and—surprise!—the person bringing the suit sues both you *and* Joe personally, on the grounds that the two of you held yourselves out as "partners." Joe is furious that he is being sued for something you did, and he turns around and sues you for "indemnification" because you and he agreed that he was only an independent contractor.

Do you see the pickle you are in here? Whenever someone is working with you as an independent contractor, it is *essential* that you let everyone you come into contact with know that that person is not an employee or partner.

EMPLOYEE OR INDEPENDENT CONTRACTOR?

Independent contractors are a lot cheaper than employees, but with independent contractors, you don't have any control over their activities. What you really want (admit it, now) is the ability to direct and control someone's activities without having to pay employment taxes and benefits, and without giving that person all the rights that employees are entitled to by law.

What is the solution to this dilemma?

Answer: "There isn't any."

Whenever you start working with someone, you have to make a determination whether that person is going to be an employee or an independent contractor. And you better get this right. The IRS is ruthless when it comes to auditing employers who attempt to claim that their "employees" are really "independent contractors."

The "Indentured Servant" 1099

The IRS has identified twenty criteria for determining if someone is an employee, and there is no "bright line" test. If, on balance, an individual meets a significant number of these criteria, the IRS will consider that person an employee. If you think someone's an independent contractor, but . . .

> ➤ They don't work for anyone else but you (or, as a practical matter, can't because you are requiring them to work sixty or more hours per week).
> ➤ You pay them a regular salary, with benefits.
> ➤ You can tell them what to do, when to do it, where to do it, and how to do it.
> ➤ You give them office space, equipment, a telephone, and/or access to your administrative staff.
> ➤ There's no real difference between the way they work and the way your other employees work . . .

Then, the IRS will view this person as an employee!

What Does It Mean to "Direct and Control" Someone?

The key test is whether you can direct or control a person's activities when she is working for you. If you can, then that person is your employee. If you can't, then the individual is an independent contractor.

The number of hours the person works is not relevant. You can have an employee working for you one day a week or one week a year (think of the college kids who work at retail stores over the December holidays).

Here's a simple way to deal with this issue (although—truth be told—it isn't a hundred percent reliable in all cases). Ask yourself: "While this person is working for me, do I have the ability to interrupt this person's work flow? Can I say to this person, 'Stop working on that project because I need you to do something else for the next couple of hours; you can go back to that later.'" If the answer is yes, that person is likely an employee and you should act accordingly. If the answer is no—you can give that person a deadline for a particular project, but she has the ability to prioritize her workload between now and the deadline date—that person is likely to be an "independent contractor."

What If the Person Agrees with the "Independent Contractor" Status?

It doesn't matter—the IRS has the power to disregard the agreement and look at what actually happens between you and the person. If it looks like a duck, quacks like a duck, and waddles like a duck, don't tell the IRS it's an independent contractor.

What Happens If I Make a Mistake and the IRS Catches Me?

I cannot make the point strongly enough: You have to take the time to get this right, because the IRS is ruthless when it audits in this area. If you make a mistake, you will be liable for *all* unpaid employment taxes due from the date you first started working with the person, plus interest and penalties. Even worse, if the "independent contractor" lives in another state, you may be subject to that state's sales, use, and other business taxes on the theory that your business is "doing business" from an illegal office there (i.e., the contractor's home).

The Bottom Line

If you are not sure whether that person you're working with is an employee or an independent contractor, ask your accountant or lawyer for advice. If you really, truly can't afford a lawyer or accountant, you can ask the IRS to make this determination for you by filing IRS Form SS-8, "Determination of Worker Status for Purposes of Federal Employment Taxes and Income Tax Withholding,"

• When Do You Give Someone a 1099? •

If someone worked for you as an independent contractor, and you paid that worker more than $600 during the year, you must send that worker an IRS Form 1099 no later than January 31 (postmark date) of the following year, and send copies to the IRS and your state tax authority by no later than February 28 or 29 of the following year, along with IRS Form 1096 (basically a "cover letter" for the 1099).

Technically, that means *every* independent contractor, including lawyers, accountants, other professionals, drop shippers, and people who give you stuff to sell on eBay (see Chapter 14). But you can use some discretion here. The people who absolutely must get 1099s are people you do not think are intelligent, disciplined, or honest enough to report your payments as income on their tax returns. Sending someone a 1099 insulates you from liability if that someone decides to "play games" and hide income from the IRS.

If you send a 1099 form out late, you will have to pay a $50 penalty to the IRS for each overdue 1099. You will also incur the wrath of your contractor, who probably has already filed her tax return and now has to amend it to attach your 1099.

NOTE: You cannot download Forms 1096 and 1099 from the IRS website and send photocopies to people. This is one of the few cases where the IRS requires you to use the actual "paper" form. You can get them from your nearest IRS field office (look in the telephone book under the blue "Government" pages), and don't wait until January 30 to do so.

available as a free download from the IRS website (www.irs.gov). But realistically, I think it's a waste of your time to do this. What are the odds, after all, that the IRS will tell you the person is an "independent contractor" if there's even the slightest doubt?

HOW TO HIRE EMPLOYEES

Employees have rights, and those rights begin even before you hire them! A lot of people in this world really don't know how to interview job candidates, so they make a lot of truly boneheaded mistakes. Entire books have been written on this subject, but here are a few simple rules for the vast majority of eBay sellers who will be hiring no more than one or two employees.

Employee Interview "Do's"

> ➤ Clearly state that employment is "at will" and may be terminated at any time, for any reason.

> ➤ Use open-ended questions to get the candidate talking.

> ➤ Make sure the candidate has the legal right to work in the United States, and fill out Form I-9 (available as a free download from www .uscis.gov/graphics/formsfee/forms/i-9.htm).

Employee Interview "Don'ts"

> ➤ Do not ask any question designed to reveal the candidate's age, sex, race, creed, color, religion, or national origin.

> ➤ Do not make inquiries about marital status, disabilities, or military discharge.

• Can You Search a Candidate's • Background on the Internet?

There's nothing legally wrong with conducting an Internet search using the candidate's name, looking at university sites, or cruising news archives or postings to chat groups and blogs. The problem here is that the information you will see online may not be reliable, or relevant, to the position for which the candidate is being considered.

For example, what if you see a blog from the candidate's former romantic partner describing in exquisite detail the candidate's—uh—preferences?

If you use the Web to check out job applicants, always confirm the information with the candidate in a follow-up interview or phone call, and don't let your final decision hinge on what you find out over the Internet.

Also, be prepared for questions from the candidate about your own background—Internet searches are a two-way street, after all.

➤ Do not make personal comments about the person's wardrobe or appearance (e.g., "Nice turban, Abdul. Tell me, how long does it take to put that on in the morning?").

After the Interview

➤ _Check the candidate's references._ It's estimated that about one-third of job applicants lie about their experiences and educational achievements on their resumes or job applications. Fearful of reprisals from former employees, many companies will not give detailed reference information, so the HR department is likely to limit its answers to verifying dates of employment, title, and salary. For best results, try to circumvent the HR department and go directly to the candidate's former supervisor, whom you might find in a chatty mood. If the supervisor says, "I only give good references," and doesn't elaborate, or if she damns the candidate with faint praise ("Yeah, Cliff worked here, he showed up on time, he was okay, I couldn't say anything really bad about him"), take the hint and don't make the offer.

➤ _Run background checks._ Before you do so, you may be legally required to get the candidate's consent first. Even if you get the candidate's consent, you are not allowed to engage in a "fishing expedition" or to ask questions that are otherwise prohibited by law. For highly sensitive positions, consider hiring a private investigator. Just about every state has a professional association of private investigators; just type "private investigator association" into your favorite search engine and you'll find your state's association website on the first couple of result pages.

➤ _Do drug testing._ Because state laws are all over the place, you will need to talk to an employment lawyer before requiring a candidate to submit to any sort of drug or alcohol test. To find a brief description of your state's drug testing regulations, go to the U.S. Department of Labor's SAID website at www.drugtest-info.com/laws/index.html. For detailed information, though, you will have to subscribe to an online database such as DTState Laws (http://lawsinhand.dtstatelaws.com, currently $149 for a one-year subscription).

SOME SPECIAL SITUATIONS

Let's consider three situations in particular: student interns, foreign students, and handicapped candidates.

Student Interns

Your local community college may be the best place to find temporary or part-time employees for your eBay business. Students are usually eager to learn and may be willing to work for less than minimum wage.

Check with your state labor department to make sure your student interns are legally able to work. Most states prohibit the employment of minors—other than your own children—under the age of sixteen, whether students or not, and the rules for minors between the ages of sixteen and twenty-one are all over the map. Some states, such as California, also have laws limiting the number of hours full-time students can work in an internship each week. Your local college's student employment or job placement department should be able to educate you on the rules that apply in your area.

Also, keep in mind that since student interns are almost always teenagers, you stand *in loco parentis*—"in the place of their parents"—whenever they are working for you. Expect to spend a significant portion of time dealing with their personal, romantic, academic, and other traumas; be willing to forgive and forget the occasional immature behavior teens will engage in; and comfort yourself in knowing that you are helping your fellow human beings "bridge their way to adulthood."

Foreign Students

You have posted an advertisement for a part-time employee to help with your eBay business. The next day you are visited by a young man wearing a flowing white robe and turban and sporting a chest-length beard, who introduces himself as Abdul, an Asian exchange student at your local college.

What do you do now, hot shot?

Well, first of all, you cannot discriminate against this person. If he meets the job qualifications you have indicated in your ad, you may have to give him a shot. When interviewing him, do not ask questions that demonstrate you are thinking about his race, religion, ethnicity, or country of origin.

But what if he isn't legally allowed under the terms of his student visa to work for you? Now, that's a different matter—then you can't hire him.

The best advice here is to ask the student to introduce you to his school's "international student adviser." Every college that receives federal funding (and that's just about all of them) is required to have a person on staff who is familiar with the rules regarding student visas. That person should be able to tell whether the student can work for you at all, or whether there are any other restrictions that apply, such as the number of hours per week the student can legally work.

One especially tricky situation involves foreign students from Middle Eastern countries. Under the USA Patriot Act, you may be required in certain circumstances to have your employees sign a sworn affidavit that their names do not appear on the government's list of known terrorist operatives. (To see the entire list, with more than 325,000 names, go to the National Counterterrorism Center at www.nctc.gov.)

The trick here, of course, is asking for such an affidavit without discriminating against a candidate because he comes from the Middle East. If you do plan to make your employees sign an "antiterrorism" affidavit, make sure *all of them do*—even the blonde, blue-eyed exchange student from Norway.

Handicapped Candidates

You have posted a job listing for a truck driver, and a man with a prosthetic arm—say, a veteran of the war in Iraq—applies for the job. What do you do?

Here's the *wrong way* to handle this candidate: "Didn't you read my ad? How the heck are you supposed to drive a truck with only one arm?" By responding this way, you are focusing on the individual's disability, which is prohibited under the Americans with Disabilities Act.

Here's the *right way* to handle this candidate: "As you know, this position will require you to drive a truck for long hours going to and from our suppliers. This is an essential function of the position. Are there any circumstances that, either with or without a reasonable accommodation, would prevent you from performing this essential function?"

Don't get me wrong; I'm not saying you have to hire this person, who clearly misread your ad. But you may be forced to evaluate whether the position can be performed by someone with a prosthetic arm and, if necessary, restructure the position as a "reasonable accommodation" to his disability.

For example, let's say you have a position that is 90 percent clerical work and 10 percent driving a forklift around your warehouse. Since the individual with the prosthetic arm can almost certainly perform the clerical work that is 90 percent of the job, you may have to "restructure" this job to eliminate the forklift part (you would continue doing this work yourself or assign that job to someone else) so that this candidate could qualify for the position.

"EMPLOYEES ARE EXPENSIVE," OR DEALING WITH EMPLOYMENT TAXES

The IRS is delighted when you hire your first employee because now, in addition to the income and self-employment taxes you pay on your own income (see Chapter 8), you have to pay employment or "payroll" taxes on your employees' wages as well.

There are five federal and state employment taxes, as follows:

➤ Withholding of federal and state income taxes
➤ Federal Social Security tax (also known as FICA)
➤ Federal Medicare tax
➤ Federal unemployment tax (FUTA)
➤ State workers' compensation and/or disability fund payments

There's one important point about federal employment taxes you have to know: The IRS looks at these as "the government's money," payable as soon as each employee earns a paycheck. *If you are so much as one day late making these payments, the IRS will come down on you like the hammers of hell!*

If the thought of doing this paperwork makes you ill, then you should hire someone to do it. If you have one or two employees, your bookkeeper may be willing to help you out. Any more than that, you should use a payroll service such as PayChex (www .paychex.com) or ADP (www.adp.com)

Withholding of Federal and State Income Taxes

First of all, technically speaking, there is no such thing as a "withholding tax." Your employees are required to pay federal and state income tax on their wages, but the government doesn't trust them (or you) to make the required payment on April 15 of each year. The government knows that, given the chance, your employees will blow all of that money at the racetrack (or buying stuff on eBay they don't need). Also, the government needs the money sooner than you do, so it can do all of the wonderful things government does for all of us.

So the government requires *you* (as the employer) to withhold income taxes from the paychecks of employees (but not independent contractors). When employees are first hired, they submit IRS Form W-4 telling you, in effect, how much you should withhold from their paycheck.

Social Security (FICA) and Medicare Taxes

Social Security tax pays for benefits under the old-age, survivors, and disability insurance part of the Federal Insurance Contributions Act (FICA). Medicare tax pays for benefits under the hospital insurance part of FICA. You withhold part of these taxes from your employees' wages, and you pay a matching amount yourself (with pretax dollars). You file quarterly reports with the IRS on Form 941.

The employee tax rate for Social Security is currently 6.2 percent (amount withheld), and the employer tax rate is also 6.2 percent (12.4 percent total), on the first $94,200 of wages earned.

The employee tax rate for Medicare is 1.45 percent (amount withheld), and the employer tax rate is also 1.45 percent (2.9 percent total). There is no wage base limit for Medicare tax; all covered wages are subject to Medicare tax.

The total FICA and Medicare tax bill for each of your employees comes to about 15.3 percent of that employee's taxable wages.

Federal Unemployment Tax (FUTA)

The federal unemployment tax is part of the federal and state program under the Federal Unemployment Tax Act (FUTA) that pays unemployment compensation to workers who lose their jobs. You report and pay FUTA tax separate from Social Security and Medicare taxes and withheld income tax. You pay FUTA tax only from your own funds. *Employees do not pay this tax or have it withheld from their pay.*

You report FUTA taxes on Form 940, Employer's Annual Federal Unemployment (FUTA) Tax return, or if you qualify, you can use the simpler Form 940-EZ instead.

State Unemployment Compensation and/or Disability Payments

In addition to federal unemployment tax (FUTA), you are also required in just about every state to make periodic contributions to your state's workers' compensation fund. In a handful of states, there's also a "disability fund" you have to make periodic payments to.

Here's an important point a lot of my law clients learn the hard way: If you are dealing with a payroll service such as PayChex or Automatic Data Processing (ADP), make sure they sign you up for state unemployment compensation and disability fund payments at the same time they sign you up for federal and state payroll taxes. Often third-party payroll services overlook this step, and things go along swimmingly until you get that nasty letter from your state's labor department accusing you of violating "workers' comp laws" by failing to register. If your payroll service can't help you with this matter, make sure your accountant takes care of it for you.

And for You and Your Partners . . . Self-Employment Taxes

Self-employment (SE) tax is a Social Security and Medicare tax primarily for individuals who work for themselves (e.g., sole proprietors, partners in a partnership, members of a limited liability company, and shareholders of a subchapter S corporation, with some exceptions).

You pay SE tax if you have self-employment income of $400 or more during a tax year. You figure your SE tax yourself and file Schedule SE to your Form 1040 each year.

The amounts are the same as they would be if you were an employee. The idea is to prevent a self-employed person from having an unfair tax advantage over an employee in identical circumstances.

Is There Any Tax Advantage to Hiring Family Members?

There is no tax benefit to hiring your spouse or parents. They are treated the same as other employees. If you employ your spouse, you can save about $56 a year in federal unemployment tax (FUTA), but that's about it.

You can, however, provide health insurance and other employee benefits to a spouse who works for you and take the full deduction (see Chapter 9). By hiring your spouse, you can also go on business trips together and deduct your spouse's meals and lodging along with your own.

Now, hiring your kids is another matter. If your children work in your business and each of them makes less than $5,000 a year, they don't pay income taxes (unless they have income from investments). If each of your children makes more than $5,000 a year, they pay taxes, but at a much lower rate than you do. If your child is under age 18, you don't have to withhold or pay Social Security or Medicare taxes on her income. If your child is under 21, you don't have to pay federal unemployment tax (FUTA), either.

So there is a benefit to hiring your kids, *provided they are truly employees* and are actually working in the business. Therefore:

> ➤ Make sure you keep records (such as time sheets) showing the time they worked.

> ➤ Make sure their compensation is "reasonable." No ten-year-old should be making $200 an hour, no matter how smart he is.

> ➤ Make sure they fill out the same employment paperwork a grown-up would, including IRS Form W-4 and Form I-9, the immigration form certifying that they are legally able to work in the United States.

"EMPLOYEES HAVE RIGHTS," SO COMPLY WITH THEM

Employees in the United States are not only expensive; they also have legal rights. Lots of them. Let's go over some of the more important ones.

The Right to Overtime Pay

If an employee makes less than $450 a week or $23,660 a year, you must pay overtime if the employee works more than forty hours a week, unless the person falls into one of several "exempt" categories under the law.

The Right to Benefits

Among other things, you must:

> ➤ Give your employees time off to vote, serve on a jury, and perform military service.

> ➤ Provide up to twelve workweeks of unpaid, job-protected leave to eligible employees (if you have more than fifty employees) for certain family and medical reasons within any twelve-month period, under the federal Family and Medical Leave Act (FMLA).

> ➤ Contribute to state short-term disability programs in states where such programs exist.

The Right to Workers' Compensation Insurance

In almost all states, you are required to provide workers' compensation insurance for your employees in the amounts mandated by law. In two states (New Jersey and Texas), workers' compensation insurance is elective, but if you opt out of the system, you lose certain defenses if an employee is injured on the job.

The Right to Unemployment Compensation

In almost all states, you have to make periodic contributions to the state's unemployment compensation system. Contributions are normally based on the amount of wages paid, the amount contributed to the unemployment fund, and the amount that discharged employees have been compensated with from the fund. Any state tax imposed on employers (and certain credits on that tax) may be credited against the federal unemployment tax.

The Right Not to Be Sexually Harassed

Under federal law, you are not required to have a sexual harassment policy, but you should have one. There are two types of sexual harassment:

> ➤ *The "Quid Pro Quo."* The employer asks an employee or a job applicant for a sexual favor in return for employment or some job benefit.
> ➤ *The "Hostile Work Environment."* A supervisor, coworker, or customer makes unwelcome sexual comments or remarks, or suggestively touches or acts in a sexually inappropriate way toward an employee, or maintains "an environment generally conducive to" such behavior (e.g., permitting X-rated calendars on cubicle walls or in the lunchroom).

The Equal Employment Opportunity Commission (EEOC) provides guidelines suggesting the key elements that should be included in a sexual harassment policy. They include:

> ➤ A clear explanation of the prohibited conduct
> ➤ Assurance that employees who make complaints or participate in an investigation of a complaint will be protected against retaliation

> A clear description of the complaint process
> Assurance that the employer will protect the confidentiality of complaints to the extent possible
> A complaint process that provides prompt, thorough, and impartial investigation
> Assurance that the employer will take immediate and appropriate corrective action when an investigation determines that harassment has occurred

The Right to Work in a Safe Environment

Under the federal Occupational Safety and Health Act (OSHA), you are required to provide a place of employment that's "free from recognized hazards that are causing or are likely to cause death or serious physical harm to employees."

OSHA applies to any business that is engaged in interstate commerce. Each state has an agency (funded mostly by the federal office of OSHA) that offers free, on-site consultations, so you don't have to pore over pages of federal regulations on health and safety in the workplace.

MAKING SURE YOU COMPLY WITH LABOR AND EMPLOYMENT LAWS

There are a lot of federal and state employment laws you have to deal with, and it's hard to summarize them because they vary from state to state and by the size of employer. A company with only ten employees has one set of rules to comply with, but when it grows to twenty-five employees, a whole new set of rules kicks in.

You could easily spend weeks or months of your life learning how to comply with employment laws, but there are two "tools" that will help you comply with federal and state employment regulations without becoming an expert on the law.

Your Employee Manual

The minute you have more than one or two employees, you should have your lawyer draft an "employee manual" describing your employment policies and procedures. Depending on where you live, an attorney should be able to draft a manual for a fee somewhere in the range of $1,000 to $2,000, maximum, as long as you don't request a lot of specific provisions. Keep in mind that your employee manual is a "contract"—your employees will be legally entitled to whatever you put in your manual. You can change what is in your manual, but only by giving notice of the change to *all* of your employees. If you don't follow the rules in your own manual, you have only yourself to blame if an employee sues you.

The "Lunchroom Poster"

Both federal and state employment laws require you to inform your employees of their rights under the law. This is commonly done by having a poster prepared describing all of their legal rights and posting it in a public place where they're likely to see it— usually the company lunchroom or a bulletin board outside the bathrooms.

There are several companies that will prepare this poster for you. The industry leader is G. Neil & Company (www.hrone.com). If you go to their website, click on "Workplace Communication," then click on "Posters," and you will be prompted for information about your company—where it's located, what industry it's in, how many employees you have, and so forth. When you finish the online questionnaire, the website will generate and ship to you a lunchroom poster that is custom-tailored to your business, for a fee that is usually less than $50.

Want to learn more about the federal and state employment laws that apply for your business? Go to the G. Neil website, order a poster for your business, and when it arrives—*sit down and read it!* You will be amazed how much information can fit onto a single piece of paper.

FIRING AN EMPLOYEE

Let's not sugarcoat this. Firing an employee—looking a fellow human being in the eye and telling him that he no longer has a source of income—is one of the hardest things you will ever do in life. Maybe Donald Trump finds it easy to say "You're Fired" every week on his reality TV show, but hey, that isn't real life, is it?

In the real world, if you aren't careful, you can get sued.

Under the law in almost all states, employment is "at will" unless you guarantee someone a term of employment. This means that you can terminate their employment at any time, with or without a reason, unless you have guaranteed (in writing) that they will be employed for a specific period of time. Your only obligation is to pay them for work they performed up to the day you escorted them out of the door. *But* . . . if an employee thinks you are being unfair, you may be sued for "wrongful termination."

In general, it's time to fire employees when . . .

➢ They are not performing up to your expectations.

➢ They are violating the law.

➢ They are dragging down your performance or the morale of other employees. ("If Cliff can get away with thus-and-such, why should I be killing myself?")

➢ You simply cannot afford to keep them.

In these situations, the survival of your business depends on your finding a way to get rid of the employee in a way that doesn't expose you to legal liability for wrongful termination.

Rule 1: No Surprises

Wrongful termination lawsuits happen most often when employees aren't aware that they are about to be fired because you sent them inconsistent signals. One of the easiest ways to get yourself sued by an employee is to give her a series of raises and bonuses and then, without warning, fire her "for cause."

You should carefully document the employee's performance, highlighting any performance issues. You should then give the employee a warning (preferably with a witness present) and a chance to turn things around. Follow up with periodic reviews—lawyers call these fee-fi-fo-fum meetings because with each meeting it is clearer and clearer to the employee that he's "on the way out." Keep detailed records of these meetings.

Keep alert to changes in the employee's work or personal life that could affect the timing of termination. A client of mine once had an employee who was "nothing but trouble." She showed up late every day, took overly long breaks, and spent more time chatting with the other employees than getting her work done. With my advice and guidance, my client held a series of fee-fi-fo-fum meetings with the employee and documented them carefully. But, on the day my client was scheduled to terminate the employee, she walks in the front door and announces to everyone in the store, "Hey, everybody, congratulate me! I just found out last night I'm pregnant!"

The client had the good sense to call me and ask, "Cliff, does this change anything?" Oh, you bet it did. If my client had fired the employee at that moment, the employee could have argued that it was "retaliation" for her pregnancy announcement. Fortunately, the employee married her boyfriend a couple of weeks later and quit her job of her own accord.

The Exit Interview

Have a witness present (preferably a big, strong one) during this meeting, because you never know what disgruntled employees will say or do when they're fired. Explain the performance you expected and the steps you took to help the employee meet that goal, and then explain why the employee has not met that expectation. Do not be vague or emotional, and don't give in to the candidate's emotions. Have a box of Kleenex at the ready.

> ➢ Keep the meeting short, and to the point. The less you say, the better.
> ➢ Fire someone on a Monday, not a Friday. Why? Because that way he won't "stew" over the weekend thinking about how unfairly he has been treated.

➢ Protect your business before you break the news. Right before the exit interview, lock the employee out of the computer system so he can't go back to his desk, erase all your files, and change all of their passwords.

➢ Ask for the return of the office and company car keys.

➢ Escort the employee out of the office immediately after the interview, with perhaps a short visit to her desk to clear out any personal items. Do not let the ex-employee hang around and poison your relationship with other employees.

➢ If you are worried about personal safety, have a building security guard present to escort the employee out of the building.

Finally, keep a bottle of V.S.O.P. brandy in your desk drawer, and take a sip from it after the employee leaves the building. Believe me, you will need it as much as, if not more than, your ex-employee will.

AFTER YOU FIRE SOMEBODY

Two more issues have to be dealt with in the aftermath of your firing one of your employees—unemployment claims and the potential for workplace disruption.

Handling Unemployment Claims

In most states, when a terminated employee files for unemployment benefits, you will be invited to a "hearing" to offer any objections to the information the ex-employee has provided on his application for benefits. Talk to an employment lawyer before you agree to participate in such a hearing. They can be time-consuming, and, in many states, the ex-employee will receive benefits no matter what you say.

If you do attend the hearing, be careful what you say about terminated employees because it will be "on the record," and they can use it as evidence in a wrongful termination suit.

When in doubt, *don't challenge the claim*. You have little to lose. Even though you are deemed to have accepted the ex-employee's version of events for purposes of the unemployment claim, you can still raise defenses in court if the ex-employee sues you for wrongful termination.

Avoiding Disruptions in the Workplace

Once you have fired someone, it's essential that you get your workplace back on track and moving forward in a positive direction. You should:

> ➤ Explain the termination promptly to other employees, to avoid rumors. But don't go into detail about the reasons for the employee's termination, because if your statement isn't a hundred percent correct, the ex-employee could sue you for "defamation of character" (see Chapter 7).

> ➤ Reassign the employee's duties promptly to other employees.

> ➤ Limit the ex-employee's contact with other workers so he can't "poison the well" and turn them against you.

COMMON QUESTIONS

Q. *My husband and I are equal partners in an LLC. Last year I began giving him a salary of about $2,000/month for six months. The salary was taken out through a payroll service, with FICA and Medicare, SDI, and unemployment insurance withheld and half paid by us. I failed to do research on the proper handling of paying ourselves if we are in an LLC. Is it true that my husband cannot be an employee of the LLC if he owns 50 percent of the LLC? What are the tax consequences of my mistake?*

A. Generally, the partners in an LLC do not receive a salary, because they are not employees. What they receive instead is a percentage of the LLC's profits and losses each year (in this case, 50 percent each). Any money they take out of the LLC checking account for their own use is considered a "draw" or "advance" against their percentage share of profits. If their percentage share comes to more than $400 per year, they must pay self-employment taxes—FICA, Medicare, and state disability insurance (SDI)—as well as income taxes. If their percentage share comes to more than $1,000 a year, then they must "estimate" their income and self-employment taxes and pay in quarterly installments.

I'm not, however, aware of any law that says that LLC members can't "voluntarily" withhold taxes from their periodic draws in order to avoid having to pay quarterly estimated taxes. Ask your accountant about this matter. As for consequences, you will have to calculate your husband's 50 percent share of the LLC's profits during 2006 (whether or not it was actually paid to him), determine the total federal and state taxes he *should* have paid on that income, subtract all amounts withheld by your payroll service, and determine the amount of taxes (including any interest and penalties if he was "underwithheld") due on the balance. Oh, and don't forget you still owe taxes on *your* 50 percent share of the profits. . . .

Q. *Do I issue 1099s or W-2s to employees who are family members?*

A. If your family members are truly "employees" (i.e., you direct and control their activities during working hours, and they don't work for anyone else), you should have sent them W-2s by January 31. By sending them out now, you will incur a $50 late filing penalty for each W-2.

If your accountant thinks you have a shot at treating them as "independent contractors," you should send a Form 1099 to each individual if you paid her more than $600 total last year. Again, you will incur a $50 late filing penalty for each 1099. If you treat them as independent contractors, make sure the tax savings are greater than the deductions you are passing up. Your accountant can help you with these calculations.

There are some wonderful deductions, though, for business owners who hire family members, especially minor children. See IRS Publication 15, Employer's Tax Guide.

Q. *I am a very small sole proprietor and have provided over $600 in products to twelve customers in 2006, but I have only received one 1099 to date. Am I responsible for the customers who have not mailed me the 1099? Some of my customers have sent me W-9 forms, but I haven't responded because I don't want them to know my Social Security number. My accountant told me I may be penalized for not responding to a request for a W-9 form. I am ready to mail my tax returns, but I don't know if I should mail them in without the 1099 forms from my customers. What should I do?*

A. You must, of course, report *all* income your customers paid you and pay taxes on it, whether or not they sent you a 1099 form, but you are not required to attach 1099s to your tax return if your customers forgot to send them to you. Just attach the ones you did receive to your Form 1040 and off you go. It is your customers who should be concerned that they didn't send you 1099s. If you fail to report income you received from them and are later audited by the IRS, they may get caught up in your audit.

The W-9 question is a bit trickier. Form W-9, which is a "Request for Taxpayer ID Number," is usually sent to independent contractors and others who must receive a 1099 at the end of the year. If someone sends you a W-9 form, you must fill it out and return it within thirty days. Otherwise, your customer may be required to withhold 31 percent of the interest, dividends, and certain other payments they make to you—it's called "backup withholding." Furthermore, you may be subject to a $50 penalty from the IRS for failing to provide a W-9 upon demand.

I understand completely your reluctance to give your Social Security number out to your customers. To avoid that, get a federal tax identification number for your business and use that on any W-9 forms you have to sign. Better yet, form a corporation for your business—that way your customers won't have to send you 1099s at all, making you both very happy.

CHAPTER 13

Doing Business Internationally

I could write a whole book on the legal and tax issues involved in international sales. Here are some of the most common pitfalls for eBay sellers who stick their toes across national boundaries. (For more detailed information, see the resources recommended in the sidebar.)

AVOIDING A "LOCAL PRESENCE"

In early 2006, a French court imposed thousands of euros in fines on a U.S.-based eBay seller for "operating a business without a license" in France.

The seller was a professional art dealer who sold about 470 art objects on eBay's auction site in France. The auction pages were clearly targeting French customers, since they appeared almost exclusively on eBay France and not any of eBay's other overseas sites and all auction descriptions were in the French language (as, indeed, they are required to be on eBay France).

Under French law, anyone who sells things on a regular basis in France while "taking measures to make profits and using the proceeds to make a living" is a "commercial vendor" and is subject

• Some Requiring Reading for International Sellers •

Thousands of books have been written on selling overseas, but here are five very basic books that should be in the library of every eBay seller:

eBay Global the Smart Way, by Joseph T. Sinclair and Ron Ubels (New York: AMACOM, $19.95). It's the first book (so far) to bear exclusively on the things eBay sellers must do to generate overseas sales and make foreign customers happy.

Importing into the United States: A Guide for Commercial Importers, by the U.S. Customs Service (Books for Business, Chicago, IL, $12.95). A concise, easy-to-read summary of U.S. import regulations, written by the folks who wrote the regulations.

A Basic Guide to Exporting, by the U.S. Department of Commerce (Passport Books, out of print). It hasn't been updated since 1998, but that's okay, since the basic structure of U.S. export law hasn't changed much since then (although some of the details have). It's out of print, but you should be able to pick up a used copy for under $5 from the major bookselling websites or from used-book sites such as www.alibris.com. If you can't find a hard copy anywhere, the entire text is published online at www.export.gov.

Export/Import Procedures and Documentation, by Thomas E. Johnson (New York: AMACOM, $68.00). Intended as a training manual for "big company" employees engaged in international trade, this is an indispensable guide for eBay-ers who sell internationally. What I love about this book is that not only does it show you all of the U.S. customs forms, but it gives numerous examples of how to correctly (and incorrectly) fill them out. A hefty price tag, but worth it.

Import/Export from Home: An Introductory Course in International Trade for the Home Worker, by David Buch (BookSurge Publishing, Charleston, SC, $15.99). Very easy to read and focused on the special needs of home-based businesses, which the vast majority of eBay sellers are.

to all laws, regulations, and taxes that French businesses have to comply with. By this description, someone who travels to the United States and buys goods with the sole purpose of reselling them in France on eBay for a profit would be considered a commercial vendor, and the fact that the "someone" was a U.S. citizen and is operating from a home office on U.S. soil makes no difference.

Now, before you toss all of your Edith Piaf records and start ordering "freedom fries" at the local Mickey D's, you should be aware that most European and Asian countries have laws similar to the French. Basically, if you are selling on a foreign website and are targeting citizens of the host country, you are legally doing business there and will be subject to all laws and taxes that country imposes on its domestic businesses.

So how do you avoid a "local presence"?

➢ Run your eBay auctions exclusively on the U.S. site. If French buyers find your auction and bid on your item, they'll be operating in the United States, not the other way around. This is the safest way to avoid a "local presence" charge, but of course it will deny you the benefits of selling to people who shop exclusively on eBay's overseas sites.

➢ Run your eBay auctions on more than one of eBay's overseas sites, and have your auction descriptions appear in several languages, one below the other, so that you do not appear to be "targeting" customers in a particular country.

➢ Don't post every one of your auctions on eBay's overseas sites. List only those items you think will have a strong local interest in that country.

➢ Avoid "blitz e-mails" and other direct marketing techniques that are targeting customers in a particular country.

➢ Make sure you don't violate any other laws in the host country that put your business on the radar screen of foreign law enforcement authorities. The art dealer in the French eBay case first came under scrutiny by French police when one of his vases for sale on eBay turned out to be stolen.

➢ Find an eBay seller in the host country and have him handle your overseas auctions as your agent or distributor in the host country. This person is already complying with all local laws, rules, and regulations (you hope) and can tell you what you need to do and when. To find such a person, go to the eBay home page, click on the Community tab, then click on the Groups tab, then click on the International prompt (in the Regional section). There, click on the seller's group for the country you wish to sell in and post a "local distributor wanted" message. Be sure to check the feedback rating of anyone who responds.

IMPORTING MERCHANDISE INTO THE UNITED STATES

Importers carry a lot of legal responsibility for merchandise they bring into the country. Here' s what you need to know to comply with U.S. import requirements,

Customs Duties and Regulations

A customs duty, sometimes known as a tariff (which is a list of duties a country imposes on imports), is basically a tax on imported goods. Every country, including the United States, taxes imports. However, they do so inconsistently, as the primary motive behind duties is to protect domestic manufacturers from overseas competition, and some industries need more protection than others do.

If you are importing goods that have a value of U.S. $200 or more, are not exempted by a trade treaty between the United States and the country of origin (such as the North American Free Trade Agreement or NAFTA, which eliminates duties between the U.S., Canada, and Mexico), and are subject to a customs duty (not all goods are), you will have to pay a duty in order for the goods to clear U.S. customs. The complete schedule of U.S. tariffs, known as the Harmonized Tariff Schedule, is published at www.usitc.gov/taffairs.htm, but be sure to update your eyeglass prescription before you look at it.

A better approach is to associate your business with a customs broker. These folks make it a point to know the ins and outs of getting goods into and out of the country (they are often on a "first-name basis" with local customs officials, and don't think that doesn't help get things done). They are well worth the fees you pay them. For an online directory of customs brokers, go to:

> ➤ U.S. Department of Agriculture's search service (www.ams.usda.gov/tmd/freight/custom_broker.htm)
> ➤ National Customs Brokers & Forwarders Association of America website (www.ncbfaa.org/scripts/search.asp)

➢ Your favorite search engine (type "[your state] customs broker" and see who turns up)

If the goods you are importing require a license to be sold in the United States (think alcohol, tobacco, drugs, and firearms), you will also need an import license to bring these goods into the country.

Finally, keep in mind that there are some goods (called "restricted goods") that you simply cannot bring into this country for any reason for health, safety, or antiterrorism reasons. Counterfeit items (such as name-brand product knockoffs), "products made with forced labor," "radio frequency products," and postage stamps (!) are all on the restricted list.

In just about every country, it is the responsibility of the importer or purchaser—the person bringing goods into the United States—to comply with U.S. customs regulations, duties, and tariffs. This means that if your vendor fails to fill out its customs forms properly, the goods will be held up at the U.S. port of entry and you will have to spend a significant amount of time (or a significant amount of money hiring a customs broker in that port city to help you) getting the goods through customs.

Currency Laws

U.S. currency laws require that cash amounts above $10,000 be declared at customs when the money enters or leaves the country. It is also illegal to conspire with couriers to bring in lesser amounts when the total exceeds the $10,000 figure, a process called "smurfing."

Marking Requirements

Every article of foreign origin imported into the United States must be marked in a conspicuous place as legibly, indelibly, and permanently as the nature of the article will permit, and in such a manner as to indicate to the ultimate purchaser in the United States the name of the country of origin of the article. The country of origin must also be reported on the customs entry documentation. Customs regulations require the commercial invoice to include the country of origin of the merchandise.

It is absolutely crucial your foreign suppliers are aware of U.S. Customs marking requirements. As an importer, it is your responsibility to know where your goods are made and by whom.

What is an acceptable country of origin marking? The marking must be in English (goods from a NAFTA country may be marked with the name of the country of origin in English, French, or Spanish). The name of the country may not be abbreviated unless the abbreviation unmistakably indicates the country's name. For example, "Gt. Britain" is acceptable for Great Britain. "PRC" is not acceptable for the People's Republic of China, but "P.R. China" is acceptable. "ROC" is not acceptable for Republic of China (Taiwan). ISO country codes, such as "NL" for the Netherlands, should not be used because they do not unmistakably indicate the country of origin to the ultimate purchaser. In this case, either "Holland" or "Netherlands" is acceptable. If the foreign spelling is close enough to the English spelling so there is no doubt of the origin, then that is acceptable. Examples are "Brasil" and "Italia."

What about documentation that states the country of origin as EC, EEC, EU, European Community or European Union? U.S. Customs regulations define a "country" as "the political entity known as a nation." The European Union is an organization of sovereign states. It is not a nation with full political union. Each country in the EU still has independent status. Please ensure your documentation states the actual country of origin, such as Spain, and not "EU," and your goods are marked accordingly.

What are the penalties for unmarked or incorrectly marked goods? If the article is not marked at the time of importation, it must be properly marked, exported, or destroyed under customs supervision prior to liquidation. Otherwise, the goods will be subject to 10 percent additional marking duties. Customs may demand redelivery for items not properly marked. If an importer does not comply with a demand for redelivery, customs may assess liquidated damages up to three times the value of the merchandise.

Foreign Trade Zones

To encourage international trade, Congress has designated more than 230 geographic areas—at least one in every state, and some not even near an ocean or major waterway—as "foreign trade zones." If you locate your eBay business or warehouse space within one of these zones, you get significant savings and deferrals of U.S. Customs duties and import tariffs.

Without a zone, if a manufacturer or processor imports a component or raw material into the United States, it is required to pay the import tax (duty) at the time the component or raw material enters the country. However, a foreign trade zone is considered to be outside the commerce of the United States and the U.S. Customs territory. So, when foreign merchandise is brought into a foreign trade zone, no customs duty is owed until the merchandise leaves the zone and enters the commerce of the United States. Only then is the merchandise considered imported and the duty paid. If the imported merchandise is exported back out of the country, no customs duty is ever due.

You can find a thorough description of the foreign trade zone program, as well as the locations of all foreign trade zones in the United States, at www.foreign-trade-zone.com.

Watch Your Use Taxes!

Any goods you import from overseas for your own consumption—as opposed to inventory you plan to sell on eBay—will be subject to use tax in your state. The customs department is required to make available to "law enforcement authorities" information about goods you bring into the United States if the declared value is greater than $500. Since your state tax authority is probably a law enforcement authority, they have the right to search you out of the customs department database and send you a bill for overdue

• A "Use Tax" Horror Story •

Once upon a time, there was a gentleman in Connecticut who loved collecting antiques. In 1999, this gentleman purchased a nineteenth-century wall clock on eBay's U.K. site from a dealer located in London. The gentleman's winning bid was U.S. $2,000. The item was shipped promptly, payment was made via PayPal, and the parties left positive feedback for each other on eBay's Feedback Forum.

But this gentleman did not live happily ever after.

In the summer of 2005, the gentleman received a letter from the Connecticut Department of Revenue Services that read as follows:

Dear Sir:

It has come to our attention that in May 1999 you brought into this country an antique nineteenth-century wall clock from [name and address of dealer], London, England, having a declared value of U.S. $2,000. As you know, the State of Connecticut requires a 6 percent use tax be paid on any item purchased overseas if no Connecticut sales tax was paid on the item and the item was purchased for your own consumption and not for resale.

If this item was purchased for resale, please send this office a copy of Connecticut resale exemption certificate Form _____ within 30 days.

If you have already paid Connecticut state use tax on this item, please send this office within 30 days a copy of your 1999 Connecticut state income tax return with the "personal use tax" box highlighted to show the amount of tax paid.

If you did not pay Connecticut state use tax on this item, please send this office within 30 days the sum of $635.52 in payment of all taxes, interest, and penalties that should have been paid on this item.

If we have not received any of the above submissions within 30 days, please be advised that we will commence legal action in the Superior Court of the State of Connecticut to recover all taxes, interest, and penalties due on this purchase.

Very truly yours,

Now, you are saying to yourself, "Hey, wait a minute! Six percent of $2,000 is only $120. What is that extra $515.52 all about?" It's interest and penalties on the $120 tax payment over the six years elapsed between 1999 and 2005.

The gentleman paid the tax (he is, after all, a gentleman), but swore he would no longer buy antiques from overseas dealers unless the price was at least 6 percent below retail.

"use tax" if they think you haven't already paid it. (And of course you haven't, have you?)

EXPORTING MERCHANDISE TO OTHER COUNTRIES

There are far fewer restrictions on exports than there are on imports, but they do exist. They include:

1. *Export Regulations/Licenses.* Basically there are two requirements:
   - ➤ You cannot sell anything to anyone in Cuba, North Korea, or any other country with which the United States does not do business generally.
   - ➤ You cannot export certain technology (such as computer software) to many countries overseas without an export license if the technology could potentially have military or terrorist applications.

2. *Antidiversion Clause in Shipping Documents.* To help ensure that U.S. exports go only to legally authorized destinations, the U.S. government requires a destination control statement on shipping documents. Under this requirement, the commercial invoice and bill of lading (or air waybill) for nearly all commercial shipments leaving the United States must display a statement notifying the carrier and all foreign parties (the ultimate and intermediate consignees and purchaser) that the U.S. material has been licensed for export only to certain destinations and may not be diverted contrary to U.S. law. Exceptions to the use of the destination control statement are shipments to Canada (intended for consumption in Canada) and shipments being made under certain general licenses. The U.S. Department of Commerce, an attorney, or the freight forwarder can provide advice on the appropriate statement to be used.

The minimum antidiversion statement for goods exported under Commerce Department authority is: "These commodities, technology, or software were exported from the United States in accordance with the Export Administration Regulations. Diversion contrary to U.S. law is prohibited."

3. *Antiboycott Regulations.* The United States has an established policy of opposing restrictive trade practices or boycotts fostered or imposed by foreign countries against other countries friendly to the United States. This policy is

implemented through the antiboycott provisions of the Export Administration Act enforced by the Department of Commerce and through the Tax Reform Act of 1977 enforced by the Department of the Treasury.

In general, these laws prohibit U.S. persons from participating in foreign boycotts or taking actions that further or support such boycotts. The antiboycott regulations carry out this general purpose by:

a. Prohibiting U.S. agencies or persons from refusing to do business with blacklisted firms and boycotted friendly countries pursuant to foreign boycott demands

b. Prohibiting U.S. persons from discriminating against, or agreeing to discriminate against, other U.S. persons on the basis of race, religion, sex, or national origin in order to comply with a foreign boycott

c. Prohibiting U.S. persons from furnishing information about business relationships with boycotted friendly foreign countries or blacklisted companies in response to boycott requirements

d. Providing for public disclosure of requests to comply with foreign boycotts

e. Requiring U.S. persons who receive requests to report receipt of the requests to the Commerce Department and disclose publicly whether they have complied with such requests

4. *Antibribery laws.* It is unlawful for a U.S. firm (as well as any officer, director, employee, or agent of a firm, or any stockholder acting on behalf of the firm) to offer, pay, or promise to pay (or to authorize any such payment or promise) money or anything of value to any foreign official (or foreign political party or candidate for foreign political office) for the purpose of obtaining or retaining business. It is also unlawful to make a payment to any person while knowing that all or a portion of the payment will be offered, given, or promised, directly or indirectly, to any foreign official (or foreign political party or candidate for foreign political office) for the purposes of assisting the firm in obtaining or retaining business. "Knowing" includes the concepts of "conscious disregard" and "willful blindness."

There is an exception to the antibribery provisions for "facilitating payments for routine governmental action."

A person charged with a violation of the antibribery provisions of the Federal Corrupt Practices Act (FCPA) may assert as a defense that the payment

• Exceptions to Antibribery Provisions •

The statute lists the following examples: obtaining permits, licenses, or other official documents; processing governmental papers, such as visas and work orders; providing police protection, mail pickup and delivery; providing phone service, power and water supply, loading and unloading cargo, or protecting perishable products; and scheduling inspections associated with contract performance or transit of goods across country. "Routine governmental action" does *not* include any decision by a foreign official to award new business or to continue business with a particular party.

was lawful under the written laws and regulations of the foreign country or that the payment was associated with demonstrating a product or performing a contractual obligation.

Firms are subject to a fine of up to $2 million; officers, directors, employees, agents, and stockholders are subject to a fine of up to $100,000 and imprisonment for up to five years. The attorney general can bring a civil action against a domestic concern (and the Securities and Exchange Commission against an issuer) for a fine of up to $10,000. Any officer, director, employee, or agent of an issuer, or stockholder acting on behalf of the firm, who willfully violates the antibribery provisions can also be charged. Under federal criminal laws other than the FCPA, individuals may be fined up to $250,000 or up to twice the amount of the gross gain or gross loss if the defendant derives pecuniary gain from the offense or causes a pecuniary loss to another person.

DEALING WITH VALUE-ADDED TAXES (VAT OR GST)

The United States is one of the few countries on Earth that does not impose a tax on wholesale transactions—as pointed out in Chapter 8, state sales taxes are imposed on retail transactions only.

Most countries, however, have some sort of value-added tax (VAT) or general sales tax (GST). Unlike a sales tax, VAT is levied on the "value added" to goods and services as they pass through each stage of the production process. In most countries, each business in the manufacturing chain pays the tax when it sells its goods to the next business in the chain, just like a sales tax, but is allowed to claim a credit for the VAT it paid when it bought the raw materials, work-in-progress, or supplies from the previous business in the chain. By imposing a tax on receipts but then allowing a credit for VAT taxes collected at earlier stages of production, the credit-invoice VAT taxes the "value added" by each business.

To further complicate things, some countries (such as Canada) impose VAT at both the national and state (provincial) levels.

Why should you care about VAT? For two reasons:

1. The VAT on imported goods is paid by the buyer and levied by the tax authority in the country where the buyer resides. So, if you are *selling* goods on eBay to people in countries that have a VAT, you do not have to collect and remit it as you would sales taxes, but you should warn potential buyers that their purchases may be subject to VAT, or else they will have a nasty surprise when the goods arrive. Then they'll post negative feedback about you on eBay. A simple statement in your Terms and Conditions should do the job. For example: "Purchasers in countries other than the United States may have to pay VAT, GST, and other taxes on this item; please contact your accountant or tax adviser to find out the impact of these taxes before you bid on this item."

2. If you are *buying* goods in another country for resale on eBay, your vendor may be tempted to charge you VAT or GST, or build it into his wholesale price. If he does, cheer up: Most countries have a procedure to reimburse you for any VAT or GST you were not required to pay, but you will have to learn to fill out some fairly complicated forms (sometimes written in English-as-a-second-language). You'll also have to deal with some of the pettiest bureaucrats the world has to offer.

REPATRIATION LAWS

One of the oldest laws known to the human race is that "a thief cannot pass good title to anything." If my mom's house was robbed ten years ago and I see that you are selling her heirloom bracelet on eBay, it doesn't matter one bit that you didn't know the bracelet was stolen, or that the person you bought it from did not know, in good faith, the person she bought it from was a thief. Under the law in just about every state, if I can prove that bracelet was the one stolen from my mom, I can put a stop to your auction and demand the immediate return of the bracelet. Any recourse you have is against the thief, who of course by this time is either long gone or in prison somewhere.

What if, however, the item in question was not stolen recently, but was dug up by a grave robber over a hundred years ago?

If you are selling antiquities of any kind on eBay, there's a good chance that someday in the not-too-distant future you will receive a nasty letter from a U.S. law firm claiming that the item was stolen from the country of origin and demanding its immediate return. Some examples:

➤ The Italian Culture Ministry brought a criminal lawsuit against the directors of the J. Paul Getty Museum in Los Angeles seeking recovery of several Etruscan vases that were illegally dug up and smuggled out of the country more than fifty years ago.

➤ Greek cultural authorities are seeking return of the marble friezes that once adorned the four sides of the Parthenon in Athens, even though these items were removed and transported to Great Britain in the early 1800s by Lord Elgin precisely because the British government did not think the Greek government at the time was stable enough to safeguard these priceless treasures. The so-called Elgin Marbles are today the most visited exhibit in the British Museum in London, and the Greek government has gone as far as to build a glass pavilion next to the Parthenon to house them once they are eventually returned.

➤ A number of prominent Jewish families have sued to recover works of art stolen from their families by the Nazis during the Holocaust.

➤ Great Britain recently passed a complex treasure trove law requiring weekend "metal detector" hobbyists to submit any coins or antiquities they find to the British government for evaluation before selling them on the open market. If the government determines that the items belong in a museum, they are required to pay the finder only a small percentage of the item's market value.

➢ The government of the People's Republic of China has passed regulations requiring the return of any Chinese antique that was exported from the country at any time without a proper export license.

The list goes on and on. While attempts by foreign governments to repatriate items that have special significance as part of a country's "cultural patrimony" have not yet impacted the eBay community (the targets of the lawsuits so far have been museums and leading auction houses such as Sotheby's and Christie's), it is only a matter of time before an eBay seller has an auction pulled because eBay received a nasty letter from a foreign government's U.S. law firm demanding repatriation of the item offered for sale.

If you are selling antiquities on eBay, what can you do? The short answer is "not much," short of avoiding the antiquities market altogether. Here are a couple of tips that may help:

➢ If you are selling antiquities, stay away from "high end" goods. It's highly unlikely that a foreign government will pursue people on eBay who are selling arrowheads, Roman coins (unless, of course, they were dug up in Great Britain), potsherds, and other commonly dug up items. If, however, someone asks you to sell a "genuine Byzantine mosaic" . . . well, that's another story.

➢ If you are selling an antiquity that has been in your family for a long time, draft a letter describing the circumstances under which it was acquired, and stating that it has been in your family for XXX years. This letter is called a "provenance letter," and it will protect you at least to the extent that anyone accuses you of being the person who illegally dug up and brought the item to the United States. When the letter is finished (be sure to have your signature notarized by a local notary public), offer the letter as part of the goods being auctioned, and quote the letter verbatim in your auction description.

➢ If you are selling an antiquity that someone else has asked you to sell, have the seller prepare a provenance letter and offer it for sale as part of the

• What About Native American Artifacts? •

When most people think of antiquities, they think of items having to do with classical civilizations such as Greece, Rome, Egypt, the Mayas of Mexico, or the Incas of Peru. But there is a series of laws in the United States, dating back to 1906 (thank you, Teddy Roosevelt), affording similar protection to artifacts that were illegally dug up from Native American sites around the United States. Generally, items excavated from Native American sites may not be removed from those sites without:

* An antiquities permit from the U.S. Department of the Interior
* A permit from the "land manager" having jurisdiction over the site

If whoever sold you a Native American artifact cannot produce either of these documents on demand, you may be in a heap of trouble when you sell it on eBay.

If the item consists of human remains or "funerary objects" that may have religious significance to a Native American tribe, it cannot be sold under any circumstances but must be repatriated to the tribal authorities upon demand.

Not sure if that "genuine Navajo blanket" has religious significance? You can contact the Repatriation Office of the National Museum of the American Indian in Suitland, Maryland (telephone: 301-238-1540), who will put you in touch with the appropriate person in the Native American tribal government who deals with such matters. There's a good chance your item will be confiscated, but if the tribal authorities don't think there's a problem with a particular item, they will send you a letter or certificate to that effect—and wouldn't that be a great thing to include in your auction description for the item?

A useful summary of the laws governing repatriation of Native American artifacts can be found online at http://bcn.boulder.co.us/environment/cacv/cacvregs.htm. For more information about the Repatriation Office of the National Museum of the American Indian and the services it offers to antiquities dealers, go to www.nmai.si.edu, click on the Outreach tab, then on the Repatriation link.

auction "lot" you are selling on eBay. If the seller knows the person from whom he acquired the antiquity, politely ask the seller to get a provenance letter from that person as well.

➤ Have the antiquity reviewed by an established, reputable dealer in antiquities and get an opinion as to the likelihood of it being a "cultural patrimony" item you will have to repatriate to the country of origin. Any dealer who is a member of the London-based Antiquities Dealers Association (www .the-ada.org), the National Antique & Art Dealers Association of America (www.naadaa.org), or the Antique Dealers Association of California (www .antiquedealersca.com) should fit the bill. Avoid dealing with "antiquities experts" who advertise in the back pages of popular magazines such as *Archaeological Digest* or *Biblical Archeology Review,* because many of these folks are not dealing in genuine antiques but rather in what are euphemistically called "genuine replicas."

DEALING WITH OVERSEAS FRAUD

Think you've been ripped off by someone in Belorussia? There are a number of ways to proceed.

As pointed out in Chapter 6, eBay does not like to get involved directly in disputes between buyers and sellers. Doing so would be inconsistent with eBay's role as a "marketplace" or "playing field" on which transactions occur between independent parties.

There is one significant exception. A couple of years ago, eBay formed a Global Law Enforcement Operation team to crack down on international auction fraud operations. This team works on both eBay- and PayPal-related criminal cases and works with law enforcement in three key areas:

1. It supports ongoing investigations conducted by law enforcement by collecting, analyzing, and presenting critical evidence in response to an official request. Oftentimes eBay's investigators are required to testify in trials.

2. It initiates and prepares cases found through member reports and internal reports.

3. It travels the globe to train law enforcement officials on trends and techniques.

eBay has more than sixty fraud investigators in the United States, Ireland, and Germany, and plans to add additional investigators in Asia. Team members that specialize in educating law enforcement officials are strategically located in Asia, Western and Eastern Europe, and the United States where they can meet regularly with law enforcement agencies to discuss trends and work on solutions. There have been arrests for fraud on eBay in Romania, India, and throughout the United States. Once these case stories become public, they can be found on the Police Blotter, which can be found on eBay's Security and Resolution Center (accessible from the bottom of any eBay page).

If you think you have been defrauded on eBay by an overseas buyer, you cannot deal with the Global Law Enforcement Operation team directly, since it deals only with law enforcement officials and agencies. You have two options:

1. File a complaint with your local police department, with a request that they contact eBay's Global Law Enforcement Operation team to pursue the matter. (The Security and Resolution Center, which is available at the bottom of any eBay page, links to Law Enforcement and Third-Party Resources.)

2. File a complaint with the FBI's Internet Crime Complaint Center, known as IC3. IC3's mission is to serve as a vehicle to receive, develop, and refer criminal complaints regarding cybercrime. The IC3 (ic3.gov) gives the victims of cybercrime a convenient and easy-to-use reporting mechanism that alerts authorities of suspected criminal or civil violations.

Keep in mind that only law enforcement officials can prosecute a fraud complaint with eBay's fraud investigators. If you are not a law enforcement official, you must use eBay's or PayPal's dispute resolution processes as described in Chapter 6, or bring a civil action against the buyer or seller in state court. Pretending to be a law enforcement official in an effort to get eBay's attention to your alleged fraud complaint can get you in hot water, so don't even think about it!

INTERNATIONAL SALES CONTRACTS

Appendix F is a typical International Sales Contract, prepared by the International Chamber of Commerce, for use by manufacturers who are selling to overseas wholesalers or retailers for resale in the latter's country.

This contract is governed by the U.N. Convention on Contracts for the International Sale of Goods (CISG). The CISG is based on U.S. sales law; however, many overseas vendors will want to have the laws of their own country apply in the event of any dispute.

COMMON QUESTIONS

Q. *What are some do's and don'ts for eBay sellers when it comes to customs documents?*

A. You don't need to be specific on the declaration, when it comes to the contents. If you sell an antique mechanical bank, for example, it is sufficient to declare the contents as "coin bank."

The declared value is, however, very important.

You do not have to declare the value your item sold for on eBay if the winning bid is greater than the actual retail value. So, for example, if you bought something at retail for $20 and it sold on eBay for $90, you would declare $20 on the customs form. If the item sold below what you paid for it, it is okay to declare the winning bid amount on the customs form.

You should not, however, declare a "zero" value for any item; that's a red flag for customs officials overseas, and they are then free to set a customs value themselves. In many cases the buyer will end up having to pay more duty/taxes than necessary. You should also exclude shipping and handling costs from the declared value.

If you include an invoice in the package to the buyer, the best invoice to supply is a copy of the auction listing or an invoice generated through the eBay system. Ensure that the value you indicate on the enclosed invoice matches the information on the customs form. The customs authorities at destinations do not really require an invoice, since they will go by the customs form. Customs will, however, request an invoice from the buyer if the value stated on the customs declaration seems unbelievable (for example, a laptop computer with a value of $10).

Q. *What is the U.N. convention governing the sale of goods, and why do so many people say in their contracts that it doesn't apply?*

A. The U.N. Convention on Contracts for the International Sale of Goods (CISG) was adopted by the United States on January 1, 1988. If applicable to a given transaction, the CISG "fills the gaps" in international sales contracts and sets forth the rights and obligations of the buyer and seller. However, the CISG provides that express contractual provisions take precedence over the default provisions of the CISG. Thus, a seller and buyer remain free to specify whatever law or terms they wish to apply to their transaction, and they may exclude altogether the application of the CISG to their contractual relationship. Since most exporters want to have their own country's law apply in case of a dispute, they generally disclaim the CISG in their standard form sales contracts.

Selling Other People's Stuff

For every person in the United States selling products on eBay, there are at least 10,000 people who wish they could but don't have the time, patience, or "computer savvy" to learn how to sell on eBay. If you are not looking for ways to help these people make money while cleaning out their attics, basements, and garages, you are missing out on one of the most exciting and profitable "sources" for items to sell on eBay.

Also, a lot of local businesses would love to get rid of their surplus, excess, or obsolete inventory in a way that wouldn't involve "junking" it and writing it off, but they don't have the time, budget, or personnel to set up an "eBay sales division" internally. Your eBay business could well help these businesses "outsource" their eBay sales in a way that benefits both you and the company.

There are special legal and tax rules you have to learn, though, when you are selling other people's stuff on eBay. If you are working with a wholesaler or overseas manufacturer, you will have to decide whether you wish to operate as an agent or a distributor. You will also need to learn a bit about "drop shipping" and consignment sales, especially when that little old lady walks into your shop with a "genuine Tiffany lamp" she wants you to sell on eBay.

AGENTS VS. DISTRIBUTORS

You know you have reached a milestone in building your eBay business when other people start calling you and asking you to help sell their things on eBay. For example, a number of U.S.-based "eBayers" make a significant living by helping overseas eBay sellers do business in the United States.

Whenever you are selling products on behalf of other people on eBay (for money, of course), you are acting either as their "agent" or their "distributor," and there's a significant legal difference between these two roles.

1. *Agents.* An agent is someone who helps someone else generates sales, but without taking possession of the seller's goods. The agent helps sellers find buyers and introduces buyers to the seller, but the seller deals directly with the customer after that point in time.

   So, for example, when you work with a "drop shipper," you are acting as the drop shipper's agent. You create the auction page for the drop shipper's stuff, you do all the listing work, and you answer the buyers' e-mail questions. If the merchandise sells, you contact the drop shipper and they take care of all the shipping, packaging, returns, etc. You never see, touch, or smell the merchandise. You keep a percentage of the winning bid as your commission and remit the rest to the drop shipper. That's an agent relationship.

   In return for helping a seller "find" customers, the agent receives a commission that is either a fixed fee or a percentage of the sales price. Just about all commissioned sales representatives, brokers, and other intermediaries are agents in the eyes of the law.

2. *Distributors.* Unlike an agent, a distributor actually takes possession of the goods being sold. So, for example, you buy a containerload of bobblehead dolls from a manufacturer in Korea, you pay the manufacturer the wholesale price at the time of delivery, you store them in your basement, and you sell them one at a time on eBay, hopefully for a profit. That is a distributor relationship. Unlike agents, who are paid either a fixed fee or a percentage of the sales price as their commission, distributors get to keep 100 percent of the profit they make when selling the goods at retail (or to another whole-

saler). Of course, unlike an agent, the distributor also has to incur costs to store or warehouse the goods in a safe and clean place, and to deal with all issues involving shipping, handling, and postage.

The legal distinction between a distributor and an agent becomes more clear when we describe the two most common situations in which eBay sellers sell other people's stuff on eBay—"consignment" and "drop shipping" arrangements.

CONSIGNMENT SHOPS AND TRADING ASSISTANTS

Consignment sales are a funny animal in the legal world. When you take goods on consignment, you stand in a very special legal relationship with both the seller and the buyer (i.e., the person to whom you sell the seller's goods).

Halfway Between an Owner and a Tenant

The best way to explain the concept of consignment is to illustrate it, using a piece of land as an example. (It's a lot easier to use real estate as an example than an antique mechanical bank or a bobble-head doll, but the same rules would apply.) Pick up two pencils from your desk and hold them in your hand. Call one of the pencils "ownership" and the other pencil "possession." Now pretend that the two pencils represent property rights—the legal rights you have to an acre of land.

When you are holding both the "ownership" and the "possession" pencils in your hands, you own the acre of land and can do whatever you want with it. You can build a house on the piece of land, you can sell it to someone else, or you can let it lie undeveloped for twenty years, waiting for a shopping center developer to express an interest in it. It's yours to dispose of any way you wish (within the limits of the law, of course—you can't build a brothel on that land if that "use" would violate local zoning laws).

Now take the "possession" pencil and give it to someone you love and cherish (because you will need to ask for it back—this is only a game, after all). You are still holding the "ownership" pencil, but your loved one now holds the "possession" pencil. That makes your loved one a "tenant" of our imaginary acre of land, and you the "landlord." If we were talking about an item of personal property (such as an antique) instead of real estate, your loved one would be called the "bailee" and you would be called the "bailor." (Isn't the law a wonderful thing?) You still have the right to sell the land to someone else, but neither you nor the purchaser of the land can do anything that would interfere with the right to "possess" the land you have given to your loved one. As long as your tenant pays the rent and obeys the terms of the lease, he can do whatever your lease allows him to do. So, if your lease grants the tenant "quiet enjoyment" of the land for ten years, you can still sell the land to a developer, but the developer cannot build a skyscraper on the land until the ten-year lease term is up (or the tenant stops paying rent).

A consignment relationship falls somewhere between owning something and just leasing it. When you take goods on consignment for someone (called a "consignor"), you have possession of the goods but not ownership—just like the tenant of a piece of land. But, unlike a tenant, in a consignment arrangement the "possessor" also has the power to sell the goods to someone else and pass the owner's "ownership" to that someone. Once the possessor (that's you) enters into a binding contract to sell the goods to a buyer (such as a successful eBay auction, which is a binding contract), the owner/consignor *must* transfer title to the buyer and can no longer take back the goods. If they do, then the owner/consignor has "breached the contract" and you can sue the owner/consignor for damages.

Your Consignment Agreement

You should never, ever, *ever* take goods for consignment on a "handshake" basis. You absolutely must have a written agreement with the owner/consignor of the goods. Why? Because under the law of most states, "unless the parties agree otherwise," the owner/

consignor of goods can terminate the relationship at any time before a binding sales contract has been entered into. You better make darn sure the "parties agree otherwise" or you could end up with a mess on your hands!

Here's how. Let's say you take an antique mechanical bank from me for consignment and put it up for sale on eBay in a seven-day auction. The bank attracts several bids and the price goes up to $4,000 within two days of posting. On day three of the auction, someone approaches me and offers me $10,000 for the bank, which I know to be worth only about $5,000. I decide to sell to this person and call you on the phone to tell you the wonderful news that "you don't have to do anything on eBay with that bank, after all; I've found a buyer, and I'm terminating the consignment."

Guess what? Unless we have a written agreement that says I can't sell the bank to anyone else until the auction is concluded, I have every right to do what I've just done, and you cannot sue me for anything. You will have to "pull" the auction on eBay and face negative feedback from the frustrated bidders, who probably didn't even know you were selling the bank on consignment for someone else.

What Should Your Consignment Agreement Say?

Appendix D is a simple form of Consignment Agreement that is specifically tailored to eBay consignment sales. Note specifically the following conditions:

➤ A provision that allows the eBay seller to terminate the agreement at any time if the seller "smells a rat," but does not allow the owner/consignor to do so until all of the consigned goods have been sold on eBay

➤ A provision allowing the eBay seller to return the goods to the owner/consignor if the seller determines that the merchandise "just won't sell"

➤ A provision allowing the eBay seller a "breakage" fee for unsold goods

➤ A provision obligating the owner/consignor to "follow through" on any successful auctions

➤ A provision granting the eBay seller a "sliding scale" commission that increases with the winning bid amount, but with a floor of X dollars just in case the consigned goods don't generate much interest on eBay

➤ A warranty from the owner/consignor that all of the consigned goods are "as described" and will not violate any of eBay's policies

➤ Disclaimer of warranty, limitation of liability, and "release" clauses protecting the eBay seller from liability to the owner/consignor in all circumstances, unless the eBay seller willfully "trashes" the goods

➤ A fixed termination date (usually three to six months from the date of signing), so that any consigned goods that haven't sold by that time will be returned to the owner/consignor without further obligation or liability

Reporting and Paying Income Taxes/Sales Taxes for Consignment Sales

If you are taking consignment sales, here's what the IRS wants you to do when it comes time for paying your income taxes.

First, total all of your income from selling consigned items on eBay last year. Then total all the amounts you paid the owners/consignors. Then, net the two amounts against each other and report the balance as income on your tax return. If the owner/consignor is an individual (as opposed to a corporation or LLC) and you paid the individual more than $600 during a calendar year, you will have to send the owner/consignor a Form 1099 by January 31 of the following year. Duplicate copies of the Form 1099 must also be mailed to the IRS and your state tax agency by February 28 or 29 of the following year.

What about sales taxes? Here's where things get a little tricky, especially if your owner/consignor lives in another state. Let's say you have an eBay business in Connecticut and you are contacted by someone in New Jersey who wants to sell a grand piano on eBay. You put the piano up for sale on eBay on this other person's behalf, and the piano sells. Here are the sales tax rules, regardless of whether you took possession of the piano:

➤ If the winning buyer lives in Connecticut, you have to charge Connecticut sales tax.

➤ If the winning buyer lives in New Jersey, you have to charge New Jersey sales tax and remit the tax to New Jersey.

➤ If the winning buyer lives anywhere else, you won't have to charge sales tax.

In other words, you charge sales tax if the buyer lives in the same state as either you or your owner/consignor.

You should also make sure to warn potential bidders that they may have to pay sales taxes on their winning bids by including a special notice on the eBay auction page. For example: "Note to residents of New Jersey and Connecticut: State and local sales taxes will be added to your winning bid." In many states, if you fail to give buyers that notice, you will be prohibited from adding sales taxes to their winning bids and will have to deduct the tax from your winning bid when the buyer pays you.

DEALING WITH "DROP SHIPPERS"

A popular way for smaller eBay sellers to sell goods in bulk without having to maintain large areas of storage space for their inventory is to enter into a "drop shipping" agreement with a large wholesaler.

The Basic Arrangement

Basically, drop shipping works like this: The drop shipper makes certain items of its inventory available to you for sale on eBay and allows you to download the drop shipper's logos, item descriptions, photos, and other information you will need to set up the auction page. You create the auction page and sell the item on eBay. When the auction ends, you e-mail the order to your drop shipper along with the buyer's name and address. The drop shipper sends the product directly to the buyer, with your company's name on the package, and charges you the wholesale price specified in the drop-shipping catalog or website. Anything above that price you get to keep.

As such, drop shipping is somewhere between an agent and a distributor relationship. Because you do not take possession of the goods, you are like an agent for the drop shipper. But because you pay the wholesale price and get to keep anything you make above that, you are a little bit like a distributor, since your fee might vary with each auction, even though the goods you sell are identical.

Keep in mind that a lot of people out there want you to believe they are drop-ship distributors. You need to find reputable distribution companies.

Your Drop-Shipping Agreement

The good news is that, unlike consignment arrangements, a drop shipper will almost never do business with you on a handshake basis. Drop shippers will insist on a written agreement to protect their interests, since, after all, there are just as many flaky "stockless retailers" out there as there are flaky drop shippers, and a reputable drop shipper will want to protect its reputation at all cost.

The bad news is that you will have to sign the drop shipper's standard form of agreement. Be sure to have an attorney review it before you sign. If the agreement contains terms you cannot agree to, be sure to have them changed, either in the agreement itself or in a "side letter" amendment, before you order your first item from the drop shipper. If the drop shipper refuses to make the changes you and your attorney believe are necessary, find another drop shipper. Heaven knows there are enough of them out there.

What Should Your Drop-Shipping Agreement Say?

Appendix E is a standard wholesale drop-shipping agreement, drafted in the drop shipper's favor. Note especially the following conditions:

➤ A provision requiring the drop shipper to give the eBay seller notice if its inventory of any popular item falls below X units. Because you are selling the item *before* you order it from the drop shipper, there's always a risk that the drop shipper runs out of inventory while one or more of your auctions are pending.

➢ A provision requiring the drop shipper to use its "best efforts" to notify the eBay seller of any changes in pricing, shipping, and other charges affecting items previously ordered by the eBay seller. If these change while an auction is pending, it could reduce or eliminate your profit on the transaction.

➢ A provision specifying whether the drop shipper's or the eBay seller's name, logo, and other identifying marks will appear on the eBay auction page. Some drop shippers will insist on their logo being used, while others insist that only your company name and logo appear on the eBay auction pages, to insulate the drop shipper from legal liability.

➢ A provision authorizing the drop shipper to substitute merchandise without notice to the eBay seller if, for example, the drop shipper runs out of inventory. Buyers on eBay hate it when a drop shipper ships something that's not 100 percent identical to the photo on your auction page. So, if your agreement has such a clause, you will have to notify your auction bidders that the "seller reserves the right to substitute merchandise of equal or better quality in the event of inventory shortfalls."

➢ A provision requiring you to pay a set-up fee to establish an account with the drop shipper. More established drop shippers will not require this fee, and you should be suspicious of any drop shippers that require a large up-front payment just to do business with them.

➢ A provision requiring you to pay a "monthly fee" if you do not place a minimum number of orders during a specified time period. It should be a small fee to compensate the drop shipper for the cost of maintaining an account that's not producing for them.—Section 14 in Appendix E is actually a "minimum purchase requirement," and if you were my client, I would tell you to resist this provision.

➢ A provision requiring the drop shipper to collect and pay any sales taxes if goods are sold to buyers in states where the drop shipper has a physical presence. As was pointed out in Chapter 8, you must post a notice on your auction pages saying, "Residents of [name the states]: State and local sales taxes will be added to your winning bid."

➢ A provision specifying when the drop shipper will and will not accept returns from a buyer. Keep in mind that if buyers think you are the seller (because the drop shipper's name does not appear anywhere on your auction pages), they may return merchandise to you and not to the drop shipper. If that happens when you are on vacation, as an example, you may not be able to return the goods to the drop shipper before the cutoff date spelled out in the agreement, so make sure this provision gives you sufficient "wiggle room."

➤ A provision allowing the drop shipper to change any term in the agreement with prior notice to the eBay seller (which should affect only the pricing terms).

Reporting and Paying Income Taxes/Sales Taxes for Drop-Shipping Arrangements

If you are drop shipping, here's what the IRS wants you to do when it comes time for paying your income taxes. First, total all of your income from selling drop-shipped merchandise on eBay last year. Then total all the amounts you paid your drop shippers. Then, net the two amounts against each other and report the balance as income on your tax return. If the drop shipper is an individual (as opposed to a corporation or LLC) and you paid the drop shipper more than $600 during a calendar year, you will have to send them a Form 1099 by January 31 of the following year. Duplicate copies of the Form 1099 must also be mailed to the IRS and your state tax agency by February 28 or 29 of the following year.

What about sales taxes? It gets a little tricky when your drop shipper has offices or warehouses in several states. Let's say you live in Connecticut and are selling products on eBay for a drop shipper that has business, office, or warehouse locations in Ohio, Texas, and California. If you place the drop shipper's item for sale on eBay, and the winning bidder resides in any of those four states (Connecticut, Ohio, Texas, or California), you must charge that state's sales tax and pay it to the appropriate state authority.

Or . . . you should make sure that it is clearly spelled out in your drop-shipping agreement that the drop shipper agrees, up-front, to pay sales taxes for any sales you make on eBay to residents of Ohio, Texas, and California.

Since the drop shipper is not doing business in Connecticut, you will still be responsible for collecting and paying sales taxes for drop-shipped items you sell to Connecticut residents. The drop shipper will not want to do that if it does not have a physical presence in Connecticut.

You should also make sure to warn potential bidders that they may have to pay sales taxes on their winning bids. In this example, your notice on the eBay auction page should read: "Note to residents of Connecticut, Ohio, Texas, and California: State and local sales taxes will be added to your winning bid." In many states, if you fail to give buyers that notice, you will be prohibited from adding sales taxes to their winning bids; that means you'll have to deduct the tax from *your* winning bid when the buyer pays you.

COMMON QUESTIONS

Q. *All of my consignors assure me that they are incorporated, so I don't have to send them a Form 1099 each year. Should I believe them?*

A. It's a good thing to believe, but to be 100 percent safe, you might want to consider asking them to fill out a W-9 form (a request for taxpayer ID number) when they first start doing business with you—that is, if you don't already do so. That way you'll be able to see on the face of the form if they're a corporation, and you'll have something to rely on if the IRS ever comes calling.

Q. *I earn most of my eBay revenue as a trading assistant. In the past I have reported only my net to my state for "business and occupations" tax purposes. In a recent audit they wanted me to report the gross, without a deduction for the amount I paid the owner of the property. What's your take on this?*

A. Without knowing more of the facts, I really can't say. What they probably were telling you to do was "gross out" everything—that is, report all of your income from eBay sales *and* all of the payments you made to the property owners (consignors). Technically, the amount you pay your consignors is not a "deduction"—it actually reduces the amount of taxable income you have to report to the IRS. You would still pay tax only on the "net" between the two amounts, but that is the correct way to report it.

Keep in mind you need to send 1099s to each consignor in January every year if you paid them more than $600 total in the preceding year.

Legal and Tax Concerns for the Advanced eBay Seller

If you are reading this chapter . . . congratulations! You've made it into the big leagues. You are now a Gold or Titanium PowerSeller, and an "enterprise" seller with hundreds of auctions going on eBay at any one time.

By this point you probably have a lawyer and an accountant working for you (as you can now afford their fees), but that doesn't mean you are out of the legal and tax wilderness. Here are some things to think about as you build a truly world-class eBay business.

TRADEMARKING YOUR BUSINESS NAME AND WEB ADDRESS

Remember back in Chapter 2 when we said it was probably premature for you to trademark your business name, or the name of your eBay Store? That's no longer the case now, big guy. Since you have spent a lot of time and money building a "brand name" on eBay, that brand name now has terrific value, and you should do everything you can to protect it, because if you don't, someone else could glom onto your name and force you to change yours to something a lot less profitable.

Can You Trademark a Name?

You should first talk to a lawyer specializing in intellectual property, or patents and trademarks, to find out if it is possible to trademark your business name. There are two possible reasons (among others) why it might not be possible. Either:

> ➤ Someone else has already trademarked the name, in which case you cannot continue to use the name. You'll have to change the name to something else to avoid being sued by the other person for "infringing" the trademark.

> ➤ The name is not "trademarkable," so that no one will be able to register a federal trademark for it.

Not all names are trademarkable. Names that are generic or merely describe what the company does (e.g., "Cliff's Antiques and Auctions") or that use simple words in everyday English (e.g., "Cliff Ennico and Associates") probably cannot be trademarked. You will have a much easier time trademarking your name if:

> ➤ The name uses a word that doesn't exist in the English language, such as "Xyrennhia Dolls: The Bobble-Head People."

> ➤ The name has nothing to do with the merchandise you sell on eBay. Think about it. What does "Monster" have to do with looking for jobs online? What does "Bumble Bee" have to do with tuna fish? For that matter, what does the name "eBay" have to do with buying and selling products and services online? (There are still a few people who think it's pig Latin for "bee.") These and other names are easily trademarked because they are not normally associated with the goods they are used to identify. If you are using words that are normally associated with your goods, then there's a good chance somebody else is using that word for the same purpose.

Registering a Federal Trademark: Should You Do It Yourself?

The website of the U.S. Patent and Trademark Office at www .uspto.gov allows you to register a federal trademark online, but in my opinion the site is very difficult and confusing to use. Even lawyers make mistakes sometimes when they register trademarks online using this site. The problem is that you cannot register a trademark for all types of goods—you have to identify, in a fairly specific way, the goods or services that the trademark will be used to identify. When the USPTO website prompts you to type in this information, it is looking for specific "categories" of goods and services that are identified in the U.S. Trademark Register (you do have a copy of that in your bathroom, don't you?).

If you describe your goods and services using anything other than the Trademark Register categories, the website will automatically assign your trademark to several different categories in which your description words appear, and you will get a bill for thousands of dollars in trademark filing fees that you shouldn't have to pay.

This is one of those areas of the law where you absolutely, positively have to use a lawyer. And not just any lawyer, but somebody who deals with the U.S. Patent and Trademark Office every day and knows the ins and outs of getting trademarks registered. Expect to pay between $1,000 and $2,000 for a thorough registration, plus another $1,000 or so for a thorough "trademark search" that will help you identify other trademarks that are uncomfortably close to your own. Yes, it's a lot of money, but it will reap dividends many times over as you build your business into a powerful "brand." Besides, if you are a successful eBay seller, you can afford it now!

What About Your Web Address?

I don't usually recommend trademarking your Web address or URL unless it is also your company or business name. The fact that you were assigned an Internet domain name for your URL means that nobody else can take it from you, unless of course you fail to renew it when it expires. If, however, you are using your address as a trademark (e.g., your Web address is stenciled prominently on the side of your delivery truck), then it may make sense to register it as a federal trademark.

Are State Trademarks Any Good?

In a word, "no." Most states allow you to register a trademark if your business is local and you don't think your business will cross state lines (e.g., "Cliff's Pizza" in Podunk, Connecticut, whose customers all live within a twenty-mile radius of the restaurant). It's a lot cheaper than registering with the U.S. Patent and Trademark Office, but it will protect your name only within your state's borders. As an eBay seller, your business will cross state lines the minute you post your first auction page, so don't waste any money here.

"BUSINESS OPPORTUNITY" AND FRANCHISE LAWS

If you are successful in building an eBay business, sooner or later you will get a phone call or e-mail message from someone who wants to get in on the action. While you may not want to make this person a partner, it might occur to you to let this person operate a similar business using your company name, logos, trademarks, business plan, and advertising materials and have him pay you a percentage of his sales for the privilege of using your credentials.

Resist this temptation at all costs, because you are in effect "franchising" your business, and there are a ton of legal rules you will need to comply with.

Franchises

Generally, a franchise is a contract between two people or companies. The "franchiser" is a company with a successful business plan or model that has proved successful in a number of locations. "Franchisees" are companies or individuals that want to run their own business but don't want to take on the risk of starting a business themselves. What the franchisee wants to do is to buy a successful business plan and "execute" that plan in a particular geographic area or "territory," using the successful company's name and logo. (Think of McDonald's Golden Arches and you have the idea.)

Before you can legally franchise your business, there are a number of legal hoops you have to jump through, and they are very costly and time-consuming. First, you have to prepare an offering prospectus (called a Uniform Franchise Offering Circular or UFOC) and have it approved by the Federal Trade Commission in Washington, D.C. Then, you must file your UFOC and other documents with the securities regulators in the twenty or so states that require this filing before you can solicit franchisees in their states. The legal and accounting costs alone will run you between $20,000 and $50,000, so you don't want to approach franchising casually and you shouldn't even be thinking of this kind of business arrangement until your eBay business earnings are really big.

Once you set up a franchise, you must make sure that all franchisees follow your business plan "to the letter." Franchises are all about uniformity and regimentation. If you walk into a Burger King restaurant in Maine, for example, you get exactly the same burger, décor, and overall experience as you would in a Burger King restaurant in southern California.

There are already several franchises of "eBay consignment shops," with the industry leader being iSold It, based in San Diego, California (www.i-soldit.com).

Once you begin franchising your business, you will no longer have time to sell on eBay—your income will come mainly from selling franchises to people around the country. Accordingly, do not consider franchising as a way to build your business unless you have tons of cash on hand, a strong stomach for legal details, and a burning desire to become the next Mary Kay.

Business Opportunities

A business opportunity or "B.O." (so-called because many of them exude a certain odor) is any "packaged business investment" that falls short of being a franchise, in that you don't operate under someone else's registered trademark that has a recognized value in the marketplace.

Unlike a franchiser, a B.O. seller typically exercises no control over the buyer's business operations; the buyer is not required to follow the seller's recommended "plan" for building the business. The buyer can use whatever name she likes and can do business any way she likes. She just has to buy her supplies, inventory, machinery, and equipment from you on a regular basis.

There are many different types of business opportunities, but the two most common are:

> *The "Supply" B.O.* You sell raw materials to someone; they make something out of it in their spare time and then sell it back to you at a specified wholesale price so you can resell it at a profit. (The "Raise Chinchillas in your Backyard" ads you see in the back pages of comic books are examples of this type of business opportunity.)

> *The "Vending Machine" B.O.* You sell vending machines or other equipment and supplies to someone; they rent the machines for $1 a year to local businesses, keep them stocked with merchandise they buy from you at wholesale, and split the profits with the business where the machines are located. For example, you've seen gumball machines in a Chinese takeout restaurant. Well, they have usually been placed there by someone who bought a vending machine B.O. from the gumball company.

Once someone has bought a B.O., she is technically on her own, although the better ones will provide some sort of assistance to help buyers market their businesses. For example, in a vending machine B.O., the seller will (for a fee) help the buyer locate and select appropriate sites for the vending machines. Or the seller will recommend the buyer sign an agreement with a "site selection agency" (usually run by the B.O. seller or his brother-in-law) that will pick sites out of the local telephone directory for the buyer and charge her a fee for doing so.

The good news is that unlike franchises, business opportunities don't have to be registered with the Federal Trade Commission. The bad news is that twenty-three states require you to prepare a "disclosure statement" (basically a skimmed-down UFOC) and file that with the state securities regulators before you can legally offer your B.O. to residents of that state.

Because there has been a fair amount of consumer fraud associated with these kinds of business investments, do not consider this method of building your eBay business if you have a reputation as a "class act" on eBay. Use common sense: If business opportunities are so great, why do the vast majority of them have to use spam e-mail or comic-book advertising to get their message across? Is that the sort of image you want to create as an eBay seller?

WHEN INVESTORS COME KNOCKING ON YOUR DOOR

As our friends in China say, "Success has a thousand fathers." When you build a really successful business on eBay, there's a good chance some multimillionaire with extremely deep pockets will come along and offer to bankroll your operation (or the cost of that new warehouse) in exchange for a piece of your business.

Great news, and one of the surest signs you have "come of age" as an eBay seller! I'm not aware that any eBay seller has made an initial public offering (IPO) of its stock, but there's no reason it couldn't happen.

Just remember that whenever you sell a piece of your company, or sell your stock, to someone who is not going to be involved in the day-to-day operation of your business (i.e., someone who will be a "passive investor" as opposed to your "business partner"), the federal and state securities laws come into play.

These laws are designed to protect consumers and other unsophisticated people against fraudulent investments. Generally, whenever you offer to sell stock in your business to an investor, you must prepare a written "prospectus" (basically a business plan on steroids), register it with the U.S. Securities and Exchange Commission and the state securities regulators in each state where you plan to peddle your stock, and deliver it to each prospective investor before you take his money. The overall cost is anywhere from $50,000 to over $100,000 in legal and accounting fees.

Unless, of course, your offering is too small for the federal and state regulators to bother with.

If you are thinking about "pitching" your business to investors, here are some tips to make sure your offering is "too small" to comply with the requirements of the federal and state securities laws:

1. *Avoid a "general solicitation" or "general advertising."* Do not broadcast to the world at large that they can become investors in your company. Do not go on eBay Radio (www.wsradio.com) and say, "Because we've been so successful, we're giving the eBay community a chance to be a part of our success; for a limited time, we are offering ten shares of stock in our company for only $30 apiece." Even if no one responds to your announcement, you have violated the law.

2. *Avoid dealing with "unsophisticated" investors.* The federal and state securities laws contain numerous exemptions for investors who are either too rich or too knowledgeable to warrant the protection of the securities laws. If the people looking to invest in your company aren't heavy hitters in your industry, or aren't rich enough to afford losing every penny they plan to invest in your company, make sure they are represented by an expert (such as an investment banker or Wall Street–type lawyer) who can evaluate your company as an investment and make the "go/no go" decision.

3. *If you must have "dummies" as investors, keep them to a minimum.* Every state securities law has an exemption for purchases of stock by less than a specified number of "unsophisticated" investors during a twelve-month period. The number varies from state to state, but is usually between five and fifteen. As long as you keep the dummies below that number, you should be okay. Sophisticated or "accredited" investors are usually not subject to the numerical limit.

4. *Don't lie to an investor, even a sophisticated one.* Even a company that never plans to make a formal "offering" of its stock can violate the securities law if it lies to its investors, or tells them only half the truth. The concept of fraud, which was described in some detail in Chapter 3, applies to your dealings with investors as well as your dealings with customers, suppliers, and other eBay community members. If you tell your investor you had $1 million in gross merchandise sales last year, when in fact you had only

$800,000 in gross merchandise sales, expect a nasty letter from your investor's attorney at some point in the near future.

5. *Don't sell yourself short.* Keep in mind that once you bring an investor on board, you have a "partner" in the business and can no longer do things without at least letting your partner know what's going on from time to time.

   The law doesn't prohibit it, but you shouldn't sell so much of your company to investors that they end up "owning" the company and bossing you around. Once outside investors own more than one-third of your company, they have rights under the corporation or limited liability company (LLC) laws in many states. In some states (such as New York), the owners of more than 20 percent of a corporation's stock can sue to dissolve the corporation if they feel the majority owners are "unduly oppressing or harassing" them, such as denying them their right to participate in the management of the corporation's business by unfair, forceful, or violent means, for example, changing the locks on the doors.

   As long as you own more than 50 percent of the company stock, you will still be running the day-to-day operations of the business, but your "minority owners" can prevent you from doing some of the most important things you want to do (which require a two-thirds vote in many states) and otherwise make your life miserable. If other people want to buy a piece of your business, keep their ownership below 20 percent, if at all possible. That way, if you want to do something the investor thinks is a bad idea, you will be able to override his objections and do what you want to do, although the law will require you to give him a "hearing" and spend at least a reasonable amount of time listening to his nagging, whining, and complaining before you prevail.

ANTITRUST LAW: IT ISN'T JUST FOR BIG COMPANIES

Antitrust? Isn't that when your business gets so big the government comes after you for monopolizing an entire industry? I can hear some of you now laughing, "Cliff, I should live so long that I have such problems! If I ever get big enough that the Justice Department sees me as a threat to the U.S. economy, rest assured I will call you for help!"

Certainly, the only time you ever read about antitrust law in the newspapers is when a large company has grown so large that it starts wielding "monopoly power" and uses it as a club to knock out smaller competitors. But antitrust law is not just for the big dogs—even small businesses can get into trouble with the antitrust authorities if they are not careful.

As a capitalist society, we rely on competition to give consumers a choice and the fairest price possible for goods and services. That's the theory, at any rate. Any conduct that prevents "full, fair, and robust" competition from happening denies consumers a choice and forces them to pay more than they should for things. So, the antitrust laws have evolved over time to prevent businesses of *any* size from engaging in "anticompetitive behavior." You can actually go to jail if you are found to be using anticompetitive practices.

Here are some of the antitrust issues you should watch out for when running an eBay business:

➤ *Price Fixing.* "Price fixing" occurs when two or more business owners in the same market agree to set their prices in stone and not compete with each other, because "the market here is so big we can all make money." Since many small business owners in similar markets talk to each other on a regular basis, price fixing can occur implicitly or even accidentally; there is no "agreement" as such to set prices, but each business copies the other's pricing patterns until there is effectively no difference between them.

The general rule here is this: Do not even discuss prices with other eBay sellers if they are selling the same type of stuff you are. And if you sell using eBay's popular Buy It Now! fixed-price feature, do not set your fixed prices based on "what everyone else on eBay is charging." (As a practical matter, price fixing doesn't happen when you use an auction format, as the auction buyers ultimately determine the final selling price.)

➤ *Tying Arrangements.* Let's say you have two products in your inventory. One sells really well; it flies out the door every day. The other one doesn't move at all; you are lucky if someone buys it on eBay below your cost, and you are almost willing to eat the shipping cost to get it out of your store.

One day you get a brilliant idea: "Hey, why don't I link these two things and require anyone who wants to buy the popular product to buy the unpopular product as well?" Good idea, except that if you are caught you will probably go to jail for violating the antitrust laws.

When you require someone to buy Product 1 in order to buy a more desirable Product 2, you are engaged in a "tying" transaction that violates the antitrust laws. A "tying" violation also occurs if you give your customers a discount on the more desirable Product 2 if they purchase Product 1, although it is less likely the antitrust authorities will enforce the rules in this case, since your customers still have a "choice" (i.e., they can either pay full price for Product 2 or get the discount by buying Product 1, too). The worst kind of "tying" violation occurs when you refuse to sell the more desirable Product 2 unless the buyer buys Product 1 as well.

➤ _Resale Price Maintenance._ If you are buying stuff from a wholesaler to sell on eBay and the wholesaler insists that you _must_ charge $XXX to your retail buyers, or you _must_ set your price within a specified price range, this is called "resale price maintenance." Basically, the antitrust laws say that a wholesaler cannot dictate the retail prices its customers can set in the open market. It is, however, okay for wholesalers to establish a "suggested retail price" to help retailers in their pricing, as long as the wholesaler doesn't refuse to do business with a retailer who refuses to go along with the suggested pricing.

➤ _Allocating Market Territories._ Picture in your mind a smoke-filled room with a bunch of gangsters right out of _The Godfather_ movies sitting around the table. The guy at the head of the table says to the others, "Okay, we got a pretty big city here, so there's plenty of room for all of us to make money. Louie, you take the South Side; Iggy, you take the North Side; Scarface, you take the East Side; and I'll take the West Side. As long as we stay out of each other's turf, there will no need for anyone to get excited." That's "allocating market territories" in a nutshell. Don't do it.

➤ _Unfair Trade Practices._ It's really hard to define an unfair trade practice, but you know one when you see one. Generally, unfair trade practices happen when some retailers or wholesalers get better deals than others, for reasons that cannot be justified by basic economics. So, for example, a wholesaler charges $10 a unit for Product X to its retailers but charges $15 a unit to you (for the same number of units—"volume discounts" are absolutely okay) because the wholesaler doesn't like the fact you are selling Product X on eBay.

Every state has an unfair trade practices law that normally consists of two sections. The first section of the law says (not in so many words, of course): "From this date forward unfair trade practices are illegal in the State of X." Yay! Raise the flag! Hard to argue with that, right? Then comes the second section: "Rather than define exactly what an unfair trade practice is, we will leave it up to the courts of the State of X to determine, on a case-by-case basis, the type of conduct that will violate this statute."

What that means is that you cannot figure out whether something is an "unfair trade practice" unless you hire an attorney who is familiar with all of the "unfair trade practice" cases that have been decided in your state and can give you a sense of how likely it is the something will be viewed as an "unfair trade practice." Even then, unless your state courts have identified the specific practice as an "unfair trade practice," anything the attorney tells you will be an educated guess, at best, and you will be taking a legal risk if you proceed with your plans. Frankly, I think your odds are better in Vegas. If you are tempted to do something and your attorney indicates there is even a slight chance it might be considered an unfair trade practice in your state, my advice is simply forget about doing it.

COMMON QUESTIONS

Q. *I have a great name for my business and don't want somebody else ripping it off. I don't want to spend thousands of dollars getting a federal trademark, though. Is there anything else I can do?*

A. Yes. You can put the letters TM next to your name. This is what lawyers call a common law trademark, and it says to someone: "I may not be able to register this name as a federal trademark, but I sure as hell look at it as a trademark, and if you even *think* about using it yourself in a similar business, I will be all over you like flies on dog poop!"

Do not, however, under any circumstances use the registration symbol (®) unless you have actually registered the name as a federal trademark. That's actually a federal crime and can land you in jail.

Q. *A number of us eBay sellers buy from the same vendor. Lately we learned that, although we all live in the same area and we all buy pretty much the* *same amount of stuff at any given time, the vendor has been charging one of us a different price. Can the vendor do that?*

A. Probably not. If it is intended to injure competition, or if it has that effect, discriminating in price is prohibited by federal antitrust law. Sellers are not allowed to charge two purchasers different prices for the same product, unless it is for a lawful purpose. For instance, a sale to dispose of damaged or perishable goods, or a "volume discount" to a retailer who buys large quantities of goods, is not considered price discrimination. On the other hand, it is unlawful for a petroleum distributor to offer the petroleum at a discount to one particular gas station but not make the same offer to everyone else.

Tools and Resources

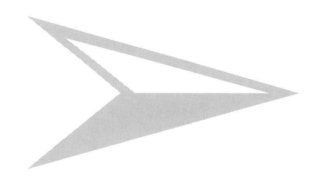

Legal and Tax Resources for eBay Sellers

BOOKS AND PUBLICATIONS

Legal Topics

This is the first book to deal exclusively with the legal issues of eBay sellers. There are a fair number of "small business law for the layman" books out there, and some of them, especially those published by the Nolo Press (www.nolo.com) are fairly good if all you want is general information about the law. However, you need to know that:

➢ None of them are eBay-specific and will contain lots of information that won't apply to your business.

➢ Much of the law differs from state to state, and you will need a good local attorney to explain to you how the "general rules" described in these books differ from the particular statutes you will have to comply with in your state.

I always ask my clients: Do you want to become a legal expert, or do you want to run your business? While a general knowledge of the law can help you anticipate legal problems before they become too serious, don't become obsessed with it. If you have a choice between a good "law book" and a book about creative new ways to source product for your eBay business, hire a good attorney to explain the law to you and buy the product sourcing book.

Tax Topics

When it comes to tax law, there is no substitute for going directly to the source. The Internal Revenue Service (IRS) publishes a number of resources that deal with specific tax topics in considerable detail. While not always the easiest literature to read, they have the advantage of being accurate and up to date (most of the time), and they all have lots and lots of specific examples and illustrations to help you figure out exactly where your business fits into the scheme of things. The most useful IRS publications for eBay sellers are:

> ➤ IRS Publication 15, "Employer's Tax Guide"
> ➤ IRS Publication 334, "Tax Guide for Small Business"
> ➤ IRS Publication 463, "Travel, Entertainment, Gift, and Car Expenses"
> ➤ IRS Publication 505, "Tax Withholding and Estimated Tax"
> ➤ IRS Publication 535, "Business Expenses"
> ➤ IRS Publication 587, "Business Use of Your Home"

All IRS publications are available as free downloads from the IRS website (www.irs.gov). Just click on Forms and Publications for a complete listing of publications by number.

In addition, there are three "private label" tax books worth investing in:

422 Tax Deductions for Businesses and Self-Employed Individuals, by Bernard B. Kamoroff, CPA (Willits, CA: Bell Springs Publishing, $18.95). Whenever you need a quick answer to whether something is deductible or not, this is the all-time classic.

J. K. Lasser's 1001 Deductions and Tax Breaks: The Complete Guide to Everything Deductible, by Barbara Weltman (New York: John Wiley & Sons, $16.95). Much more thorough than Kamoroff's book, although not as easy to read. Be sure to use only the current version, since this book is updated every few years to reflect changes in the tax law.

Tax Loopholes for eBay Sellers, by Diane Kennedy and Janelle Elms (New York: McGraw-Hill, $24.95). Focuses on deductible expenses and tax planning strategies for the more sophisticated eBay seller.

Newsletters, Magazines, and Newspaper Columns

The eBay Seller's News, published by eBay PowerSeller Skip McGrath of Anacortes, Washington, is a free monthly e-mail newsletter. To sign up, go to www.auction-sellers-resource.com. You'll probably find out more about McGrath's other information products as well, especially as your business grows beyond the "occasional sales" stage.

Entrepreneur magazine publishes a special "eBay Startup Guide" once a year, usually in the spring, right before the annual eBay Live! convention. It contains many useful legal, tax, and other articles that are custom-tailored for the eBay community. To order the current issue for $3.99, go to www.entrepreneur.com, click on the Magazine Subscriptions link, and click on the "Click Here to Order Entrepreneur's eBay Startup Guide" prompt.

The author of the book you are reading, Cliff Ennico, has his own weekly syndicated newspaper column, "Succeeding in Your Business." Known as the "Ann Landers of the business world," he frequently responds to legal and tax-related e-mail questions from eBay sellers. For this week's column, go to www.entrepreneur.com (the website of *Entrepreneur* magazine) and type "Ennico" into the search engine box. To find all of the author's past eBay-related columns, type in the search "Ennico eBay."

SOFTWARE PRODUCTS

eBay Accounting Assistant is probably the best single accounting or bookkeeping software program for eBay sellers. It integrates with QuickBooks and is available from eBay for free if you have a subscription to eBay Stores, Blackthorne, Blackthorne Pro, Selling Manager, or Selling Manager Pro.

KeepMore.net is a full-service online bookkeeping, accounting, and tax preparation software program that lives on the Internet, not on your personal computer. It is available for a monthly subscription of $19.95, an annual subscription of $199, or a "lifetime" subscription of $999. (For more information, go to www.keepmore.net.)

TurboTax Personal and Business for eBay Sellers helps you handle your entire federal and state tax return, including Schedule C (for income from online selling and other businesses) and any income from investments, retirement, and rental properties. Available for $59.95 (federal return) plus $29.95 (state return). For more information, go to www.taxcenter.turbotax.com/taxproducts/turbotaxebay.

TurboTax Expense Pro is designed to help eBay sellers (and others) keep track of their deductible business expenses. Great for Schedule C filers who don't want to use TurboTax Personal and Business for eBay Sellers to prepare their entire tax return. For more information, go to www.turbotax.com and type "Expense Pro" into the site's search engine.

INTUIT'S "EBAY TAX CENTER"

Intuit Corp., which publishes the Quicken, QuickBooks, and TurboTax software products for small businesses, has spent a lot of time and money creating a Tax Center for eBay Sellers. Here, you'll find a wealth of tax-related information and answers to specific tax questions.

Intuit also has a team of "tax experts" (mostly CPAs) based in Omaha, Nebraska who spend all their time answering tax questions raised by TurboTax users—for free. Go to the main site at www.taxcenter.turbotax.com, and click on the Ask an Expert prompt.

"DO IT YOURSELF" INCORPORATION WEBSITES

Before using any do-it-yourself site to set up your eBay selling business, be sure to reread Chapter 2, as very few Web resources can provide the services that a good local attorney or accountant can.

Having said that, two incorporation sites stand out from the pack:

> ➤ BizFilings.com, based in Madison, Wisconsin (800-981-7183)
> ➤ MyCorporation.com, based in Calabasas, California (888-692-6771), which is owned by Intuit Corp., the maker of the TurboTax software

GOING TO THE SOURCE: EBAY'S WEBSITE

The "Community" Section on eBay

For the reasons listed in the Introduction to this book, eBay does not like to give legal and tax advice to its community members, or endorse anyone who does (including me). If you click on the Community tab on eBay's home page you will be exposed to a wealth of information about just about every aspect of doing business on eBay, but you won't see a discussion board or chat room devoted to legal and tax topics.

That, of course, will not stop the eBay community from seeking free legal and tax advice online. If you comb through the discussion boards, chat rooms, and answer center carefully enough, you will find hundreds of postings from eBay members dealing with legal and tax issues. Be careful, though. Most of the information in eBay's Community section is being posted by eBay sellers who do not have a professional legal or tax background, and much of the legal and tax advice you will find here is misleading or just plain *wrong* (although sincere and well-intentioned). Generally, you shouldn't follow any advice you get from eBay's Community pages without confirming it first with a local attorney or accountant.

ONE EXCEPTION: You can find some decent legal and tax information in the eBay Community Workshops. Go to the eBay home page, click on the Community tab, then Discussion Boards. Follow the right-hand column about halfway down the page and click on the Workshops prompt. You will see a list of online workshops hosted by some of the best eBay and e-commerce experts in the United States. The eBay Community Workshops dealing with legal and tax issues are probably the best and most reliable source of legal and tax information on the eBay website. (Full disclosure: Quite a few are hosted by the author of this book.)

THE "HELP" SECTION ON EBAY

Go to the eBay home page, click on the Help tab, and you will find extensive information about doing business properly on eBay. This is by far the best place to keep on top of eBay's many policies. Click on the Help tab, then click on the Rules and Policies prompt for a complete list of eBay's policies. Familiarizing yourself with eBay's policies and user restrictions can help you to avoid or solve a lot of legal-related problems down the road.

By clicking the Live Help prompt on eBay's home page, you can set up a dialogue with an eBay customer representative who will help you answer any question you can't answer by reviewing the site's Help section. But be forewarned: Customer reps are not lawyers or tax advisers, and they *will not* answer legal or tax questions.

THE EBAY UNIVERSITY

The education team at eBay sponsors a series of live seminars (usually on Saturdays) around the country to help eBay sellers get better at what they do. In 2005, they added an "eBay for Business" program (taught in part by the author of this book) to help eBay sellers with their legal, tax, and organizational questions. To find out when this program will be offered in your area, go to http://pages.ebay .com/university/classes.html and click on Choose a City under the eBay for Business course description.

The annual eBay Live! convention also features many programs on legal, tax, and other issues eBay sellers have to deal with. To find out where this year's convention will be held, go to www.ebay.com/ebaylive. It's not free, but the cost of attending eBay Live! is a deductible business expense (see Chapter 9).

FINDING A LOCAL PROFESSIONAL

When you get right down to it, there is absolutely no substitute for finding a good accountant *and* a good business lawyer (you need both) to help you with one-on-one advice that's tailored to your specific needs.

How to find one?

For lawyers, it's easy: You can go to www.findlaw.com, click on Search for Local Lawyers and follow the prompts. (Here's a tip: When selecting the "type of practice" choose "Internet law—cyberspace" rather than "corporate law"—that will get you closer to a business lawyer who is comfortable dealing with e-commerce issues).

Or you can contact your local bar association. Just about every county in the United States has one, and sometimes for a small fee, the local bar association will provide a list of small business lawyers with offices in your zip code.

Now, what about finding a good accountant? By selling on eBay you are, by definition, a "retailer." Why not introduce yourself to several brick-and-mortar retailers in your area and ask them which accountants they use? That's often the best way.

You can also contact your state's society of certified public accountants. Type "[your state] CPA society" into your favorite search engine to find its website. Every state has a society of CPAs, and some societies even have a "find a CPA" feature on their websites, allowing you to search for accountants by zip code.

You can also go to www.cpadirectory.com, the largest online database of CPAs in the United States. (Tip: When filling in the search boxes, select Small Business for "services provided," and Electronic Commerce for "industries serviced.")

When it comes to finding good local professionals, nothing beats good old-fashioned word-of-mouth. One of the best ways to find good professionals to help you build your eBay business is to get other eBay members in your area to recommend good attorneys and accountants. Go to the eBay home page, click on the Community tab, then click on Group Center. From there, click on Regional, then click on your state. Select the largest eBay "group" within your state and post a question asking for referrals of local lawyers and accountants who have done good work for other eBay members. Be sure to include your town and city name as well as your zip code. If the same name crops up more than once, this lawyer or accountant is probably the best candidate.

Sample "Terms and Conditions" for eBay Auction Pages

[NOTE: When preparing an eBay auction page, you are allowed to fill in certain information about your sales policies. To make sure nothing has been overlooked, though, consider adding this "General Terms and Conditions" section to all of your eBay auction pages.]

GENERAL TERMS AND CONDITIONS

Unless we state otherwise on a particular eBay auction page, all of _____'s eBay auctions are subject to the following general terms and conditions. PLEASE DO NOT BID on any of our items without first reading these terms and conditions, as once you have placed a bid you will be bound by them.

Condition; Item Description. We have done our best to reveal the material condition of the offered piece in sufficient detail. We are not experts in this type of merchandise; accordingly, if any item is not "as described" in our auction page, your sole recourse is to ask for a refund under our "Return and Refund Policy," described below. In no event will we be responsible for any defects in condition that are either disclosed in our item description or are clearly depicted in our auction photos. WE DISCLAIM ANY AND ALL WARRANTIES, EXPRESS OR IMPLIED, REGARDING ANY ITEM SOLD ON EBAY, INCLUDING BUT NOT LIMITED TO THE WARRANTIES OF MERCHANTABILITY AND FITNESS FOR A PARTICULAR PURPOSE.

Photos. We are not professional photographers. Colors may appear slightly different to each bidder due to individual monitor settings on your personal computer. For that

305

reason, colors may vary slightly between what you see on your screen and the product you receive. We are not responsible for slight variations in color, and will not accept returns based on this except in extraordinary circumstances where it can be clearly proven that the discrepancy was our fault.

Return and Refund Policy. If you feel an item has been incorrectly described on our auction page, please e-mail us within _____ (____) days after the auction closing and explain why you feel that way. If we agree, you will return the item to us in exactly the condition it was in when we delivered it to a "common carrier," including all original tags. When we receive the item back from you, we will refund your winning bid amount, less sales tax, shipping, and delivery charges, promptly but in no event later than _____ (____) days after we receive the item. If any item is returned to us in a condition different from the condition it was in when we delivered it to a "common carrier," or if we believe in good faith that the item returned is not the same as the item we shipped to you, we will notify you and return the item to you without a refund.

Except for the above return and refund policy, ALL SALES ARE FINAL. Requests for returns or refunds made after _____ (____) days following an auction closing date will be honored only in our sole discretion based on compelling evidence that we were at fault.

Payment. Unless we indicate otherwise in a particular auction page, we accept personal checks, cashiers' or bank checks, money orders (bank or U.S. Postal Service), and PayPal. Orders paid by personal check will not ship until your check clears—normally this will take twenty (20) days, but we will ship sooner if our bank notifies us that your check has cleared. Interest on all payments not received within _____ (_____) days after an auction closing date will bear interest at eighteen percent (18%) per annum or the highest rate allowed by the law of the State of _____, if less.

Shipping and Handling Charges. The winning bidder, if located in the United States, will pay a "shipping and handling charge" of $_____ for priority mail, delivery confirmation, highly protective packaging, and loving handling. This fee is based on our actual costs of shipping and handling, and complies with all eBay policies regarding such fees. The winning bidder, if located outside of the United States, will pay the actual shipping charges we incur, which must be paid in full before we ship. If you have a preferred method of delivery, we will be happy to use it as long as you let us know within _____ (____) days after an auction closes and agree to pay the fee charged by that carrier. Otherwise we will use the carrier we are most comfortable using based on our prior experience with similar items.

Shipping Schedule. We typically ship _____ times a week, but all overnight packages will go out within _____ business days of receipt of payment.

Insurance. We offer insurance as an option on all of our auctions. If we do not offer insurance as an option on any auction, you may nonetheless ask us to insure delivery for an additional fee. We will determine the additional fee and notify you before shipping. We will not refund your money if items are lost, damaged, or destroyed in transit unless you buy insurance (see below).

Risk of Loss. We pack all items with great care, and will assume all risk of loss until we deliver the item to a "common carrier" (such as the U.S. Postal Service, UPS, Federal Express, or Airborne Courier). In the unlikely event that the item is lost, damaged, or destroyed before we deliver it to a "common carrier," our only liability or obligation to you will be to refund promptly any monies we have received from you. In such event you agree not to post "negative" or "neutral" feedback for the transaction, and neither will we. We will provide proof of delivery to a "common carrier" to you upon your request, along with tracking numbers if the "common carrier" has given them to us.

At the moment we deliver the item to a "common carrier," risk of loss in the item shifts from us to you. This means that you, from that moment forward, assume any risk of loss to the item from any cause or circumstance whatsoever, whether or not within your control. We strongly recommend that you purchase insurance for items over $_____ or whatever amount represents an unacceptable loss to you, because if you opt not to insure, WE WILL NOT BE RESPONSIBLE FOR ANY LOSS, THEFT, OR DAMAGE TO ANY ITEM AFTER DELIVERING THE ITEM TO A "COMMON CARRIER" AS DESCRIBED ABOVE.

Sales and Use Taxes. State and local sales taxes will be added to your winning bid if you live in any of the following states: _____ , _____ , and _____ . If you believe in good faith that you are exempt from sales tax, we will not waive sales tax unless you furnish to us a completed and signed "resale exemption certificate" in the form required by your state's tax authority.

Note to Overseas (Non-U.S.) Buyers. Your purchase may be subject to Value-Added Tax (VST), General Sales Tax (GST), customs duties, and other taxes, payments, and impositions required by the law of your country. Please consult with your accountant or tax adviser before bidding in any of our auctions. The laws of your country may prohibit you from buying or importing our items; be sure to check with your attorney before bidding on any item that may be illegal in your country. We are not a "commercial vendor" in any country other than the United States of America, and are accordingly not obligated to comply with any laws, rules, license requirements, or regulations in your country unless we are advised otherwise by our legal counsel. All payments must be made in U.S. Dollars, and we will not accept any other currency. The U.N. Convention on Contracts for the International Sale of Goods shall not apply to any of our auctions or sales on eBay.

Restricted Bidders. We will not honor bids from eBay members with a feedback rating of less than _____ or a feedback rating that is less than ____% positive. We will not honor bids from residents of the following countries: _____ , _____ , and _____ . We will reject bids from any person who was a "nonpaying buyer" (see below) in any of our previous auctions. If you fall into any of these categories, please do not bid on any of our items.

Bid Retractions. Once you have placed a bid in one of our auctions, "your bid is a legal contract" and you may not retract it for any reason without our permission, which we may withhold in our sole discretion. Please DO NOT BID until you have all of the information you need about an item; if you have already bid on an item before requesting additional information, you will not be allowed to retract your bid based on the additional information we provide you.

Nonpaying Buyers. We do not tolerate nonpaying buyers (NPBs). If you are the winning bidder and you fail to contact us within _____ days after an auction closes, or if you fail to tender all funds due to us within _____ days after an auction closes, we will presume you are a nonpaying buyer, your purchase will be canceled, you will receive "negative feedback" from us on eBay's Feedback Forum, and you will be barred from ever bidding again on our auctions.

If you are planning to go on an extended vacation or business trip when the auction closes and will not be able to communicate with us within the above time periods, please contact us in advance and let us know so that we do not mistakenly treat you as a nonpaying buyer.

Auction Termination. We reserve the right to terminate any auction prior to the closing date for any reason. In that event we will notify each bidder, and let them know whether and when the item will be reposted. If an auction ends at any time during any eBay outage (regardless of eBay policy or classification), the auction will be canceled and the item reposted at a later time. In that event we will use our best efforts to notify all bidders via e-mail of the new auction posting.

Communications to Seller. All communications to us should be sent to the following e-mail address: _____. We will use our best efforts to respond to all e-mail communications within twenty-four (24) hours of receipt. Any additional information we provide you about a particular item may, at our discretion, be posted to our auction page or otherwise made public for the benefit of all bidders.

Disputes. In the event of any dispute involving one of our eBay auctions, you agree to submit the dispute to eBay's SquareTrade mediation service before leaving "negative" or "neutral" feedback for us on eBay's Feedback Forum or pursuing any other legal remedy. By bidding in any of our auctions, you irrevocably agree that any dispute, conflict, or controversy between you and _____ [name of seller] will take place only in a court of law located in _____ County, State of _____ , United States of America, and will be governed by the laws of the State of _____ that apply to contracts between residents of that State.

Employment "Offer Letter" for Part-Time/Temporary Employee

Cliff's Antiques, Inc.
[Address]

[*Date*]
[*Name and Address of Employee*]
Dear Mr./Ms. [*Name*]:

We are pleased to offer you a part-time/temporary position with [*Name of Employer*] ("Employer") as [*title of position*]. Specifics of our offer are as follows:

1. You will be employed by Employer on a part-time basis subject to the terms of this letter, with monthly performance reviews, and shall have the title of [*title of position*].

2. You will work on _____ and _____ [days of week, for example, "Monday, Wednesday, and Friday"] of each week, except holidays, for _____ (___) hours each day beginning at _____ A.M. and ending on _____ P.M. If you wish to reschedule your working hours or days, you must obtain the approval of [*name of immediate supervisor*] in advance. You will perform such tasks as shall be assigned by [*name of immediate supervisor*] and such tasks as are usually and customarily performed by persons holding the title of [*title of position*].

3. You will be compensated at the rate of _____ dollars ($_____) per hour (or per day), before withholding of federal and state income taxes, Social Security, Medicare, unemployment insurance, and other customary deductions, payable on Friday of each week. You will not be paid for holidays or any day on which you did not actually perform work.

4. You will not be entitled to vacation, sick days, or personal days with pay during the term of your employment. All requests for unpaid time off (other than holidays observed by all of Employer's employees) must be approved in advance by [*name of immediate supervisor*].

5. You will be entitled to participate in such employee benefits, if any, as Employer offers to all of its part-time employees, but Employer is not obligated to provide any such benefits at any time. If Employer requests that you travel as part of your duties, you will be reimbursed for _____ percent (_____%) of your reasonable and documented travel and living expenses incurred in the course of your employment, but any expense in excess of _____ dollars ($_____) must be approved in advance by [*name of immediate supervisor*].

6. You will be employed on an "AT WILL" basis. That is, the terms of your employment shall continue unless terminated by either you or Employer. Termination by Employer may be with or without cause, at any time. The terminating party shall give the other party three working days' notice prior to any termination. Employer reserves the right to pay the equivalent of three days of your salary in lieu of this notice requirement.

7. All work that you perform for Employer will be performed in our offices or as mutually agreed otherwise.

8. Your employment is to be considered exclusive to Employer. While you are employed by Employer, you will not engage in any employment or other activity that would conflict with your obligations to Employer, and you will not work for any individual or company that directly or indirectly competes with Employer.

9. During the course of your employment you will learn information about the Employer, its products, services, suppliers, and customers that the Employer desires to be kept strictly confidential at all times. You agree that, during your employment and at all times thereafter, you will not disclose any such information to anyone other than Employer, or use such information in any way other than to perform your duties for Employer. You also agree that during the term of your employment and for a period of two (2) years afterward, you will not solicit or accept business from any of our vendors whose identities you learned about while you were an employee of ours. Your agreements in this paragraph 9 will survive the termination of your employment for any reason, and may be enforced by Employer at any time during or after the term of your employment.

10. This Agreement is governed by the laws of the State of [*name of state*], and you agree that any action, claim, lawsuit, or proceeding relating to this Agreement will be commenced exclusively in the courts of the State of _____ located in _____ County.

If the terms of this offer are acceptable to you, please indicate below by signing and returning one copy of this letter to us. This offer is conditioned upon a satisfactory check of your references.

Mr./Ms. [*Name*], we are looking forward to having you join [*Name of Employer*], and are sure that you will find your new career challenging and rewarding.

Sincerely,
[*Name of Company*]
By: [*Name of Signatory*]
Signature: _____
ACCEPTED AND AGREED TO AS OF: [*Date*]
[*Name of Employee*]
Signature: _____
Social Security No.: _____

Agreement for Consignment Sales on eBay

THIS AGREEMENT is made as of ＿＿＿＿＿＿＿, 20＿ between Cliff's Antiques, Inc., a corporation organized and existing under the laws of the State of ＿＿＿＿＿＿ having an office at ＿＿＿＿＿＿＿ ("Cliff's Antiques"), and ＿＿＿＿＿＿, an individual residing at ＿＿＿＿＿＿＿ ("you" or "Seller").

1. **Services.** By signing this Agreement you authorize Cliff's Antiques to provide the following services in accordance with the terms and conditions of this Agreement: to (i) receive and store the goods more particularly described on the attached Exhibit "A" (the "Goods"); (ii) list, offer, and sell the Goods on eBay; (iii) deliver the Goods to the buyer, if any; (iv) collect the sales price from the buyer; (v) deduct Cliff's Antiques' sales fee; and (vi) forward the remainder of the sales price to Seller in accordance with the terms below (collectively, the "Services").

2. **Binding Bids.** Cliff's Antiques will list the Goods for sale on eBay in such manner as Cliff's Antiques may determine in its sole discretion. Seller is obligated to complete the transaction with the highest bidder upon the listing's completion, unless there is an exceptional circumstance, such as (a) the buyer fails or refuses to pay for the Goods, or (b) Cliff's Antiques cannot authenticate the buyer's identity. In such event, Seller authorizes Cliff's Antiques to relist the Goods for sale on eBay in such manner as Cliff's Antiques may determine in its sole discretion.

3. **Unsold Goods.** Should the Goods fail to sell after being listed on eBay, Seller hereby authorizes Cliff's Antiques to relist such unsold Goods ("Unsold Goods") on eBay at such time and in such manner as Cliff's Antiques may determine in its sole discretion. If, in its sole discretion, Cliff's Antiques determines at any time that any Unsold Goods cannot be sold on eBay, Cliff's Antiques may terminate this Agreement with respect to such Unsold Goods only and require that Seller pick them up at Cliff's Antiques' business address at ＿＿＿＿＿＿ during business hours. Seller shall pick up any such Goods

within _____ (_____) working days after receipt of notification from Cliff's Antiques that such Goods have failed to sell. Seller agrees that if Seller fails to pick up any such Unsold Goods within _____ (_____) working days, Cliff's Antiques will deliver the goods to the Seller at Seller's expense. The parties agree that Cliff's Antiques will be entitled to a minimum fee of _____ dollars ($_____) per listing, for listing any Unsold Goods under this Agreement ("Breakage Fee"), and that Breakage Fee may be deducted from the proceeds of sale of any of the other Goods or invoiced to Seller each month; each such invoice to be payable within _____ (_____) days of receipt by Seller.

4. **Payment to Seller.** As consideration for the Services, Seller agrees Cliff's Antiques will be entitled to collect a sales fee ("Sales Fee") according to the following formula: either (i) _____ percent (_____%) of the first $_____ of the price for which the Goods are sold on eBay (the "Sales Price"), plus _____ percent (_____%) of the next $_____ of the Sales Price, plus _____ percent (_____%) of the remaining Sales Price over $_____; or (ii) _____ dollars ($_____), whichever amount is greater, plus the applicable fees charged by eBay and PayPal, both of which can be found on their respective websites. Following receipt by Cliff's Antiques of the Sales Price from the winning bidder ("Buyer"), Cliff's Antiques is authorized by Seller to deduct the Sales Fee from the monies received and forward the remainder to Seller, at the address listed at the beginning of this Agreement, within _____ (_____) days from the date of receipt of the Sale Price of the last item that sells from the consignment of Goods contemplated by this Agreement.

5. **Fund-Raising Program.** Seller has the option of requiring Cliff's Antiques to donate a portion of the Sales Price of each of the Goods, not to exceed _____%, to charity under eBay's "Giving Works" program. By choosing this option, the Seller acknowledges that (i) Cliff's Antiques is not a charitable organization; (ii) Cliff's Antiques is not providing tax advice to the Seller, and the Seller is expected to rely on his own tax adviser as to all tax effects of such donations on the Seller; (iii) the Seller is relying on the certification of the chosen organization as to its qualifying as a charitable organization and not on Cliff's Antiques in that regard; and (iv) Cliff's Antiques will not provide an acknowledgment as to any special status for tax-reporting purposes but only evidence that it made a payment to the desired organization on the Seller's behalf, and the Seller must rely on receiving a written acknowledgment from the charity directly if it needs or wants one.

6. **Bailment Relationship.** The relationship between Cliff's Antiques and the Seller is that of bailor and bailee, in which the bailor (Seller) deposits his personal property (Goods) with the bailee (Cliff's Antiques) for the purpose of listing and selling the Goods to third parties through eBay. Nothing contained herein will be construed as creating any agency, partnership, employment, or other form of joint enterprise between the parties.

7. **Title and Risk of Loss.** Title and risk of loss for the Goods remains with Seller until such time as the Goods are delivered to a carrier for delivery to the Buyer. Title and risk of loss will not transfer to Cliff's Antiques at any time. Title to Goods shipped will pass directly from Seller to Buyer.

8. **Seller's Warranty of Goods.** Seller warrants that (i) Seller has all the necessary rights and authorization to produce and distribute the Goods and to permit Cliff's Antiques to offer, sell, and deliver the Goods to any third party; (ii) the Goods and the rights

granted under this Agreement do not infringe the proprietary or intellectual property rights of any third party; and (iii) all descriptions of the Goods set forth on Exhibit "A" are truthful, accurate, and complete in all respects. Seller represents and warrants that description of the Goods and that the Goods will not: Be false, inaccurate, or misleading; Be fraudulent or involve the sale of counterfeit or stolen items; Violate any law, statute, ordinance, or regulation (including, but not limited to, those governing export control, consumer protection, unfair competition, antidiscrimination, or false advertising); Be defamatory, trade libelous, unlawfully threatening, obscene, or contain child pornography or be otherwise adult in nature or harmful to minors.

9. **Breach.** Without limiting other remedies, Cliff's Antiques may immediately remove all listings of the Goods from eBay, temporarily suspend, indefinitely suspend, or terminate the Services and refuse to provide future services to Seller if (i) Seller breaches this Agreement; (ii) Cliff's Antiques is unable, despite its commercially reasonable efforts, to verify or authenticate any information Seller provides to Cliff's Antiques about any of the Goods; (iii) Cliff's Antiques believes that Seller's acts or omissions may cause financial loss or legal liability for Seller or Cliff's Antiques; or (iv) Cliff's Antiques suspects that Seller (by conviction, settlement, insurance, or escrow investigation, or otherwise) has engaged in fraudulent activity or any crime involving moral turpitude in connection with the Goods, Cliff's Antiques, or eBay.

10. **Indemnity.** Seller agrees to indemnify and hold Cliff's Antiques and (as applicable) its parent, subsidiaries, affiliates, officers, directors, members, employees, and agents, harmless from any claim or demand, including but not limited to reasonable attorneys' fees and disbursements, made by any third party due, connected to or arising out of Seller's breach of this Agreement, Seller's violation of any law or the rights of any third party, or any acts or omissions of Seller in connection with the Goods or the business relationship contemplated hereby.

11. **Warranty Disclaimer.** Cliff's Antiques provides its Services "as is" and without any warranty or representation as to the Services, express, implied, or statutory. Cliff's Antiques specifically disclaims any implied warranties of title, merchantability, fitness for a particular purpose, and noninfringement. Some states do not permit a disclaimer of implied warranties, so the foregoing disclaimer may not apply to Seller.

12. **Waiver of Consequential Damages.** IN NO EVENT WILL CLIFF'S ANTIQUES BE LIABLE TO SELLER FOR ANY INCIDENTAL, CONSEQUENTIAL, EXEMPLARY, INDIRECT, SPECIAL, OR PUNITIVE DAMAGES ARISING OUT OF THIS AGREEMENT OR ITS TERMINATION, REGARDLESS OF THE FORM OF ACTION (INCLUDING NEGLIGENCE AND STRICT PRODUCT LIABILITY) AND IRRESPECTIVE OF WHETHER CLIFF'S ANTIQUES HAS BEEN ADVISED OF THE POSSIBILITY OF ANY SUCH LOSS OR DAMAGE.

13. **Liability Cap.** Cliff's Antiques' liability, and the liability of its employees, agents, and suppliers to Seller or any third parties, in any circumstance, is limited to the greater of (i) the estimated value of the applicable Goods, as stated on the attached Exhibit "A," or (ii) $100. Some states do not allow the exclusion or limitation of incidental or consequential damages, so the above limitation or exclusion may not apply to Seller.

14. **Release.** Seller releases Cliff's Antiques and eBay (and Cliff's Antiques' officers, directors, shareholders, members, employees, and agents) from any damages (actual and consequential) of every kind and nature, known and unknown, suspected and unsus-

pected, disclosed and undisclosed, arising out of, resulting from, or in any way connected with the Services, unless such damages were directly and solely caused by the willful misconduct of Cliff's Antiques, its employees, or agents.

15. **Term.** The term of this Agreement will commence upon _____ , 20___ and, unless terminated earlier in accordance with the terms of this Agreement, will continue until all Goods accepted for listing by Cliff's Antiques under this Agreement are sold and delivered, returned to Seller, or disposed of in accordance with section 3, but in no event more than _____ (_____) days from the _____, 20___. This agreement may be terminated by Cliff's Antiques without notice, for any reason or no reason, at any time.

16. **Survival of Certain Terms.** The following sections will survive the termination of this Agreement for any reason: the attached Exhibit "A," and sections 3, 5, 6, 7, 8, 9, 10, 11, 12, 13, 15, and 16. All other rights and obligations of the parties will cease upon termination of this Agreement.

17. **General.** This agreement will be governed in all respects by the laws of the United States of America and the State of _____ as such laws are applied to agreements entered into and to be performed entirely within the State of _____ between residents of such State. All notices or requests will be in writing and will be sent by fax, or signing for receipt of delivery if sent by courier. Notices will be sent to the parties at the address set forth at the beginning of this Agreement. The failure of either party to require performance by the other party of any provision hereof will not affect the full right to require such performance at any time thereafter; nor will the waiver by either party of a breach of any provision thereof be taken or held to be a waiver off the provision itself. In the event that any provision of this Agreement will be unenforceable or invalid under any application law or be so held by applicable court decisions, such unenforceability or invalidity will not render this Agreement unenforceable or invalid as a whole and, in such an event, such provisions will be changed and interpreted also as to best accomplish the objectives of such unenforceable or invalid provision within the limits of applicable law or applicable court decisions. This agreement, and the exhibits thereto, constitute the entering of an agreement between the parties with respect to the subject matter hereof. This agreement supersedes, and the terms of this Agreement govern, any prior or collateral agreements with respect to the subject matter thereof, with the exception of any prior confidentiality agreements between the parties. This Agreement may only be changed by mutual agreement of both parties in writing.

IN WITNESS WHEREOF, the parties hereto have signed this Agreement as of the first above-stated date.

Cliff's Antiques, Inc.
By: _____
    Cliff Ennico, its President
[Name of Seller]
By: _____
    Print Name: _____
    Print Social Security No.: _____ [You will need SSN in order to send the Seller
    a Form 1099 at the end of the year.]

Wholesale "Drop Shipping" Agreement

THIS WHOLESALE DROP-SHIP AGREEMENT (the "Agreement"), effective _____, 2____ ("Effective Date"), is made and entered into by and between _____ , a [corporation/partnership/limited liability company] organized and existing under the laws of the State of _____ located at _____ (the "Drop Shipper"), and _____ , a [corporation/partnership/limited liability company] organized and existing under the laws of the State of _____ located at _____ (the "eBay Seller").

RECITALS

eBay Seller desires to sell and promote the products offered by Drop Shipper, and Drop Shipper grants eBay Seller a nonexclusive license to use the product images, product descriptions, and other marketing materials that may be provided from time to time. eBay Seller agrees not to sell, convey, or otherwise distribute any images, descriptions, or marketing materials owned by Drop Shipper unless it is for the express purpose of promoting Drop Shipper's products.

NOW, THEREFORE, in consideration of the mutual covenants and conditions herein contained, and for other good and valuable consideration, the receipt and sufficiency of which are hereby acknowledged, the parties agree as follows.

1. **Term.** eBay Seller and Drop Shipper agree that the term of the Agreement shall commence on the effective date and shall continue for a period of ____ months, and will be renewed automatically for a subsequent term if notice to cancel or nonrenew is not received in writing by Drop Shipper ____ days prior to the expiration of the original term.

2. **Termination.** Either party may terminate the agreement by providing _____ days' prior written notice to the other party by regular mail or e-mail to the current address on record. Drop Shipper may terminate this Agreement immediately and declare all sums due hereunder immediately due and payable in the event of any breach by eBay Seller.

3. **Drop Shipper Provided Services.** Drop Shipper will provide a website at _____ with product images and descriptions for eBay Seller to copy and use in eBay Seller's promotional materials, website, or other means of advertising. Additionally, Drop Shipper will provide a Web-based shopping cart, payment forms, and other means for eBay Seller to purchase a product to be shipped to eBay Seller's customer.

4. **Products.** Drop Shipper agrees to manufacture or contract with manufacturers that will produce and supply goods to eBay Seller of various types, sizes, and prices. Drop Shipper agrees to maintain a sufficient supply of goods of each type, size, and price to fulfill orders placed by eBay Seller from time to time, and will notify eBay Seller when its inventory of any particular item falls below _____ units.

5. **Pricing.** Drop Shipper agrees to sell its products to eBay Seller at discounts ranging from _____% to _____% off the suggested retail price. Suggested retail prices are the prices the Drop Shipper will normally display on the website in the event retail customers wish to purchase. eBay Seller is encouraged to mark up the wholesale prices so that eBay Seller makes an acceptable profit.

6. **Advertising.** eBay Seller may advertise using Drop Shipper's product images, descriptions, or other marketing materials in any lawful manner or means while this Agreement is in force.

7. **Account Setup.** eBay Seller agrees to fill out all information required on the Retail Setup Form located at _____ [Drop Shipper's Web address], which includes a valid credit card, eBay Seller address, contact information, website, and logo. Within _____ business days, Drop Shipper will provide to eBay Seller a Login ID and initial password. eBay Seller agrees to login within _____ days and change the initial password before placing an order.

8. **Order Processing.** eBay Seller is expected to use the provided Login ID and password to login to the Drop Shipper to place orders. The eBay Seller will select the desired product(s), enter the customer's shipping address, enter in a gift message if desired, and then enter in a valid billing address and credit card information. The credit card will be authorized before any shipment occurs. After the credit card has been authorized, the order will be processed and sent to the Supplier for fulfillment. eBay Seller agrees to pay all product costs, shipping, and applicable taxes at the time of order by using a valid payment method indicated on the site. Currently, Drop Shipper accepts [types of acceptable payment], but payment methods are subject to change at any time.

9. **Shipping.** Drop Shipper will ship products in accordance with the Shipping Rates & Policy posted on the Drop Shipper website. It is understood by eBay Seller that the Shipping Rates & Policy may be amended from time to time as conditions and carrier rates change. Drop Shipper will use its best efforts to notify eBay Seller of any such changes affecting items previously ordered by eBay Seller.

10. **Use of eBay Seller's Logo.** eBay Seller grants a nonexclusive license to Drop Shipper to use its logo or a likeness of its logo on the packing materials, gift message, or

other documents shipped with an order. Drop Shipper agrees to make every attempt to include the logo in every shipment on behalf of the eBay Seller but will not be required to reship, cancel, or reimburse in the event a shipment is made without eBay Seller's logo.

11. **Substitutions.** Drop Shipper will make its best efforts to supply products as represented on the Drop Shipper's website. Drop Shipper, however, will occasionally substitute ingredients, packing materials, containers, or decorations, when necessary, to fill an order for a product. Drop Shipper will not be required to make an adjustment in price for eBay Seller or communicate substitutions. Drop Shipper will attempt to use a higher-value item or items when it is necessary to substitute.

12. **Billing.** eBay Seller authorizes Drop Shipper to charge the Credit Card submitted via the Retail Signup Form for any fees, interest, charges, or chargebacks incurred by eBay Seller under this Agreement. Decline of any supplied credit card will result in the loss of eBay Seller's wholesale discount or, at Drop Shipper's sole discretion, will result in immediate termination of this Agreement.

13. **Setup Fees.** eBay Seller agrees to pay a setup fee in the amount of $_____ in order to establish a wholesale account with Drop Shipper.

14. **Monthly Fees.** There are no monthly fees associated with maintaining a wholesale account with the Drop Shipper, except in the event that eBay Seller fails to order more than $_____ of product from the Drop Shipper website each month. In the event that eBay Seller fails to order more than $_____ in a month, for that month the difference between what was ordered and $_____ shall be due and charged to the credit card on file within _____ days of the end of the month.

15. **Sales Taxes.** Drop Shipper will make its best efforts to collect and remit to the proper taxing authority all sales taxes for Internet sales that ship to a _____ [state] address, where applicable. eBay Seller agrees to collect, report, and remit all taxes to the correct tax authority for all business transactions, sales, or revenue stemming from its activities. eBay Seller further agrees that Drop Shipper is not obligated to determine whether a sales tax applies and is not responsible to collect, report, or remit any tax information arising from any transaction outside of _____ [state].

16. **Return Policy.** Drop Shipper will honor returns to its Returns Center for _____ days from the date of receipt during which customer may return undamaged and unused product for any reason. All returns must be sent to "Returns Center," located at _____ [address] at the customer's expense. For deliveries that are refused for any reason other than errors clearly attributed to Drop Shipper, there will be a $_____ minimum charge per order deducted from the refund credit to be issued to eBay Seller. Return credits will be issued within _____ to _____ days of the return to the credit card used for the original purchase.

17. **Incorrect Order Records.** If the apartment/suite number is not included or a bad postal code is provided and reshipping is required, there will be a reshipping charge equal to and in addition to the original shipping charge added to the eBay Seller's credit card. There will be a $_____ restocking fee for all packages returned to Drop Shipper because of a bad address being supplied.

18. **Participation.** Drop Shipper shall have the right to deny participation to any applicant or eBay Seller in this wholesale drop-ship program for any reason.

19. **Limitation of Liability.** Drop Shipper shall in no way be liable to eBay Seller for any use of images, text, or marketing advice provided by Drop Shipper. eBay Seller attests to having independently evaluated the desirability of participating in Drop Shipper's wholesale/drop-shipping program and is not relying on any representation, guarantee, or statement other than what has been set forth in this Agreement. Drop Shipper will not be liable for indirect, special, or consequential damages, or any loss of revenue, profits, or data arising in connection with this Agreement, even if Drop Shipper has been advised of the possibility of such damages. Further, Drop Shipper's aggregate liability arising with respect to this Agreement will not exceed the total commissions paid or payable to eBay Seller under this Agreement. In addition, we make no representation or warranty that the operation of Drop Shipper's website will be uninterrupted or error-free, and we will not be liable for the consequences of any interruptions or errors.

20. **Publicity.** eBay Seller shall not create, publish, distribute, or permit any written material that makes reference to Drop Shipper without first submitting such material to Drop Shipper and receiving its consent.

21. **Confidentiality.** Except as otherwise provided in this Agreement or with the consent of the other party, each of the parties agrees that all information, including, without limitation, the terms of this Agreement, business and financial information, customer and vendor lists, and pricing and sales information, concerning Drop Shipper or eBay Seller, respectively, shall remain strictly confidential and secret and shall not be utilized, directly or indirectly, by such party for its own business purposes or for any other purpose, except and solely to the extent that any such information is generally known or available to the public through a source or sources other than such party hereto or its distributors.

22. **Independent Contractors.** Drop Shipper and eBay Seller are independent contractors and nothing in this Agreement will create any partnership, joint venture, agency, franchise, sales representative, or employment relationship between the parties. eBay Seller will have no authority to make or accept any offers or representations on Drop Shipper's behalf.

23. **Representations and Warranties of eBay Seller.** eBay Seller hereby represents and warrants to Drop Shipper as follows:
   (a) This Agreement has been duly and validly executed and delivered by eBay Seller and constitutes eBay Seller's legal, valid, and binding obligation, enforceable against eBay Seller in accordance with its terms.
   (b) The development, operation, and contents of eBay Seller's website does not infringe upon the copyright, trademark, or any other right of any person or entity.

24. **Independent Investigation.** eBay Seller acknowledges that it has read this Agreement and agrees to all its terms and conditions. eBay Seller understands that Drop Shipper may at any time (directly or indirectly) solicit customer referrals on terms that may differ from those contained in this Agreement or operate websites that are similar

to or compete with eBay Seller's website. eBay Seller has independently evaluated the desirability of entering into this Agreement and is not relying on any representation, guarantee, or statement other than as set forth in this Agreement.

25. **Assignment.** This Agreement and the rights and obligations hereunder may not be assigned by eBay Seller without prior written consent of eBay Seller.

26. **Reservation of Rights.** Drop Shipper reserves the right to monitor eBay Seller's websites and auction listings at any time to determine whether they are in compliance with this Agreement.

27. **Governing Law; Venue.** This Agreement will be governed by the laws of the United States and the State of _____, without reference to rules governing choice of laws. Any action relating to this Agreement must be brought in the federal or state courts located in the State of _____, and eBay Seller irrevocably consents to the jurisdiction of such courts. eBay Seller may not assign this Agreement, by operation of law or otherwise, without Drop Shipper's prior written consent. Subject to that restriction, this Agreement will be binding on, inure to the benefit of, and enforceable against the parties and their respective successors and assigns. Drop Shipper's failure to enforce eBay Seller's strict performance of any provision of this Agreement will not constitute a waiver of Drop Shipper's right to subsequently enforce such a provision or any other provision of this Agreement.

28. **Modifications to Agreement.** Drop Shipper retains the right to modify this Agreement at any time. If any modification is unacceptable to eBay Seller, upon _____ days' prior written notice eBay Seller may terminate the agreement. Continued participation will constitute acceptance of the modifications.

29. **Severability.** If any provision or section of this Agreement shall be deemed unlawful, void, or for any reason unenforceable, then that provision or section shall be deemed severable from these terms and conditions and shall not affect the validity and enforceability of any remaining provisions.

30. **Miscellaneous.** This Agreement is governed by _____ [state] law, and may not be extended, amended, or changed in any way except by a written instrument signed by both eBay Seller and Drop Shipper. This Agreement contains the entire agreement of the parties relating to the services eBay Seller will provide the Drop Shipper, and supersedes any and all prior and contemporaneous agreements and understandings relating thereto.

IN WITNESS WHEREOF, the parties have caused this Agreement to be duly executed and delivered as of the above-stated date.

[Name of Drop Shipper]
By: _____
Print Name: _____
Title: _____

[Name of eBay Seller]
By: _____
Print Name: _____
Title: _____

International Sales Contract (Manufactured Goods Subject to Resale)

[NOTE: This contract is recommended by the International Chamber of Commerce or ICC.]

A. SPECIFIC CONDITIONS

These Specific Conditions have been prepared in order to permit the parties to agree to the particular terms of their sale contract by completing the spaces left open or choosing (as the case may be) between the alternatives provided in this document. Obviously, this does not prevent the parties from agreeing to other terms or further details in Box A-16 or in one or more annexes.

SELLER CONTACT PERSON
Name and address

_____ _____

_____ _____

_____ _____

BUYER CONTACT PERSON
Name and address

_____ _____

_____ _____

_____ _____

The present contract of sale will be governed by these Specific Conditions (to the extent that the relevant boxes have been completed) and by the ICC General Conditions of Sale (Manufactured Goods Intended for Resale), which constitute Part B of this document.

SELLER
signature

_____

place _____ date _____

BUYER
signature

_____

place _____ date _____

A-1. Goods Sold

_____

_____

Description of the Goods
[If there is insufficient space, parties may use an annex.]

A-2. Contract Price (Art. 4)
Currency: _____

Amount in numbers: _____   Amount in letters: _____

A-3. Delivery Terms
Recommended terms (according to Incoterms 1990: see Introduction, §5)

_____ **EXW** Ex Works named place: _____

_____ **FCA** Free Carrier named place: _____

_____ **CPT** Carriage Paid To named place of destination: _____

_____ **CIP** Carriage and Insurance Paid To named place of destination: _____

_____ **DAF** Delivered At Frontier named place: _____

_____ **DDU** Delivered Duty Unpaid named place of destination: _____

_____ **DDP** Delivered Duty Paid named place of destination: _____

Other terms (according to Incoterms 1990: see Introduction, § 5)

_____ **FAS** Free Alongside Ship named port of shipment: _____

_____ **FOB** Free On Board named port of shipment: _____

_____ **CFR** Cost and Freight named port of destination: _____

_____ **CIF** Cost Insurance and Freight named port of destination: _____

_____ **DES** Delivered Ex Ship named port of destination: _____

_____ **DEQ** Delivered Ex Quay (duty paid) named port of destination: _____

Other delivery terms:
CARRIER (where applicable)
NAME AND ADDRESS   CONTACT PERSON

_____   _____

_____   _____

_____   _____

A-4. Time of Delivery
Indicate here the date or period (e.g., week or month) at which or within which the Seller must perform his delivery obligations according to clause A.4 of the respective Incoterm (see Introduction, § 6)

_____

_____

A-5. Inspection of the Goods by Buyer (Art. 3)
_____ Before shipment place of inspection: _____

_____ Other: _____

A-6. Retention of Title (Art. 7)

_____ YES

_____ NO

A-7. Payment Conditions (Art. 5)
_____ **Payment on open account (art. 5.1)**

Time for payment (if different from art. 5.1) _____ days from date of invoice.
Other: _____

_____ Open account backed by demand guarantee or standby letter of credit (art. 5.5)

_____ **Payment in advance (art. 5.2)**

Date (if different from art. 5.2): _____ Total price _____% of the price

_____ **Documentary Collection (art. 5.5)**

_____ D/P Documents against payment _____ D/A Documents against acceptance

_____ **Irrevocable documentary credit (art. 5.3)**
_____ Confirmed _____ Unconfirmed

Place of issue (if applicable): _____ Place of confirmation (if applicable): _____

Credit available: Partial shipments: Transhipment:
_____ By payment at sight _____ Allowed _____ Allowed
_____ By deferred payment at: _____ days
_____ Not allowed _____ Not allowed
_____ By acceptance of drafts at: _____ days
_____ By negotiation

Date on which the documentary credit must be notified to Seller (if different from art. 5.3)
_____ days before date of delivery _____ other: _____

_____ **Other:** _____
(e.g., cheque, bank draft, electronic funds transfer to designated bank account of Seller)

A-8. Documents
Indicate here documents to be provided by Seller. Parties are advised to check the Incoterm they have selected under A-3 of these Specific Conditions. (As concerns transport documents, see also Introduction, § 8.)

_____ **Transport documents:** indicate type of transport document required _____
_____ **Commercial Invoice** _____ **Certificate of origin**
_____ **Packing list** _____ **Certificate of inspection**
_____ **Insurance document** _____ **Other:** _____

A-9. Cancellation Date
TO BE COMPLETED ONLY IF THE PARTIES WISH TO MODIFY ARTICLE 10.3.
If the goods are not delivered for any reason whatsoever (including force majeure) by (date) _____ the Buyer will be entitled to CANCEL THE CONTRACT IMMEDIATELY BY NOTIFICATION TO THE SELLER.

A-10. Liability for Delay (Art. 10.1, 10.4, and 11.3)
TO BE COMPLETED ONLY IF THE PARTIES WISH TO MODIFY ART. 10.1, 10.4, OR 11.3.

Liquidated damages for delay in delivery shall be:
_____% (of price of delayed goods) per week, with a maximum of _____% (of price of delayed goods)
or:
_____ (specify amount)

In case of termination for delay, Seller's liability for damages for delay is limited to _____% of the price of the nondelivered goods

A-11. Limitation of Liability for Lack of Conformity (Art. 11.5)
TO BE COMPLETED ONLY IF THE PARTIES WISH TO MODIFY ART. 11.5.

Seller's liability for damages arising from lack of conformity of the goods shall be:
_____ limited to proven loss (including consequential loss, loss of profit, etc.) not exceeding _____% of the contract price;
or:
_____ as follows (specify):
_____

A-12. Limitation of Liability Where Nonconforming Goods Are Retained by the Buyer (Art. 11.6)
TO BE COMPLETED ONLY IF THE PARTIES WISH TO MODIFY ART. 11.6.

The price abatement for retained nonconforming goods shall not exceed:
_____% of the price of such goods
or:
_____ (specify amount)

A-13. Time-Bar (Art. 11.8)

TO BE COMPLETED ONLY IF THE PARTIES WISH TO MODIFY ART. 11.8.
Any action for nonconformity of the goods (as defined in article 11.8) must be taken by the Buyer not later than _____ from the date of arrival of the goods at destination.

A-14(a), A-14(b). Applicable Law (Art. 1.2)

*TO BE COMPLETED ONLY IF THE PARTIES WISH TO SUBMIT THE SALE CONTRACT TO A NATIONAL LAW **INSTEAD OF CISG**.* The solution hereunder is **not** recommended (see Introduction, § 3).

(a) This sales contract is governed by the domestic law of _____ (country).
To be completed if the parties wish to choose a law other than that of the Seller for questions not covered by CISG.
(b) Any questions not covered by CISG will be governed by the law of _____ (country).

A-15. Resolution of Disputes (Art. 14)

The two solutions hereunder (arbitration or litigation before ordinary courts) are alternatives: parties cannot choose both of them. If no choice is made, ICC arbitration will apply, according to art. 14.
_____ **ARBITRATION** _____ **LITIGATION (ordinary courts)**
_____ ICC (according to art. 14.1). In case of dispute the courts of
Place of arbitration _____ (place)
_____ Other _____ (specify) shall have jurisdiction

A-16. Other: _____

B. GENERAL CONDITIONS OF SALE

Art. 1 General

1.1 These General Conditions are intended to be applied together with the Specific Conditions (Part A) of the International Sale Contract (Manufactured Goods Intended for Resale), but they may also be incorporated on their own into any sale contract. Where these General Conditions (Part B) are used independently of the said Specific Conditions (Part A), any reference in Part B to Part A will be interpreted as a reference to any relevant specific conditions agreed by the parties. In case of contradiction between these General Conditions and any specific conditions agreed upon between the parties, the specific conditions shall prevail.

1.2 Any questions relating to this Contract which are not expressly or implicitly settled by the provisions contained in the Contract itself (i.e., these General Conditions and any specific conditions agreed upon by the parties) shall be governed:

(a) by the United Nations Convention on Contracts for the International Sale of Goods (Vienna Convention of 1980, hereafter referred to as CISG), and

(b) to the extent that such questions are not covered by CISG, by reference to the law of the country where the Seller has his place of business.

1.3 Any reference made to trade terms (such as EXW, FCA, etc.) is deemed to be made to the relevant term of Incoterms published by the International Chamber of Commerce.

1.4 Any reference made to a publication of the International Chamber of Commerce is deemed to be made to the version current at the date of conclusion of the Contract.

1.5 No modification of the Contract is valid unless agreed or evidenced in writing. However, a party may be precluded by his conduct from asserting this provision to the extent that the other party has relied on that conduct.

Art. 2 Characteristics of the Goods

2.1 It is agreed that any information relating to the goods and their use, such as weights, dimensions, capacities, prices, colors, and other data contained in catalogs, prospectuses, circulars, advertisements, illustrations, price-lists of the Seller, shall not take effect as terms of the Contract unless expressly referred to in the Contract.

2.2 Unless otherwise agreed, the Buyer does not acquire any property rights in software, drawings, etc. which may have been made available to him. The Seller also remains the exclusive owner of any intellectual or industrial property rights relating to the goods.

Art. 3 Inspection of the Goods Before Shipment

If the parties have agreed that the Buyer is entitled to inspect the goods before shipment, the Seller must notify the Buyer within a reasonable time before the shipment that the goods are ready for inspection at the agreed place.

Art. 4 Price

4.1 If no price has been agreed, the Seller's current list price at the time of the conclusion of the Contract shall apply. In the absence of such a current list price, the price generally charged for such goods at the time of the conclusion of the Contract shall apply.

4.2 Unless otherwise agreed in writing, the price does not include value-added tax (VAT) and is not subject to price adjustment.

4.3 The price indicated under A-2 (Contract Price) includes any costs which are at the Seller's charge according to this Contract. However, should the Seller bear any costs which, according to this Contract, are for the Buyer's account (e.g., for transportation or insurance under EXW or FCA), such sums shall not be considered as having been included in the price under A-2 and shall be reimbursed by the Buyer.

Art. 5 Payment Conditions

5.1 Unless otherwise agreed in writing, or implied from a prior course of dealing between the parties, payment of the price and of any other sums due by the Buyer to the Seller shall be on open account and time of payment shall be 30 days from the date of invoice. The amounts due shall be transferred, unless otherwise agreed, by teletransmission to the Seller's bank in the Seller's country for the account of the Seller, and the Buyer shall be deemed to have performed his payment obligations when the respective sums due have been received by the Seller's bank in immediately available funds.

5.2 If the parties have agreed on payment in advance, without further indication, it will be assumed that such advance payment, unless otherwise agreed, refers to the full price, and that the advance payment must be received by the Seller's bank in immediately available funds at least 30 days before the agreed date of delivery or the earliest date within the agreed delivery period. If advance payment has been agreed only for a part of the contract price, the payment conditions of the remaining amount will be determined according to the rules set forth in this article.

5.3 If the parties have agreed on payment by documentary credit, then, unless otherwise agreed, the Buyer must arrange for a documentary credit in favor of the Seller to be issued by a reputable bank, subject to the Uniform Customs and Practice for Documentary Credits published by the International Chamber of Commerce, and to be notified at least 30 days before the agreed date of delivery or at least 30 days before the earliest date within the agreed delivery period. Unless otherwise agreed, the documentary credit shall be payable at sight and allow partial shipments and transshipments.

5.4 If the parties have agreed on payment by documentary collection, then, unless otherwise agreed, documents will be tendered against payment (D/P) and the tender will in any case be subject to the Uniform Rules for Collections published by the International Chamber of Commerce.

5.5 To the extent that the parties have agreed that payment is to be backed by a bank guarantee, the Buyer is to provide, at least 30 days before the agreed date of delivery or at least 30 days before the earliest date within the agreed delivery period, a first demand bank guarantee subject to the Uniform Rules for Demand Guarantees published by the International Chamber of Commerce, or a standby letter of credit subject either to such Rules or to the Uniform Customs and Practice for Documentary Credits published by the International Chamber of Commerce, in either case issued by a reputable bank.

Art. 6 Interest in Case of Delayed Payment

6.1 If a party does not pay a sum of money when it falls due, the other party is entitled to interest upon that sum from the time when payment is due to the time of payment.

6.2 Unless otherwise agreed, the rate of interest shall be 2% above the average bank short-term lending rate to prime borrowers prevailing for the currency of payment at the place of payment, or where no such rate exists at that place, then the same rate in the State of the currency of payment. In the absence of such a rate at either place, the rate of interest shall be the appropriate rate fixed by the law of the State of the currency of payment.

Art. 7 Retention of Title

If the parties have validly agreed on retention of title, the goods shall remain the property of the Seller until the complete payment of the price, or as otherwise agreed.

Art. 8 Contractual Term of Delivery

Unless otherwise agreed, delivery shall be "Ex Works" (EXW).

Art. 9 Documents

Unless otherwise agreed, the Seller must provide the documents (if any) indicated in the applicable Incoterm or, if no Incoterm is applicable, according to any previous course of dealing.

Art. 10 Late-Delivery, Nondelivery, and Remedies Therefor

10.1 When there is delay in delivery of any goods, the Buyer is entitled to claim liquidated damages equal to 0.5% or such other percentage as may be agreed of the price of those goods for each complete week of delay, provided the Buyer notifies the Seller of the delay. Where the Buyer so notifies the Seller within 15 days from the agreed date of delivery, damages will run from the agreed date of delivery or from the last day within the agreed period of delivery. Where the Buyer so notifies the Seller after 15 days of the agreed date of delivery, damages will run from the date of the notice. Liquidated damages for delay shall not exceed 5% of the price of the delayed goods or such other maximum amount as may be agreed.

10.2 If the parties have agreed upon a cancellation date in Box A-9, the Buyer may terminate the Contract by notification to the Seller as regards goods which have not been delivered by such cancellation date for any reason whatsoever (including a force majeure event).

10.3 When article 10.2 does not apply and the Seller has not delivered the goods by the date on which the Buyer has become entitled to the maximum amount of liquidated damages under article 10.1, the Buyer may give notice in writing to terminate the Contract as regards such goods, if they have not been delivered to the Buyer within 5 days of receipt of such notice by the Seller.

10.4 In case of termination of the Contract under article 10.2 or 10.3, then in addition to any amount paid or payable under article 10.1, the Buyer is entitled to claim damages for any additional loss not exceeding 10% of the price of the nondelivered goods.

10.5 The remedies under this article are exclusive of any other remedy for delay in delivery or nondelivery.

Art. 11 Nonconformity of the Goods

11.1 The Buyer shall examine the goods as soon as possible after their arrival at destination and shall notify the Seller in writing of any lack of conformity of the goods within 15 days from the date when the Buyer discovers or ought to have discovered the lack of conformity. In any case the Buyer shall have no remedy for lack of conformity if he fails to notify the Seller thereof within 12 months from the date of arrival of the goods at the agreed destination.

11.2 Goods will be deemed to conform to the Contract despite minor discrepancies which are usual in the particular trade or through course of dealing between the parties, but the Buyer will be entitled to any abatement of the price usual in the trade or through course of dealing for such discrepancies.

11.3 Where goods are nonconforming (and provided the Buyer, having given notice of the lack of conformity in compliance with article 11.1, does not elect in the notice to retain them), the Seller shall at his option:
- **(a)** replace the goods with conforming goods, without any additional expense to the Buyer, or
- **(b)** repair the goods, without any additional expense to the Buyer, or
- **(c)** reimburse to the Buyer the price paid for the nonconforming goods and thereby terminate the Contract as regards those goods.

The Buyer will be entitled to liquidated damages as quantified under article 10.1 for each complete week of delay between the date of notification of the nonconformity according to article 11.1 and the supply of substitute goods under article 11.3(a) or repair under article 11.3(b) above. Such damages may be accumulated with damages (if any) payable under article 10.1, but can in no case exceed in the aggregate 5% of the price of those goods.

11.4 If the Seller has failed to perform his duties under article 11.3 by the date on which the Buyer becomes entitled to the maximum amount of liquidated damages according to that article, the Buyer may give notice in writing to terminate the Contract as regards the nonconforming goods unless the supply of replacement goods or the repair is effected within 5 days of receipt of such notice by the Seller.

11.5 Where the Contract is terminated under article 11.3(c) or article 11.4, then in addition to any amount paid or payable under article 11.3 as reimbursement of the price and damages for any delay, the Buyer is entitled to damages for any additional loss not exceeding 10% of the price of the nonconforming goods.

11.6 Where the Buyer elects to retain nonconforming goods, he shall be entitled to a sum equal to the difference between the value of the goods at the agreed place of destination if they had conformed with the Contract and their value at the same place as delivered, such sum not to exceed 15% of the price of those goods.

11.7 Unless otherwise agreed in writing, the remedies under this article 11 are exclusive of any other remedy for nonconformity.

11.8 Unless otherwise agreed in writing, no action for lack of conformity can be taken by the Buyer, whether before judicial or arbitral tribunals, after 2 years from the date of arrival of the goods. It is expressly agreed that after the expiry of such term, the Buyer will not plead nonconformity of the goods, or make a counterclaim thereon, in defense to any action taken by the Seller against the Buyer for nonperformance of this Contract.

Art. 12 Cooperation Between the Parties
12.1 The Buyer shall promptly inform the Seller of any claim made against the Buyer by his customers or third parties concerning the goods delivered or intellectual property.

12.2 The Seller will promptly inform the Buyer of any claim which may involve the product liability of the Buyer.

Art. 13 Force Majeure
13.1 A party is not liable for a failure to perform any of his obligations in so far as he proves:

    (a) that the failure was due to an impediment beyond his control, and

    (b) that he could not reasonably be expected to have taken into account the impediment and its effects upon his ability to perform at the time of the conclusion of the Contract, and

    (c) that he could not reasonably have avoided or overcome it or its effects.

13.2 A party seeking relief shall, as soon as practicable after the impediment and its effects upon his ability to perform become known to him, give notice to the other party of such impediment and its effects on his ability to perform. Notice shall also be given when the ground of relief ceases. Failure to give either notice makes the party thus failing liable in damages for loss which otherwise could have been avoided.

13.3 Without prejudice to article 10.2, a ground of relief under this clause relieves the party failing to perform from liability in damages, from penalties and other contractual sanctions, except from the duty to pay interest on money owing, as long as and to the extent that the ground subsists.

13.4 If the grounds of relief subsist for more than 6 months, either party shall be entitled to terminate the Contract with notice.

Art. 14 Resolution of Disputes

14.1 Unless otherwise agreed in writing, all disputes arising in connection with the present Contract shall be finally settled under the Rules of Arbitration of the International Chamber of Commerce by one or more arbitrators appointed in accordance with the said Rules.

14.2 An arbitration clause does not prevent any party from requesting interim or conservatory measures from the courts.

Index

eBay the Smart Way

The definitive series on eBay—exclusively from AMACOM
Comprehensive and easy to use!
Affordably priced—a lot of information, all for $25 or less!

eBay the Smart Way: Selling, Buying, and Profiting on the Web's #1 Auction Site by Joseph T. Sinclair $17.95

eBay Business the Smart Way: Maximize Your Profits on the Web's #1 Auction Site by Joseph T. Sinclair $24.95

eBay Photography the Smart Way: Creating Great Product Pictures That Will Attract Higher Bids and Sell Your Items Faster by Joseph T. Sinclair, Stanley Livingston $19.95

eBay Inventory the Smart Way: How to Find Great Sources and Manage Your Merchandise to Maximize Profits on the World's #1 Auction Site by Joseph T. Sinclair, Jeremy Hanks $19.95

Building Your eBay Traffic the Smart Way: Use Froogle, Datafeeds, Cross-Selling, Advanced Listing Strategies, and More to Boost Your Sales on the Web's #1 Auction Site by Joseph T. Sinclair $17.95

eBay Global the Smart Way : Buying and Selling Internationally on the World's #1 Auction Site by Joseph T. Sinclair, Ron Ubels $19.95

eBay Motors the Smart Way: Selling and Buying Cars, Trucks, Motorcycles, Boats, Parts, Accessories, and Much More on the Web's #1 Auction Site by Joseph T. Sinclair, Don Spillane $17.95

Check out www.amacombooks.org/ebay for more details on all these helpful titles!